50 American Biographies

50 American Biographies

HBJ Harcourt Brace Jovanovich, Publishers
Orlando San Diego Chicago Dallas

Editorial Advisory Board

Lloyd Chorley
C.K. McClatchy High School
Sacramento, California

Thomas DiBacco, Ph.D.
American University
Washington, D.C.

Adrian Davis
Redford High School
Detroit, Michigan

Anne Bauer Setchel
Brookland Middle School
Henrico County Schools
Richmond, Virginia

Jesse de la Rosa
Brown Junior High School
McAllen, Texas

Richard L. Terry
Chairperson—Social Studies
Linton High School
Schenectady, New York

Contributing Writer

Leonard Philip Poggiali
School Administrator and
  English Teacher
Fayetteville-Manlius
  High School
Manlius, New York

Original edition written by Helen Miller Bailey

Illustrations by Stacey Cooper

Copyright © 1989 by Harcourt Brace Jovanovich, Inc.

All rights reserved. No part of this publication may be reproduced or transmitted in any form or by any means, electronic or mechanical, including photocopy, recording, or any information storage and retrieval system, without permission in writing from the publisher.

Requests for permission to make copies of any part of the work should be mailed to: Copyrights and Permissions Department, Harcourt Brace Jovanovich, Publishers, Orlando, Florida 32887

ACKNOWLEDGMENT
Grateful acknowledgment is made to Joan Daves for permission to reprint from "I Have a Dream" speech by Martin Luther King, Jr. Copyright © 1963 by Martin Luther King, Jr.

Printed in the United States of America

ISBN 0-15-371590-1

CONTENTS

PART I:	BEGINNINGS	1
	John Smith	2
	Anne Hutchinson	9
	Paul Revere	15
	Mercy Otis Warren	21
	Haym Salomon	27
	Phillis Wheatley	32
	Benjamin Franklin	38
	Tecumseh	44
	Daniel Boone	49
	Noah Webster	55
PART II:	EXPANSION AND TURMOIL	61
	Sequoyah	62
	John James Audubon	67
	Sam Houston	72
	Dorothea Dix	78
	Harriet Tubman	85
	Clara Barton	90
	Ulysses S. Grant	96
	Robert E. Lee	103
	Frederick Douglass	110
	Samuel L. Clemens	117

PART III	**INVENTION AND REFORM**	**123**
	Emily Dickenson	124
	Andrew Carnegie	130
	Susan B. Anthony	136
	Joseph Pulitzer	143
	Thomas Alva Edison	149
	Samuel Gompers	156
	Frederic Remington	162
	Booker T. Washington	168
	Jane Addams	175
	William E.B. Du Bois	182
PART IV	**HARD TIMES**	**189**
	Will Rogers	190
	Mary McLeod Bethune	197
	Robert Goddard	204
	George Gershwin	210
	Franklin D. Roosevelt	215
	Frank Lloyd Wright	222
	Richard Byrd	228
	Louis Armstrong	234
	Jackie Robinson	240
	Georgia O'Keeffe	247
PART V	**BROADER HORIZONS**	**251**
	John Glenn	252
	John F. Kennedy	260
	Martin Luther King, Jr.	267
	Maria Tallchief	274
	Roberto Clemente	278
	Luis Alvarez	285
	Shirley Chisholm	289
	Cesar Chavez	295
	Christa McAuliffe	301
	Sandra Day O'Connor	305

50 American Biographies

PART I: BEGINNINGS

The earliest experiences of settlers in America were both dangerous and exciting. Early British attempts to settle the New World met with little success. Their settlement at Roanoke mysteriously disappeared. In fact, it was at Jamestown that the British finally established their first permanent settlement in the area that would later become the United States of America. It is at Jamestown that this chronicle begins, with the knowledge and skill of John Smith.

Throughout the next decades, more and more settlers came to the New World. French, British, and Spanish settlements became common along the east coast of North America. Some came for political reasons; some came to escape religious persecution. Still others simply came for the excitement of conquering a new territory.

By the 1700s, the British colonies in the New World numbered thirteen. Because Great Britain was separated from the colonies by the huge Atlantic Ocean, differences in lifestyle and policies were bound to arise. Little by little, the colonies grew restless under the rule of a British government that, they felt, did not understand them. By 1775, colonial unrest reached its peak. The result was the American Revolution. By winning the revolution, the colonists declared to all nations that they, too, considered themselves a nation.

The years following the American Revolution were filled with hope, expectancy, and turmoil. There were many disagreements as to how the new nation should be governed. Finally, in 1788, the Constitution of the United States of America was approved by the states.

Safe now from the rule of other countries, and secure in the government policies of the United States, the citizens could look forward with confidence to the tasks of exploring, expanding, and shaping the United States of America.

JOHN SMITH

Soldier, explorer, author, founder of the first permanent English settlement in North America; born in England in 1580 and died there in 1631

Like other boys growing up in the 1580s, John Smith longed for adventure. He listened to reports about the Spanish Armada, the wars in Europe, and the exploits made by English seamen. He wanted to know more about the world outside England, where he could taste exotic foods and see people different from himself. Adventures that he would have never imagined possible awaited him.

John Smith and his parents lived on a farm in England. John attended nearby schools until he was sixteen years old. Then his parents decided that he should become an apprentice to a merchant. John traveled to the town where the merchant lived.

It did not take long, however, for John Smith to realize that he did not like being an apprentice. He had to sit at a desk all day, writing letters and doing bookkeeping chores. When John's father died in 1596, John stopped working for the merchant and sold the land he inherited from his father. He kept half of the money for himself and gave his mother the other half. He wanted a life of adventure.

John Smith heard that the Dutch Army needed soldiers. He became a soldier in the Dutch Army and for the next four years fought for

Holland against Spain. After fighting many battles, he became a skillful soldier.

When John returned to England, he was in his early twenties. The people in his town begged him to tell stories of his adventures. At first John enjoyed talking about his adventures, but he soon became bored. By the end of the summer, he was once again ready for adventure.

John Smith boarded a ship headed for Italy. There he got into a fight and was thrown overboard. He then swam to an island where two pirate ships were anchored. John joined one of the pirate ships and sailed across the Mediterranean Sea, along the coast of Africa, dropped off cargo in Egypt, and stopped in Italy. From there, John traveled to Hungary and joined a Hungarian fighting unit. Battles in the war between the Hungarians and the Turks were frequent and violent. John fought hand-to-hand combat against the Turks. During one battle, John Smith was captured by the Turks and sold as a slave. His owner put an iron collar around John's neck and threw him into the filthy slave pens. One day, he fell asleep in a pile of hay. His owner discovered him sleeping and began to beat him. John defended himself and killed his master. He put on his master's clothes, took his weapons, and escaped by horseback. He traveled only at night and finally reached Russia. From there, he decided to return home. John Smith was not yet twenty-five years old, but he had already experienced more than a lifetime's adventures.

While John was away, England had changed. King James the First, the new ruler, wanted to send explorers to North America. Investors financed the formation of two exploration companies—the London Company and the Plymouth Company. The Plymouth Company wanted to explore the north area of Virginia. The London Company preferred to establish colonies farther south. John Smith joined the London Company's expedition.

The directors of the London Company thought that vast wealth existed in the New World. They expected the explorers to find silver, gold, and jewels, as well as a shortcut to the Pacific Ocean. A shortcut would make it easier for England to trade with China and the East Indies. The directors purchased three ships for the expedition: the *Susan Constant*, the *God Speed*, and the *Discovery*. In December 1606, the ships sailed from London to the New World.

Late in April 1607, the ships landed in Virginia. The morning after they landed, the captain of the *Susan Constant* read aloud the instructions from the directors of the company. John Smith was one of seven men chosen to be on the governing council. However, because Smith had offended some of the "gentlemen" during the voyage, the captain of the ship had arrested Smith and imprisoned him below deck. John did not want to cause additional bad feelings by fighting for his right to govern. He told the others he would accept their decision, but only on a temporary basis.

The men named the settlement "Jamestown" after King James. John Smith helped cut down trees to make room for their tents. Other men cleared land so they could begin planting crops. However, not all of the men wanted to participate in the hard work. They wanted to look for gold and silver. John knew that without shelter and food, they would die. England had tried to establish other colonies in America, but all the attempts had failed. John Smith was determined to make Jamestown succeed.

While some of the men started constructing houses and a fort, John Smith and an exploring party took a small boat up a river they named the James River. One morning, they saw a group of Indians on the shore. John stood in the front of the boat and was the first one ashore. He presented the Indians with beads and they eagerly took the gifts. Soon, the two parties sat down to a meal of cornbread and roast dog. John and the men did not realize what they were eating until they were nearly done with the meal. John insisted that they not act disgusted. He realized that to survive in the New World, the settlers would have to maintain a friendly relationship with the Indians. It was important not to offend them in any way.

John Smith later took another exploration party up the James River. They stopped at a large Indian village where John began to learn their language. He found out that the town was the headquarters of a chief, named Powhatan (POW uh TAN). John spoke with him and discovered that Powhatan was the chief over many tribes in the area. As he talked with Powhatan, John Smith began to suspect that the continent was much larger than anyone thought and that they might not ever find a shortcut to the Pacific Ocean.

When the traveling party returned to Jamestown, they discovered that a band of Chesapeake Indians had made a surprise attack on the town. The Chesapeake Indians had not consulted Powhatan before the attack. The town had been unprepared for the attack and most of the settlers had been unarmed. John had always insisted that people who went outside the fort walls carry guns, but his instructions had been ignored. Luckily, only two people had been killed. He knew that someday the unfriendly Indians would return, and he insisted that they build up their defenses. Then John demanded a trial to prove his innocence of the accusations that had been made against him when on the ship from England. At the trial, he was found not guilty and was finally able to take his place on the council. John lost no time in taking charge of the colony.

John had part of the work force add two towers to the fort. He also had land cleared all around the town, making it more difficult for the Indians to make sneak attacks. John had other men cut trees into lumber. The lumber was stored in the holds of the ships. This lumber would eventually go back to England. The directors of the London Company expected to see a profit from the colony.

At the end of June, the *Susan Constant* was ready to sail back to England. The ship carried lumber and beaver and fox furs. When the ship arrived in London, the directors of the London Company were disappointed because the ship did not bring gold or jewels. They sent back two ships with provisions and a new set of instructions ordering the members of the colony to find gold.

Whenever he could, John went on exploring and trading trips. He made careful notes about the landmarks and the rivers and made maps of the areas he explored. He realized that new settlers would find this information of the unknown territory valuable.

In the fall of 1608, John Smith became the president of Jamestown. Under his supervision, the town began to flourish. He had new work schedules organized and had the men begin construction on additional houses. They expected more settlers from England at any time. The food harvest was abundant, and an extra storehouse had to be built to hold the surplus food. A high wall was added around the town for additional protection, and John Smith insisted that weekly military training be resumed.

John decided that the triangular shape of the fort was inadequate. He drew up plans for a star-shaped, five-pointed fort. The colonists began to enlarge and change the design of the fort. John Smith's idea proved to be successful and the new design became a standard design throughout the colonies. The design was still in use 150 years later.

During the evening hours, John worked on his new book. He had already sent one book to England to be published. That book was about the New World and the colony at Jamestown. His new book, *A Map of Virginia, with a Description of the Country*, was a masterpiece of cartography, or mapmaking. John Smith felt sure that this book would assure him a place in history, and it did.

Soon the ship of immigrants arrived. Two of the immigrants had a powerful effect on Jamestown; they were the first women to arrive at the all-male colony. The presence of the women signified that Jamestown was now considered a permanent settlement. The colony had become a more safe and pleasant place to live. Many of the colonists began to think of sending for their wives and girlfriends.

In 1609, another ship from England arrived. The ship contained provisions, tools, and bolts of cloth. There was also a letter for Captain John Smith from the directors of the London Company. He was in for a shock.

John Smith read the letter with disbelief. The directors criticized him for mistreating the Indians. John knew that someone must have given the directors false information. The letter also stated that King James had decided to become personally involved in Jamestown. Therefore, his own personal council would look after the colony. A new government and administration would need to be formed and the London Company would be sending a man who would become the Royal Governor. John could remain in office until the new man arrived. Then he would be removed from office. The directors showed no gratitude to John Smith or to any of the men for all they had done.

One night, while John slept, a man accidently set fire to John's gunpowder bag while lighting his own pipe. The explosion engulfed John in flames. Immediately, he jumped into the river, but he had been severely burned. The doctor at the settlement could do little to relieve his pain and for several days no one was sure that John Smith would live. When it appeared that John would live, he returned to England to seek additional medical treatment.

After John Smith left Jamestown, the colony took a turn for the worse. His presence, organization, and strength had stabilized the settlement. The new leader could not get the settlers to accept his authority. The next leader could do no better. The storehouses were low on food and there was no one left to trade with the Indians for food. No one made plans for the winter. The "starving time" was about to begin. When John Smith left Jamestown, there were approximately 573 settlers. During the winter of 1609–1610, more than 500 people died. Eventually, ships arrived from England, and the settlement was not in such great danger.

When John Smith returned to England, he was very sick and depressed. He rented rooms in a small house and saw no one but the doctor who treated him. Slowly, his health began to improve. Although his burns healed, he remained upset about Jamestown. He felt that the directors had not treated him fairly and did not understand the problems involved in setting up a town in the New World. John eventually had an opportunity to tell his side of the story to King James. After his talk with King James, Prince Henry gave a party for John Smith. He had invited the directors of the London Company. Finally, Smith was able to explain to them face-to-face the facts of the Jamestown colony. From that time, the London Company called on John Smith to advise them.

In 1612, his book, *A Map of Virginia, with a Description of the Country,* was published. The book was a success. The first printing sold out in a few days and the following printings sold out in six months. People began to realize how much John Smith knew about the New World. They began to ask and pay for his advice. He advised merchants and others interested in forming trade and exploration companies. He finally gained the fame and respect he felt he deserved.

In 1614, John Smith again set sail for America. He was in charge of an expedition to what was then called Northern Virginia. He and his crew were to bring back whale oil. A product of whale oil was needed for making perfume. John had equipped his ship with harpoons and nets, but his harpoons were not sturdy enough to kill a whale. Instead, the crew concentrated on fishing and trapping for furs. When he returned to England, the investors were pleased with the cargo.

John Smith spent the next few years launching voyages that were unsuccessful. His strength had begun to fail, yet he still wanted to assist in the colonization of America. He decided to devote himself to a new project. In 1621, he began to write a complete history of the New World to the present day. The project turned out to be six volumes and was called *The Generall Historie of Virginia, New England and the Summer Isles*. It was published in 1624 and was an immediate success.

John began to have trouble breathing and could not complete the project. On June 21, 1631, he died in his sleep. He was fifty-one years old. No one can be certain that all of his adventures and exploits occurred in precisely the manner he reported. It is certain, however, that John Smith was a hard-working soldier, knowledgeable adventurer, respected leader, and well-known author. He cared deeply about exploration and colonization in America. It is for these reasons he has been adopted as an American hero.

Directions: On a separate sheet of paper, answer the following questions about John Smith.

1. What do you think was John Smith's attitude toward the American Indians? How did this attitude affect Jamestown?

2. Why do you think Jamestown flourished under John Smith's leadership? Explain your answer.

ANNE HUTCHINSON

Puritan colonist who fought for individual freedom; born in England in 1591, died on Long Island in 1643

On a warm September Thursday in 1634, the *Griffin* sailed into Boston Harbor. The people living in four-year-old Boston ran from the Market Place and from their homes, eager to see who would come ashore. They knew that whoever their new neighbors were, their coming would affect everyone who lived in the isolated settlement.

On the deck of the ship, a middle-aged woman holding a baby stood beside a quiet man. Around the couple crowded nine more of their children, ranging in age from nineteen to three. If they found the new town ugly, they kept their feelings to themselves. Instead, each watched eagerly to be the first to spot Edward Hutchinson among the boats that were approaching the ship. The woman smiled with delight as she sighted her 22-year-old son who had come to Boston a year before. Neither Anne Hutchinson nor anyone in Boston could have foreseen the sorrow the woman and the town would bring to each other before Boston was another four years older.

Anne Marbury Hutchinson was born in the tiny English village of Alford in Lincolnshire in 1591. Her father was a clergyman who had disagreed with the Church and had been forbidden to preach. When Anne was thirteen, however, her father made peace with the Church and was given a parish in the city of London. Life in the crowded city was very different from that in peaceful little Alford. Anne no longer ran in open fields and meadows where she knew everyone she met. Instead, she walked in dark, dirty streets where overhanging houses kept out the sun and she saw only the faces of strangers. Anne began to go with her mother to care for the members of the congregation who were sick. She learned to use herbal medicines and to help women who were giving birth to children.

When Anne was twenty-one, she married William Hutchinson, who had been a neighbor in Alford. For twenty-two years they lived quiet, busy lives in Alford. William was a successful merchant and sheep farmer. During that time, Anne gave birth to fourteen children. Eleven of the children lived to go to America with their parents.

While they lived in Alford, Anne and William sometimes spent a day and a half on horseback traveling the twenty-four miles to a town called Boston. In Boston, they went as often as they could to listen to John Cotton, a Puritan preacher. Upon her return to Alford, Anne would call together a group of women and tell them what John Cotton had said in his sermons. She became a well-known teacher and many people came to hear her.

King Charles I did not trust the Puritans, and he began to persecute them. That is why John Winthrop had taken a group of Puritans to the New World in 1630 and founded the Massachusetts Bay Colony. By 1633, the Hutchinsons had decided to go to the New World so that they could follow their religious beliefs without fear. Their oldest son, Edward, went ahead to prepare the way for the rest of the family. In the night, just before Edward's ship sailed, John Cotton slipped aboard, barely escaping the King's men who were in pursuit.

Now, a year later, the family was reunited and looking forward to a new life. The Hutchinsons built a home on High Street, just across from John Winthrop's house. William became active in the business and political life of the community. Anne began to use her nursing skills to help people who were sick and women who were giving birth. People grew to love her and to depend on her.

Anne kept busy establishing a home and learning how to use new foods and herbs. On Sabbath days she would listen for the drum that called the town to worship. Then she and William would lead their family to the cold, dark meeting house, where the wind whistled through the cracks. Anne and her daughters sat on hard benches without backs on one side of the large room. William and his sons joined the men on the other side. Pastor John Wilson had returned to England to try once again to bring his reluctant wife to Boston. In his absence, John Cotton preached the two-hour sermons that would be discussed all week. Life in New Boston was not easy, but Anne found it good.

The first meetings at her house were small. A neighbor stopped by to talk about the Sabbath sermon. She liked the way Anne explained what John Cotton had meant. The next time she came, she brought a friend with her who had been puzzled by something the popular preacher had said. More women came. After a while, some of the women brought their husbands. Soon, every Thursday as many as eighty people crowded into Anne's front room. Then she began to hold meetings on Monday. These were soon just as crowded.

From his house across the High Street, John Winthrop watched uneasily as her influence increased. He loved the colony to which he had devoted his life and wanted only good for it. He feared Anne's growing power. As it was, the colony was in constant danger from King Charles and from the nearby Pequot Indians. Winthrop feared that if the experienced leaders lost control, all in the colony would be lost. He was uncertain what to do.

John Winthrop had been governor of the colony from its founding in 1630 until 1633. In the annual election in 1633, the colony had elected a new governor because they felt that Winthrop was not strict enough. Winthrop had learned his lesson well; he would soon demonstrate to the colony just how strict he could be.

For a year, Anne and her family were busy and happy. The people in the colony liked the family and respected them. Like most of the people in Boston, the Hutchinsons enjoyed listening to John Cotton's sermons. Then, in October 1635, John Wilson returned and reclaimed his church. Anne and her followers did not agree with John Wilson's sermons. They tried to have Wilson removed as pastor and John Cotton restored to the pulpit. Their effort failed, but it brought the division in the church into the open.

For a time, Anne gave up her meetings, and early in the spring, 1636, she gave birth to her fifteenth child. Anne continued to disagree with Wilson's sermons. One Sabbath day, unable to listen any longer to a message she could not agree with, she rose and led her followers from the church. She resumed the meetings in her living room.

In the spring of that year, Anne's brother-in-law, John Wheelwright, arrived from England. Wheelwright was a Puritan minister who had been forbidden to preach in England. In her meetings, Anne said that only two men in the colony preached the Covenant of Grace. Those two men were John Cotton and John Wheelwright. She said that all the other ministers preached a Covenant of Works. According to Anne, a Covenant of Grace meant that the most important thing was what a person believed. A Covenant of Works meant that the most important thing was what a person did. Even the preachers in the colony's churches had a hard time understanding the difference. Now John Winthrop knew what he had to do to regain control of the colony from Anne.

Winthrop began to meet with the preachers. They tried to find fault with Anne's teachings. They sent spies to her meetings, but they did not go themselves to hear what she said. They sent for Anne to come to John Cotton's house, and they questioned her closely. She proved that all she taught was in the Bible. John Cotton agreed with all that she said. The ministers tried to get John Cotton to change the way he preached. Cotton had trouble explaining just what he meant by what he taught. Everyone became angrier and angrier.

In an attempt to calm the situation, the churches proclaimed January 20, 1637, as a day of prayer. John Wheelwright preached a sermon on that day that some people heard as a call for civil war. In March, the General Court found Wheelwright guilty of attempting to cause a rebellion. Seventy-nine men, most of them Anne's followers, signed a protest because they did not think Wheelwright should have been found guilty.

Winthrop was elected governor in May 1637. That summer, the weather was so hot that many newly arrived settlers died of sunstroke. People chose the dangers of traveling at night rather than risk being abroad in the midday heat. Despite the heat, ministers came to Boston from all the colony churches to question John Cotton and investigate the beliefs that Anne held and taught. Early in August, the official trumpeter went on horseback from village to village, blowing his horn to call the people together. He announced to all the people that on August 30 the first synod, or gathering of the churches, ever called in New England would begin. The synod lasted nine days through the still stifling heat of late summer. When it was over, the preachers had a plan to silence Anne Hutchinson. During the following months they made their preparations.

November began with a violent, early snowstorm. The winter promised to be as cold as the summer had been hot. On November 2, 1637, the General Court met at Newtown, five miles from Anne's house. Winthrop succeeded in removing from the court all of the men who supported Anne. The first act of the Court was to sentence Wheelwright to be banished, and he left at once for New Hampshire. He preferred to risk traveling in winter to remaining any longer in Massachusetts. Banishment means that the person must go to another place to live or face imprisonment or death. One after another, Anne's supporters were given heavy fines, stripped of their rights as citizens, removed from their positions, even put in jail.

At last Anne stood alone before her nine judges and forty other accusers. She faced some of the best-educated and most powerful men in the New World. For hours she stood in the bitterly cold meeting house answering calmly and clearly the questions of the seated men. After a long time she looked as if she were about to faint, and she was allowed to sit down. The trial continued the next day. At length, Anne was declared guilty and sentenced to be banished. Hearing her sentence, Anne asked to know why she was banished. Winthrop replied in a voice like thunder that the court knew why and that was enough.

Because of the bitter weather, Anne was imprisoned at Roxbury, two miles from her home. In March she was called before the church. For hours she listened as her teachings were twisted and turned in ways she had never intended. This time, she was excommunicated, or cast out of the church. She left the meeting house with her head high and no sign of remorse on her face.

In the spring of 1638, Anne and most of her family went to live in Rhode Island. They traveled six days by canoe and on foot to go the sixty-five miles. Anne was not silenced. Less than a year later, she was preaching in public. She believed that women were as capable as men and should be as free to do what they wanted to do as men were. She thought that every person, man or woman, should control his or her own life. Her influence continued to grow and spread. Winthrop and the Boston church continued to try to silence her, but she would not give in to them.

William died in 1642, and Anne took her six youngest children to live in the Dutch settlement on Long Island. In a lonely place in Pelham Bay called Anne's Hoeck, the family built a small house. They had lived there less than a year when Anne and five of her children were killed by Indians who had decided to drive all white settlers from their hunting lands. Only ten-year-old Susanna survived.

Anne Hutchinson and her family had come to the New World in search of religious freedom. Although Anne did not find what she sought, she furthered the cause of religious freedom in America. Through her determination and courage, she showed American colonists a broader definition of the term "individual freedom."

Directions: On a separate sheet of paper, answer the following questions about Anne Hutchinson.

1. What was Anne Hutchinson's purpose in bringing her family to the Massachusetts Bay Colony?
2. Did Anne find what she sought in the New World? Explain your answer.

PAUL REVERE

Silversmith, patriot of the American Revolution; born in Massachusetts in 1735 and died there in 1815

A thirteen-year-old French boy landed on the public wharf in Boston in 1715. His name was Apollos Rivoire, and he was completely alone. His family in France were Huguenots, French Protestants, and were being bitterly persecuted at this time. His parents had sent him to America for safety. A kind uncle living on the island of Guernsey had provided enough money to pay for his trip and a ten-year apprenticeship with the best silversmith in Boston.

Apollos went to the silversmith's shop. He learned his trade well. At the end of seven years, the master silversmith died, and his widow gave Apollos his freedom in return for the sum of forty pounds. Apollos could now work for wages. By the time he was twenty-eight, he had his own silversmith shop. The town of Boston grew, and Apollos did well as a master silversmith. He married the daughter of a prosperous neighbor.

Their second child, a son, was christened Paul Revere, with the English spelling. Paul practically grew up in his father's shop. When he was eight, Paul was sent to a school for the sons of craftsmen. On the first floor of the wooden schoolhouse, he joined other boys of all ages who learned to read by shouting out passages of the Bible. On the second floor of the building another teacher taught the boys how to write and do simple arithmetic. After a few years, Paul had completed all the schooling available to the sons of craftsmen. He left the school and entered his father's shop as an apprentice.

There he learned to work with silver and with the gold and copper that his father occasionally used. When Paul was nineteen, Apollos died. Paul's mother took over the silversmith shop. Two years later, Paul left to join the British army and take part in the French and Indian War. He spent nine months as a second lieutenant in a regiment that was skirmishing with the French and their Indian allies in the upper parts of the New York colony.

When he returned home from the army, the young silversmith became master of his father's shop. He married Sarah Orne, and they lived in the house that he maintained for his mother and younger brothers and sisters. The Paul Revere House still stands in Boston, and visitors can see many of the things that this busy colonial family used in their everyday lives.

Sarah and Paul Revere had eight children. Sarah died in 1773. Several months later, Paul married Rachel Walker, a woman with five children of her own. She was a kind and loving stepmother. Business at the shop was good, and the Revere family lived better than most working-class families in the colonies. Three of Paul's sons were apprenticed in the silversmith shop. Records show that the Revere shop made silver buttons, shoe buckles, creamers, and rings of silver and gold, as well as other objects made of precious metals.

As part of his business, Revere also made engraved plates for printing illustrations. This was a new branch of the silversmith craft which Revere had taught himself. He would make a smooth metal sheet and then use fine tools to etch a design, picture, or even the words and music to songs in it. When properly inked, such a plate would transfer the design to paper pressed against it. Revere became very good at this process. His ability to engrave illustrations later helped the cause of American independence.

In 1765, after the French and Indian War was over, the British government decided to obtain part of the money needed to pay for the war by imposing a stamp tax on the colonies. This meant that all papers, such as marriage certificates, bills of sale, and newspapers, had to have a stamp on them before they were legal. This upset the colonists because they did not have a voice in the tax decision. They had no representative in the British Parliament when the tax was passed. Paul Revere was one of the first craftsmen to join the Sons of Liberty, a group of colonists who protested the stamp tax. He engraved a cartoon and a poster attacking the Stamp Act, printed a great many copies of them on cheap paper, and handed them out around the town. The Stamp Act was eventually repealed, but the colonies and the British continued to quarrel.

When British troops were quartered in Boston in 1770, a crowd rioted against them. The troops fired into the crowd and killed some of the civilians. This incident became famous as "the Boston massacre." Paul Revere was asked by the Sons of Liberty to make an engraving of the incident. In the engraving, the soldiers are lined up stiffly, all firing at once, and the townspeople seem very orderly and sad as they fall down. At the trial of some of the soldiers, it was shown that they fired in self-defense. However, this print of the "massacre" became the most popular picture in the colonies, and thousands of copies of it were sold throughout the colonies.

A lawyer, Samuel Adams, and his merchant friend, John Hancock, were the leaders of the Sons of Liberty. They thought that the other colonies should get news of the happenings in Boston, so in 1772 they organized a Committee of Correspondence to write letters and send messages to Pennsylvania, New York, and Virginia. Because he had a swift horse and had learned to ride well in the army, Revere was chosen by the Committee to carry the letters to the other towns.

Great Britain, determined to make the colonies help pay war expenses, created other kinds of taxes in the colonies. One such tax was the tax on tea. One night in 1773, the Sons of Liberty decided to throw British tea into Boston Harbor in protest against the tax on the tea. They called their protest the "Boston Tea Party." Paul Revere was nearly forty at the time, but he smeared his face with grease, put feathers in his hair, and posed as an Indian with the other conspirators. They were out all that night dumping tea into the harbor. Then, without resting, Revere saddled up his horse and started on the long road to New York and Philadelphia. His mission was to inform the Committees of Correspondence in those towns about what had happened that night in Boston. He was gone eleven days—five days riding to Philadelphia, one day resting and talking with the Committee in Philadelphia, and five days returning.

Revere rode a distance of about sixty-five miles each day over the rough winding roads and trails. When his horse grew tired, he was often able to change it for a fresh one, but there was never a fresh substitute for Paul Revere himself. He carried many of the messages in his head, so he had to talk personally with the members of the committees in New York and Philadelphia to get their reactions to the Boston Tea Party.

Revere, along with other craftsmen and shopkeepers in Boston, had pledged himself to keep watch on the British officers and men in the city. During the first weekend in April 1775, Revere and other watchers began to suspect that the British were planning to march on the villages west of Boston. Their aim was to destroy military stores that the colonists had collected at Concord. They also planned to capture John Hancock and Samuel Adams, who were then in Lexington.

On Sunday of that weekend, Revere rode twelve miles from Boston to the village of Lexington. He found Adams and Hancock at a Lexington inn and warned them that the British might try to capture them during the coming week. On the way home, Revere rode through Charlestown, a village across the bay from Boston. He spoke with patriots there and arranged to send a warning signal in case the British marched.

On April 18, 1775, the patriots in Boston learned from three different people that the British were planning to march to Concord. Paul Revere had two lanterns placed in the church tower as a signal to the patriots in Charlestown that the British were crossing the bay by boat and were marching inland to Lexington. Paul Revere went across the bay in a rowboat in the dark of night. When he landed silently in Charlestown, the patriots there loaned him the best horse in the town.

Another rider, William Dawes, also went out from Boston that night. Riding around the bay by land, he was to meet Revere in Lexington. Paul Revere's mission was to awaken Adams and Hancock and help them escape. They were the Massachusetts delegates to the Second Continental Congress in Philadelphia, and they had a trunk full of papers and letters for the Congress. Revere took time to wake every farmer and villager on the road from Charlestown to Lexington.

At one point Revere ran into two British officers. Revere's horse was faster than the officers' horses and he got away. He rode on to the Reverend Clark's house in Lexington. There he found Adams and Hancock and warned them of the danger.

After warning the men, Revere met Dawes, and they continued on toward Concord. They were joined by Dr. Samuel Prescott, a young doctor from Concord who was in Lexington that night. The three men rode on together. On the road, halfway between the two villages, British troops captured Revere and Dawes. Dawes got away without his horse. Revere was held for several hours and then released and left to walk back to Lexington. He returned to the inn where Adams and Hancock were staying.

Meanwhile, Dr. Prescott rode on to Concord to spread the alarm. The minutemen were alerted in both Lexington and Concord, and the next day when the British soldiers marched toward the village green, the colonial soldiers were ready for them. The Battle of Lexington and Concord took place, and the American Revolution began. Where was Paul Revere on that fateful day, April 19, 1775? John Hancock had asked him to take the trunk full of papers to safety. Busy slipping out the back with the valuable papers, Paul Revere hardly saw the Battle of Lexington and Concord.

Revere took a very active part in the remainder of the war, however. He acted as a colonel in the militia guarding Boston, with one of his sons serving as a lieutenant under him. When the patriots needed gunpowder, Paul Revere, the skilled craftsman, was sent to visit a powder factory in Philadelphia to learn how it was made.

When the war was finally over, Paul Revere's shop began to prosper. He and his sons imported hardware—pewter, brass, and iron shipfittings—to sell to shipowners. He wanted to make these items for himself. Revere began developing methods of casting brass and copper and soon had the biggest metal-working plant in Massachusetts. The Revere family then built a rolling mill to manufacture copper sheeting. No one else in America was able to do this at the time. The mill cost Revere $25,000—a great deal of money in those days. However, the Revere family earned the money back and much more besides when the mill began operating. The copper sheeting was used for most of Boston's merchant fleet. At this time, the Revere family also began to make church bells. In the years after the Revolution, they made more than a hundred of these bells for the rapidly growing city of Boston. Some of them can be heard ringing in Boston today.

In his old age, Paul Revere was a leading citizen of Boston. He had the time and the money to support many local charities. Paul Revere also helped his nephews and cousins finish school, and he set them up in trade or helped them open silversmith shops. He sent his youngest son to Harvard College.

Paul Revere was so proud of the Revolutionary spirit that he would never change styles with the changing times. He continued to wear the knee breeches and three-cornered hats of Washington's day. In 1815, when he was eighty, the Massachusetts Historical Society asked him to write about his ride to Lexington. This account was read by the poet Henry Wadsworth Longfellow a generation later. Longfellow turned it into his famous poem *Paul Revere's Ride*. It is because of Longfellow's poem that people usually think of Paul Revere, rather than Dawes or Prescott, when they recall that eventful night.

Directions: On a separate sheet of paper, answer the following questions about Paul Revere.

1. In what ways are the memory and handiwork of Paul Revere preserved today? Explain your answer.
2. In what ways did Paul Revere help the cause of the American Revolution? Explain your answer.

MERCY OTIS WARREN

Poet, playwright, historian, and patriot; born in Massachusetts in 1728 and died there in 1814

In 1814, the twenty-mile trip from Braintree to Boston was measured in hours. Even though it was a hot, August day, a 79-year-old man—who hardly ever left his home—rode from Braintree to Boston on a mission of truth. He was John Adams, former President of the United States. He went directly to the great Atheneum library in Boston to correct a mistake.

When he arrived, he asked to see a copy of an old play, *The Group*. This sarcastic comedy, published in 1775 without the author's name, had stirred many people to fight against the British. Nearly forty years later, in the summer of 1814, rumors claimed that *The Group* was written by a man. Adams knew better. Now, in the Atheneum library, he turned the pages of the worn pamphlet. A short time later, with quill and ink, he certified, on a page of the play itself, that the author of *The Group* was a woman, Mercy Otis Warren.

During her life, Mercy Otis Warren was well known for her writing and the role she played in the American Revolution. Besides plays, she wrote poems and a history of the Revolution. She exchanged letters with many famous men and women of her day. Her fireside warmed countless gatherings of Revolutionary heroes and heroines. Men such as Thomas Jefferson, John Adams, and Samuel Adams sought her advice. Abigail Adams, President John Adams' wife, was also a close friend.

Two hundred years later, Mercy Otis Warren is barely remembered. When she is remembered, it is as the sister of patriot James Otis or the wife of General James Warren. In her early plays, she deliberately avoided fame by not putting her name to her work. She was not sure that politics and hilarious plays were proper activities for a woman. John Adams, more than anyone outside her own family, urged her to write. He once sent a letter to Mercy's husband. Tell her, he wrote, that God has given her powers "for the good of the world" and it would be wrong not to use them.

Adams's trip to the Boston Atheneum was more than a casual gesture by an aging friend. It is true that theirs was a long friendship that began in the early stages of the American Revolution. However, after the war, political and personal differences caused them to have a bitter quarrel. For five years they did not even speak. Now Mercy's friend again, Adams traveled to the Atheneum as a final tribute to a woman he very much admired. Mercy Otis Warren died two months later on her farm in Plymouth. She was eighty-six years old.

Mercy Otis was born in 1728 in Barnstable, Massachusetts, on Cape Cod. She was the third child and first daughter of James and Mary Allyne Otis. Eventually thirteen children were born into the family, but only seven grew to adulthood. Mercy's background was Puritan. One of her mother's ancestors had come to America on the *Mayflower*. Her father's great-grandfather settled in Massachusetts in the early 1600s.

Mercy's father was a successful farmer and merchant. He was also a lawyer, county judge, and colonel. With all of his achievements, there was one thing he lacked that he demanded of his sons: a college education. To prepare for entrance to Harvard College, the two oldest sons went to study with an uncle, the Reverend Dr. Jonathan Russell. Mercy, three years younger than her brother James, and two years younger than Joseph, was allowed to trail along.

Mercy, ever hungry for learning, devoured her uncle's lessons. She feasted on the books she found in his library. She read and listened carefully to his sermons. Some biographers say that that is how she learned to write so well. The more she learned, the more she wanted to learn. Then, quite suddenly for Mercy, her schooling ended. Her brothers were ready to enter Harvard.

At that time, colleges were not open to women. James, sensing his sister's disappointment, saw to it that she continued her reading. He led her through the works of the great poets: William Shakespeare, John Milton, John Dryden, and Alexander Pope. Together they explored the ideas of great thinkers. They held many discussions. They shared an admiration for the culture of ancient Greece.

When Mercy was twenty-six years old, she married James Warren of nearby Plymouth. Like Mercy's father, James Warren was a farmer and a merchant, and he was destined for a military and political career. Like her brothers, he was a Harvard graduate. Their long, devoted marriage was filled with affection and mutual admiration. They had five sons: James, Winslow, Charles, Henry, and George.

In the restless days before the American Revolution, Mercy's brother James was regarded as the most brilliant orator and politician in Massachusetts. Suddenly, rising like a meteor in the sky, there was young James Otis stirring people up against the British. In the courts, in the old State House, in the town hall, he fought for civil rights and against injustice. He inspired many and soon became known as James Otis, the Patriot. In one stirring speech, James Otis cried out, "Taxation without representation is tyranny!" Instantly, that became a rallying cry for the Revolutionary cause.

James grew more and more angry against the Loyalists, those colonists who were loyal to Britain. James decided to seek out the Loyalists and argue with them in person. One night in 1769, unarmed, he wandered into a Loyalist coffeehouse. The moment he entered the room, someone jumped from behind to hit him over the head with a cane. Another person turned out the lights. Then in the dark, Otis was attacked with swords and clubs. Among his many injuries was a deep cut in his head.

James Otis never recovered his health. He lost control of his emotions and his thoughts. Once brilliant, James Otis was now harmlessly but hopelessly insane. He remained in the care of his family and friends until his death thirteen years later. Mercy was deeply affected by her brother's tragic beating and its effect on his patriotic contributions. After all, she had shared his views and patriotism. He was the greatest influence on her life. The terrible blow that came to James Otis pushed Mercy to produce her greatest work. She felt it was her duty to take his place.

Mercy had long been interested in writing. She had written poetry for many years. Somehow, even with her main occupation as wife and mother, she managed to find time to write. James Warren always supported his wife's writing.

Mercy felt that her greatest talent was in satire, a kind of sarcastic humor. She decided to use her talent for the revolutionary cause. Where her brother had used oratory and legal action to attack the British, she would use sarcastic poetry and plays to poke fun at their weaknesses and arouse people against them.

Three years after the attack on James, Mercy published her first play, *The Adulateur*. In her play, Mercy predicted the American Revolution. In this play and her next, *The Defeat,* she made teasing fun of Thomas Hutchinson, the Royal Governor of Massachusetts. The villian of these plays was Rapatio. Mercy's readers knew that Rapatio was Hutchinson. In the story, Rapatio was the tyrannical ruler of a make-believe country called Servia. Rapatio and his henchmen were silly, stupid, and bungling. The heroes of the play were the liberty-loving people who lived in Servia. People of Massachusetts were soon calling Thomas Hutchinson by the name *Rapatio*.

Mercy's next play was *The Group*. The new characters were Brigadier Hate-All, Judge Meagre, Sir Sparrow Spendall, Hector Mushroom, and Hum Humbug. Through tricks and jest, she continued to attack the British, and at the same time she foretold what lay ahead.

These plays were widely read and widely praised. Mercy wrote them to be read and had no intention of having them performed. The city of Boston, because of its Puritan background, had no theaters. Theater was considered sinful. The playwright herself probably never saw a play performed.

As popular and well-received as her plays were, and as important as they were for stirring people against the British, Mercy's greatest contribution still lay ahead. That would be her three-volume history with a very long title: *History of the Rise, Progress, and Termination of the American Revolution, interspersed with Biographical and Moral Observations.* She began to write her observations of people and events in 1775, in the midst of revolutionary fever. She knew so much of this exciting history firsthand. She knew the people personally. She worked on the history for thirty years. She recorded with her pen everything she saw and believed about the Revolution and its aftermath. Finally, in 1805, the long-awaited publication of her three-volume history took place.

Many people praised Mercy for her history. John Adams, on the other hand, was stung by Mercy's uncomplimentary description of him. That is why she temporarily lost his friendship.

After the American Revolution and before the publication of Mercy's history, the people of the new Republic became divided into political parties; namely, the Republican Party (ancestor of today's Democratic Party) and the Federalist Party. James and Mercy Warren were Republicans. Always concerned about civil liberties, they now differed sharply with many of their old Patriot friends. The Warrens—husband and wife—feared that the new Constitution would make the federal government too strong, that it would endanger the liberty of the people. They opposed signing the Constitution.

The other party, the Federalists, supported the Constitution. John Adams, as the second President of the United States, was a Federalist. The two parties finally compromised by adding the ten amendments to the Constitution that make up the Bill of Rights. The Bill of Rights was designed to protect the liberties that concerned Mercy and other Republicans.

Because of his quarrels with old friends, James Warren lost his political position and influence. The Warren sons had many disappointments affecting their own careers. Mercy suffered again and again because her old friend, John Adams, never stepped in to help them. Also, it seemed to her that Adams had forsaken the ideal for which the American Revolution had been fought: to protect individualliberties.

When he sat down to read Mercy's history, John Adams had no idea that she had written unkindly of him. What he read surprised and pained him. He could not stand it! He would not stand it. He wrote a letter to Mercy. She replied. Then he wrote back. For three months they wrote back and forth. Each letter became angrier and angrier. Each letter from Mercy became more and more bitter. Her pen, sharpened from years of wit, now became more and more sarcastic against Adams. Then the letters stopped altogether.

After five years, Elbridge Gerry, a friend of the Warrens and Adamses, went to Abigail Adams. He asked her help in restoring the damaged friendship. Yes, she agreed, the quarrel had gone on too long. Soon, John Adams and Mercy Warren spoke again. They wrote warmly to one another, renewing their friendship. In fact, Adams's political ideas changed. He agreed with Mercy about many things. In many ways he was now closer to the Republicans than to the Federalists.

Mercy remained in good physical and mental health throughout her life. She outlived her husband by six years and survived all but two of her sons. To her dying day, she believed in the cause of liberty, that people must govern themselves. Modern historians still use her history as an important resource about the American Revolution.

Directions: On a separate sheet of paper, answer the following questions about Mercy Otis Warren.

1. Mercy Otis Warren and her brother James Otis used words in different ways to express their political views. Explain how the words of each contributed to the cause of the American Revolution.

2. How did being a woman affect Mercy Warren's work? Explain your answer.

HAYM SALOMON

Patriot, broker, commission merchant; born in Poland in 1740 and died in 1785 in Pennsylvania

No one knows exactly when or why Haym Salomon came to America. A native of Poland, he came to New York City a few years before the American Revolution. Most of his early life is clouded in mystery. He was in his early thirties when he first appeared in New York. He knew a lot about commerce and trade, and he could speak many different languages.

When Salomon reached New York, he sought out fellow members of the Jewish faith. He joined a small but historic Jewish community. Jews originally settled in New York in 1654 when it was called New Amsterdam and its leader was Peter Stuyvesant. At the time of the American Revolution, there were only about 2,500 Jews in all the thirteen colonies—out of a total population of two and a half million people. Most of these Jews were originally from western Europe. Haym Salomon was one of very few Jews of his day who came to America from eastern Europe.

By 1776—the year of the Declaration of Independence—Salomon was already known as a patriot among the people of New York. He was a broker and commission merchant. A commission merchant was someone who brought buyers and sellers together and thereby earned a commission. Salomon wanted to do business with the American troops. In 1776, he left New York City with supplies and a letter of reference to General Philip Schuyler of the Continental Army. Salomon found the general and the army in Lake George. There Salomon saw the sufferings of the soldiers. He was appalled by their hardships. There was no standard uniform then. The men came to the army in their old farm clothes made of cloth spun and woven by the women in their families. They received no extra warm clothing for the winter. Food rations were low. Each soldier brought his own musket from home and had to cast his own bullets to fit his gun. Haym Salomon never forgot what he saw at Lake George.

When Salomon returned to New York, he found the city under British rule. The British had occupied New York City on September 15, 1776. The rabbi of the Jewish congregation had fled New York with many of his followers. Some stayed in Connecticut, but most continued to Philadelphia. Haym Salomon chose not to leave New York at this time.

In 1777, Salomon married Rachel Franks, the daughter of a wealthy Jewish merchant. Rachel's father strongly supported the colonists and, like Salomon, chose to stay in New York. Haym was thirty-seven years old when he got married. His bride was only fifteen. Soon after his marriage, Salomon was arrested as a spy by the British. They locked him up in the dreaded Provost Prison, the place where the British kept all but their highest-ranking prisoners. The cold, damp cells were vastly overcrowded and had almost no ventilation. Bad food was thrown to the prisoners, and those who were sick received no medicine. Some say that while Salomon was imprisoned, he developed a cough that he carried with him for the rest of his life.

Many of the British forces holding the city were not Englishmen. They were young farm boys from a part of Germany called Hesse. The Duke of Hesse made a deal with his distant relative, the British King. He supplied Great Britain with a large number of his subjects to help beat the Americans. These soldiers, called Hessians, could not understand their English officers, and they had little idea why they were in America.

The British jailors discovered that Salomon spoke fluent German. They released him to act as a translator and supplier for the Hessian soldiers. When he was carrying out his assignments, Salomon secretly urged the Hessians to defect and aided them with money. When Salomon became worried that the British were growing suspicious, he decided that the time had come to flee New York. On August 11, 1778, he arrived in Philadelphia. Unfortunately, he was unable to take his wife and baby with him.

Ill and needing food, clothes, and friends, Salomon went first to the synagogue. Salomon found some old friends there, and he also made new friends. Some of his friends soon helped Rachel Salomon and her infant join Haym in Philadelphia.

Salomon borrowed money from friends and became a broker and commission merchant again. He helped buyers and sellers of many different products do business with one another. Some of these products were tea, salt, hides, silk stockings, men's clothing, dry goods, almonds, raisins, and sugar. He also dealt in real estate. He excelled in learning about new kinds of trade. Soon he was able to repay his loans, and in time he was very successful.

After Salomon built up a small fortune, he approached members of the Continental Congress. He told them that he was at their disposal to help the cause of liberty. The Congress needed money to buy warm clothes and adequate food for its soldiers. The Congress also needed weapons and ammunition. However, the Continental Congress had no power to collect taxes, so it had no money with which to buy these things. France, a longtime enemy of Great Britain, was willing to offer credit to the colonists, but French credit was not cash. France sent couriers with documents called *bills of exchange*. Bills of exchange were no more than promises to pay later. The French king would pay in real money after the war. Many merchants worried that if the colonists lost the war, the French would never redeem the bills of exchange. The Congress needed to find buyers who were willing to cash the bills of exchange. They sent Robert Morris, their Superintendent of Finance, to see Salomon.

Robert Morris, a wealthy Philadelphia banker, had given away two thirds of his own fortune to the soldiers at Valley Forge. He bought food and clothing for the soldiers of Washington's tattered army. No one, however, had paid the soldiers their wages. Many soldiers were leaving to go home to beg for pay from their state legislatures. Most of the soldiers did not feel they were fighting for a unified country. They enlisted to fight for their home states—Pennsylvania or Massachusetts or Virginia. Now, all the state legislatures could do was promise the soldiers farming land after the war. No one knew how long the war would last. The soldiers wanted their wages at once.

Haym Salomon came to the rescue. In June, 1781, Morris enlisted Salomon as a broker. Since Salomon was by that time an established merchant whose credit was very good, he guaranteed the bills of exchange. He found buyers for them. In return, he agreed that his commission, or interest, would be one-half percent—a very small amount. Morris kept diaries of the government's finances. In his entries for 1781 and 1782, he mentioned Salomon's efforts more than one hundred times. Salomon became the most important money broker for the Continental government.

In the late summer of 1781, General George Washington made plans to march his small army from New York to Yorktown, Virginia. There, with the help of the French fleet, he would attack the British. The plan called for swift action, but it also required a great deal of money. Haym Salomon helped raise the money that was needed, and the army moved south to Yorktown. There Washington won the final battle of the war. He accepted the surrender of the British on October 19, 1781.

All along, Salomon was also helping many individuals who needed money, including several members of the Continental Congress. One of them was James Madison, the nation's future President, who borrowed money from Salomon on several occasions. These personal loans were often at no interest, so Salomon made no money from the transactions.

After the war, Salomon's business prospered. By the end of 1784, Salomon's business was so successful that he planned to expand it to New York where he expected to open an auction house. Then tragedy struck. On January 6, 1785, Salomon died unexpectedly. He was forty-five years old. Rachel Salomon was only in her twenties. She was left with three young children and another on the way. Many thought that Salomon died a wealthy man. Then the executors of his estate made the discovery. They found that the estate consisted mainly of old government bills of exchange that were nearly worthless. Now there were debts that had to be paid. There was little money left for the widow and her children.

Estimates of what Haym Salomon gave to the cause of the American Revolution have ranged up to more than half a million dollars. The actual amount is not known. What is known is that he was a successful merchant who gave away nearly everything he had for the cause of the American Revolution. Once Salomon wrote to Robert Morris that he believed it was a man's duty to leave his children a legacy of liberty rather than a legacy of material possessions. Haym Salomon helped provide the legacy of liberty for all Americans.

Directions: On a separate sheet of paper, answer the following questions about Haym Salomon.

1. Why do you think Haym Salomon gave so much for the cause of liberty? Explain your answer.
2. Why was it hard to raise money for the American Revolution? Explain your answer.

PHILLIS WHEATLEY

America's first black poet; born in Africa around 1753 and died in Massachusetts in 1784

One summer day in 1761, a ship named *The Phillis* sailed into Boston harbor with a cargo of African slaves. These were not ordinary slaves. They were the ill and aged rejects on a schooner that had already been to many other ports. The ship's captain had sold all the strong, healthy slaves at stops in the West Indies and the southern colonies. The captain, now anxious to cross the ocean and obtain a fresh cargo, offered the remaining slaves at bargain prices. Among the frail and sickly people who stood chained on the Boston wharf was a small girl. Her only clothing was a piece of dirty carpet.

John Wheatley, a wealthy Boston tailor and merchant, purchased the girl as a servant for his wife. On the way home, Wheatley reasoned that the girl was very young but she could be trained to be a lady's maid. The Wheatley mansion was in the heart of Boston, on fashionable King Street. Besides Mr. and Mrs. Wheatley, the family included their twin children, Mary and Nathaniel, who were eighteen years old. The household also included slaves who worked in the kitchen and house and handled the carriage and horses.

Susanna Wheatley and her children took an immediate liking to the black child. They called her Phillis, after the ship that brought her to them. "How old do you think she is?" the Wheatleys asked one another. They noticed that Phillis was losing her front teeth so they decided she was about seven years old.

When Phillis arrived in Boston, she could not speak a word of English. Almost immediately, Susanna and the twins began teaching Phillis to read and speak the language. They introduced her to other subjects as well. They quickly found that Phillis had an astonishing talent for learning. Within sixteen months, she mastered English. The family marveled at her ability. It seemed a miracle. The tiny girl, less than two years out of Africa, could read the Bible. She studied geography, history, and astronomy. She recited the poetry of John Milton. She not only read but translated Latin and Greek tales. Soon she was even writing poetry in the style of her favorite poet, Alexander Pope.

Phillis had a special position in the Wheatley family, quite different from that of their other slaves. She was not required to do heavy labor. Her chores were more delicate. She attended Susanna Wheatley and helped with light housecleaning. Furthermore, she had a room of her own in the house. The other slaves slept in the carriage house behind the mansion. Phillis ate with the family, except when there were dinner guests. Then she served the guests.

One evening, when Phillis was about fourteen years old, she served dinner to the Wheatley family and some guests. Two of the guests told a frightening tale of how they were nearly shipwrecked during a terrible storm. They narrowly escaped being cast away in the winds and rains. Phillis, lifting platters and removing plates, listened to the story. The tale went around and around in her head. As soon as her chores were done, she wrote a poem about it. The Wheatleys were very impressed with Phillis's poem. They helped her publish it. For the first time, Phillis saw her poetry in print. It was in the December 21, 1767 issue of the Newport, Rhode Island *Mercury*.

Most of Phillis's poetry marked special events. One February night, in 1770, a mob of colonial sympathizers gathered in front of the home of a Loyalist named Richardson. Loyalists were people who were loyal to the British king. Richardson, reacting with fear, ran out of his house. Armed with a gun, he fired into the mob. Christopher Snider, the young son of a poor colonist, was killed. Phillis wrote "On the Death of Mr. Snider Murder'd by Richardson." She called the boy the first martyr of the American Revolution. A few weeks later another angry mob gathered on King Street, not far from the Wheatley house. This time armed British troops came to restore order. The soldiers shot into the mob, killing five people. Phillis wrote "On the Affray in King-Street, on the Evening of the 4th of March." The event became known as the Boston Massacre.

Phillis also wrote poetry about God. She held deeply religious feelings that were encouraged by the Wheatleys. The Wheatleys and many other Bostonians were Puritans. One day Phillis went to hear a British evangelist, George Whitefield. The popular Whitefield preached throughout the American colonies, stirring people wherever he went—including Phillis. On October 2, 1770, George Whitefield died unexpectedly. Phillis was so moved that she wrote a poem, "On the Death of Rev. George Whitefield." She wrote a letter to his British patron, the Countess of Huntingdon, and enclosed the poem.

The Countess of Huntingdon was a patron of religious causes. In addition, she was very interested in the abolition of slavery. She became a friend and patron of Phillis. In 1771, the Countess had Phillis's poem about Whitefield published in London. Phillis gained an international reputation.

In August 1771, Phillis was baptized and accepted into the Wheatley family church, the Old South Meeting House. Few Africans were admitted into this church, and her acceptance there shows her special status in Boston. Through her friendships and visits with the Wheatleys' friends, including many prominent people, Phillis developed poise and confidence.

By 1772, Phillis had written so many poems that Susanna Wheatley suggested publishing a book. In those days, publishers required advance sales. In February, 1772, Mrs. Wheatley began advertising in the local Boston newspapers for subscribers for the proposed book. There was no response. People in Boston were not interested. Disappointed, Phillis, with Susanna's help, decided to turn to the Countess of Huntingdon. The Countess contacted a London bookseller. Soon he was corresponding with Phillis. Yes, he was definitely interested in publishing a book of her poetry.

The publisher had only one concern. People might not believe that an 18-year-old black slave—and a girl, at that—had written the poems. In those days, many white people believed that black people were inferior beings and were incapable of cultural achievements. Therefore, the publisher requested a letter, written and signed by important people, guaranteeing that Phillis was the author. A group of prominent Bostonians was called together. They planned to meet with Phillis and give her an oral examination. Then they would decide whether or not to sign the letter.

In 1772, Phillis met with eighteen of Boston's most important citizens, including Thomas Hutchinson, governor of Massachusetts; John Hancock, later a signer of the Declaration of Independence; and the Rev. Mather Byles, a poet and nephew of the renowned minister, Cotton Mather. There is no record of what the men asked her. They may have had her recite Latin or Greek or explain some of her poems. Whatever happened in that room, the eighteen people agreed to write and sign the letter of guarantee confirming that Phillis, John Wheatley's slave, had written the poetry.

Throughout that year, Phillis suffered from chronic asthma. The family doctor was called. He examined Phillis and suggested that she needed a dose of sea air. John and Susanna Wheatley agreed with the prescription. They asked their son, Nathaniel, to accompany Phillis on a voyage across the ocean.

On May 8, 1773, Phillis and Nathaniel sailed for London. More than a month later—on June 17—Phillis reached London. The Countess welcomed her. In fact, Phillis became the toast of London society. This was the high point of her life. She met and charmed everyone. She was the guest at banquets and received many gifts. The future Lord Mayor of London gave her a rare edition of Milton's *Paradise Lost*. The Earl of Dartmouth, the secretary of state for the American colonies, gave her a leather-bound copy of *Don Quixote*. She met Benjamin Franklin, who was in London representing colonial interests. Most important, she completed arrangements for the publication of her book.

Phillis was invited to be presented at court. The Countess urged her to accept the invitation. Just as she was agreeing, Nathaniel arrived with troubling news. Mrs. Wheatley was extremely ill in Boston. Phillis knew she must return home, to her owner. After six weeks in England, Phillis returned to Boston and regretfully missed her chance to meet the king. She sailed from England on July 26, 1773. Days later, her book of poetry appeared in London bookshops. *Poems on Various Subjects, Religious and Moral* was dedicated to the Countess of Huntingdon. Inside, on the first page, there was the letter of guarantee from the eighteen men of Boston.

Susanna lay gravely ill when Phillis returned. In October, as a final gesture toward Phillis, Susanna freed her. Phillis wrote letters to friends informing them that she was no longer a slave. On March 3, 1774, Susanna Wheatley died. Phillis was filled with sorrow. Although she had been a slave, she had enjoyed the protection and kindness of Susanna Wheatley. Thanks to the whole Wheatley family, Phillis had not endured the difficulties and suffering common to most black Americans at that time.

Phillis continued to live in the Wheatley house. Things were not the same, however. Nathaniel, loyal to the British, moved permanently to England. Mary was busy raising a family. In 1771, Mary had married John Lathrop, a minister. Soon after Susanna died, they moved into the Wheatley house on King Street.

Phillis began to write patriotic poems. In 1775, she wrote a poem to General George Washington. Phillis mailed it to him along with a letter. Washington was so pleased that he invited Phillis to visit him at his headquarters in Cambridge. She accepted the invitation.

At the beginning of 1778, John Wheatley died. Just a few weeks later, Mary also died. The break with the Wheatley family was now total. Phillis, left a legacy by John Wheatley, moved into a smaller house. At first her intention was to live alone. That plan soon changed. On April 1, 1778—one month after Mary's death—Phillis married John Peters, a free black man. Between 1779 and 1783, they had three children.

John Peters was described as very handsome, a fine writer, and excellent speaker. He dressed fashionably, wore a white wig, and carried a cane. He may have been a victim of racial injustice, or he may have been a scoundrel. He charmed Phillis as he had charmed many others. He claimed, without truth, to be a lawyer, a doctor, a barber, a baker, and a merchant. When Phillis married him, Peters began a small grocery business. That soon failed. His debts mounted. He used Phillis's money to pay them. Then he went into debt again and disappeared. Struggling to support herself and the children, Phillis took on jobs cleaning the houses for the wealthy families in Boston. She tried in vain to publish a second volume of poems.

When her husband reappeared, Phillis moved with him into a rundown apartment in a Boston slum. Again he left. Phillis became a scrub woman in a cheap lodging house. She fell ill. The hard work wore her down. The children were also ill, and two of them died.

On December 5, 1784, Phillis Wheatley and her remaining infant died. John Peters was in debtors prison. When her white friends found out what had happened, they were too late to give Phillis a proper burial. She had already been buried in an unmarked grave. She died alone, poor, and almost forgotten. She was only thirty-one years old.

For fifty years, there was little interest in the life and work of Phillis Wheatley. Then in 1834, a distant relative of the Wheatleys reminded readers about Phillis Wheatley. Margaretta M. Odell, an abolitionist, published a new edition of Phillis's poetry and a memoir about her life. Since then, many people have discovered Phillis Wheatley's poetry for themselves.

Directions: On a separate sheet of paper, answer the following questions about Phillis Wheatley.

1. What did the Wheatleys' attitude toward slavery seem to be, and how did this attitude affect Phillis Wheatley? Explain your answer.

2. Why was it fitting for an abolitionist to publish a book of Wheatley's poetry? Explain your answer.

BENJAMIN FRANKLIN

Statesman, scientist, inventor and author; born in Boston in 1706 and died in Philadelphia in 1790

Ben Franklin grew up near the Boston Harbor, a busy port in 1718. As a young boy, Ben watched the tall ships arrive from England and Holland. He watched sailors load and unload cargo, climb masts, and hoist sails. Ben Franklin wanted to visit faraway places. He wanted to go to sea.

"Absolutely not!" Ben's father would not allow it. He had already lost one son to the sea. Josiah Franklin would find a safer occupation for his youngest son. Twelve-year-old Ben knew one thing for sure. He did not want to make candles and soap like his father did. The smells were terrible and the fumes hurt his eyes. For the past two years he had worked for his father and that was enough. He wanted to make a change. His father agreed. He would help Ben find a suitable trade.

Ben Franklin was the fifteenth child in a family of seventeen children. His mother was from Nantucket Island, off the coast of Massachusetts. His father came to America from England to find religious freedom. He was a Congregationalist, a kind of Protestant. When Ben was very young, Josiah Franklin hoped his son would become a minister. With that in mind, he enrolled Ben in school at the age of eight. However, he withdrew him two years later. Money was in short supply. Besides, Josiah noticed that most of the ministers he knew were poor. Instead, he decided to train Ben for a practical trade.

Josiah Franklin knew that Ben loved to read. Long before he went to school, Ben taught himself to read. Later, he taught himself several foreign languages, history, geography, and the sciences of electricity, botany, and oceanography. Josiah decided that this son who loved books so much should learn to make them. In those days, boys learned trades by becoming apprentices to someone in the field. Josiah Franklin persuaded Ben to become the apprentice of one of his older brothers, a printer. James Franklin would teach Ben how to set type and run the printing presses. At the age of twelve, Ben Franklin signed a contract to work as apprentice to his brother until Ben was twenty-one years old.

Ben worked hard. He saved money by eating less, and then he used the money to buy books. He enjoyed learning the printer's trade. James started publishing the *New-England Courant*, a weekly newspaper. On the sly, Ben began writing humorous articles for the *Courant* that poked fun at life in New England. Ben did not use his own name. Instead he pretended the articles were by a make-believe widow, Silence Dogood. One by one, Ben slipped the Silence Dogood articles under the print-shop door. James found them and printed them. Readers loved the Silence Dogood articles. Many people bought the *Courant* just to read Silence Dogood. One day, James found out that Silence Dogood was really young Ben. He angrily refused to publish any more articles by Silence Dogood.

Ben and James argued about many things. Ben did not like working for his brother. He wanted to have his own print shop. He asked James to release him from the contract. "Never!" James refused. Ben's thoughts returned to the sea. He decided to run away.

When he was seventeen years old, Ben sold some of his books and secretly bought passage on a ship headed for New York. In New York, Ben could not find work. At the time, New York was a small town, much smaller than Boston. Someone suggested that he try the big city of Philadelphia. Ben boarded a ship for Philadelphia. When the boat got stuck in New Jersey, the impatient youth jumped ship and walked the remaining fifty miles. He arrived in Philadelphia nearly penniless, and very tired, hungry, and dirty. He felt poor, but he felt free.

Soon after Ben arrived in Philadelphia, he found a job in a print shop. Not long after, he had his own printing presses and newspaper, the *Pennsylvania Gazette*. In 1733, he decided to publish a book of weather information and household hints. He included many witty sayings about thrift and common sense. He called the book *Poor Richard's Almanack*. It became an immediate best-seller. The next year, Ben published a new edition of *Poor Richard's Almanack*. Then he published another and another. A new almanac appeared each year for twenty five years. Many of the sayings in *Poor Richard's Almanack* are still repeated today. Here are some examples: "A penny saved is a penny earned." "Never leave that till tomorrow which you can do today." "Honesty is the best policy."

Ben's first landlady in Philadelphia was Mrs. Read. After Ben settled into his printing business, he married Mrs. Read's daughter, Deborah. Ben and Deborah had two sons and a daughter. They grieved deeply when one of their sons, Francis, died from smallpox at the age of four.

With his success as a printer, Ben turned his attention to improving his city. He helped establish the first lending library in the colonies and he organized the first fire department. He worked to improve street lighting and street cleaning. Soon Philadelphia was the safest, cleanest city in the colonies. Philadelphia had no hospital. Ben raised money to build one. The city had no college. Ben helped establish the school that later became the University of Pennsylvania.

Ben thought the mail deliveries were too slow. He agreed to serve as postmaster of Philadelphia. His improvements were so great that he became deputy postmaster general for all the colonies. He established the first dead-letter office. He speeded delivery overseas and throughout the colonies.

When Ben was about forty years old, he started working with the new science of electricity. A few scientists had discovered how to create electrical shocks. They entertained people by showing off electrical charges that looked like giant spiders and made zapping noises. Electrical experiments and tricks were very dangerous. Some scientists were killed in the process.

Ben Franklin read everything he could find about electricity. He corresponded with scientists in Europe, asking questions and giving his ideas. He experimented with electrical shocks. He became convinced that lightning was a form of electricity. He decided to prove it. One day in 1752, Ben took a kite with a pointed wire. The kite had a cotton string. On the end of the string, Ben tied a metal key and a piece of silk. He knew that electricity would go through cotton but would stop at silk. He flew the kite in a thunderstorm. When he saw a bolt of lightning, Ben touched the key and felt a mild shock. That is how he proved that lightning is electricity. It is a good thing that the shock was mild. Otherwise, Ben might have been killed.

After Ben proved that lightning is electricity, he did something practical about it. He invented the lightning rod. He put one on top of his own house. Not long after, his house was saved when lightning struck the rod and not the house. Suddenly, lightning rods became very popular throughout the colonies.

Ben Franklin also invented bifocals and the Franklin stove, both in use today. The Franklin stove is a furnace that is designed to give people a safe, efficient way to heat their homes. He also designed double-duty furniture: a chair-table and a chair-step ladder. He introduced turnips and rhubarb into America. His experiments with color proved that wearing white in hot weather will keep a person cooler than wearing black. Ben was the first scientist to study the movement of the Gulf Stream in the Atlantic Ocean. While traveling across the ocean to and from diplomatic assignments, he charted courses and recorded ocean temperatures and depths. He found safer routes for ships to follow.

There were many other inventions and experiments. Ben never patented a single one. He said he wanted people to enjoy what he had invented. He wanted people to use them freely. His inventions were his contribution to everybody's well-being.

In addition to his other important contributions to America, Ben Franklin played an important role in the American Revolution. He spent sixteen years in England trying to work for the colonies and against war. When he realized that war could not be prevented, he left England and sailed to America to join in the fight for independence.

Ben returned to Philadelphia in 1775. It was a bad time in his life, filled with sorrows and failure. Despite years of work, he had not been able to prevent war. His wife had died while he was in England. His son, William, his only surviving son, decided to support the British in the war. This was the worst disappointment of all. Ben had felt very close to William. He was proud when William became colonial governor of New Jersey. Now he and his son suffered a break that would never fully mend.

Upon his return to Philadelphia, Ben found representatives from the colonies meeting there. They invited Ben to represent Pennsylvania at the Continental Congress. They asked a Virginia planter, Thomas Jefferson, to write a declaration of American independence from Great Britain. Jefferson asked Ben to suggest ways to improve the Declaration of Independence. Jefferson had written, "We hold these truths to be *sacred and undeniable*. . . ." Ben suggested changing the words to "We hold these truths to be *self evident*. . . ." Then Ben and the other delegates signed the Declaration.

Soon after the Declaration was signed, Ben returned to Europe. This time he went to France, where he successfully sought money and support for the American cause. He spent the rest of the war in

France. After the war, he was a signer of the peace treaty with Great Britain and, four years later, the Constitution of the United States. At the age of eighty-one, Ben became president of the Pennsylvania Society for the Abolition of Slavery.

During the last years of his life, Ben lived in Philadelphia in a large house with his daughter Sally and her family. He loved children, especially his grandchildren. Every day during his final illness, his granddaughter Debbie came to his bedside to recite her lessons.

Benjamin Franklin died on April 17, 1790. He was buried next to his wife in Christ Church Burial Ground in Philadelphia. People still visit Ben's grave. When they are in Philadelphia, they can go to see the hall where he and the others met to sign the Declaration of Independence and the Constitution. They can travel down Benjamin Franklin Parkway to the Franklin Institute. There they will see the nation's memorial to this great American.

Directions: On a separate sheet of paper, answer the following questions about Benjamin Franklin.

1. What do the sayings in *Poor Richard's Almanack* tell you about Benjamin Franklin? Explain your answer.
2. Some people think Benjamin Franklin was the greatest American who ever lived. Why do you think they feel that way? Explain your answer.

TECUMSEH

Shawnee war chief; born in Ohio in 1766 and died in Canada in 1813

In a forest in western Ohio, ten-year-old Chiksika (chihk SEE kuh) waited patiently with his father, Puckeshina (puhk uh SHEEN uh), in their wigwam. They lived in a Shawnee village on the Mad River, near where the city of Springfield, Ohio, stands today. Growing restless, Puckeshina walked outside, and Chiksika followed him. Puckeshina was an important Shawnee war chief. As the man and boy stood looking into the clear, starry sky, a glowing meteor swept across the sky. Their eyes were still dazzled by the light when they heard the cry of a newborn baby. The little boy born that night in 1768 to Puckeshina's wife was named Tecumseh (tuh CUHM suh), which means "Shooting Star." He was to grow up and become a great warrior and war chief. He would almost stop the westward expansion of the United States.

Tecumseh grew up during a time when there was almost constant war between the Shawnees and the American settlers. The white settlers pushed steadily westward, carving farms and homes out of the forests. The Indian tribes struggled to keep their homes and hunting lands.

When Tecumseh was six years old, his father was killed in a battle with the Virginians. Chiksika took over his young brother's training and taught Tecumseh the things a Shawnee warrior needed to know. He took the young boy on long hunting trips. Once the brothers went into western Kentucky, where there were still a few of the buffalo that had filled the forests and plains before the white settlers came. Tecumseh was excited by the hunt and raced joyfully after a fleeing buffalo. Suddenly, his horse tripped, throwing Tecumseh to the ground and breaking the boy's leg. Chiksika was able to set the broken leg, and he and Tecumseh remained where they were for several months so that the leg could heal.

During his childhood, Tecumseh had several white companions. The Shawnees sometimes captured children during raids on farms and settlements and brought them back to the villages. The captive children were brought up with the Indian children. One of these captive children was Stephen Ruddell, who was a close friend of Tecumseh. After he grew up, Stephen wrote about his life among the Shawnees and included details of Tecumseh's childhood.

Chiksika took Tecumseh on his first war party when Tecumseh was about fifteen years old. It was not a large battle, but the fighting was fierce. Chiksika was slightly wounded in the first burst of gunfire, and Tecumseh was so shocked by the blood and the noise that he panicked and ran into the forest. Though he later returned to the battle, he felt shamed by his flight.

A few months later, Tecumseh went with a small war party that ambushed American flatboats carrying settlers and supplies down the Ohio River into Kentucky. This time he proved himself to be one of the most courageous warriors in the party. He gained the respect of even the oldest and bravest warriors. He also made a decision that was to gain him the respect of his enemies as well. At that time, people who were captured by either side were often cruelly tortured to death. During the attack on the flatboats, the Indians had captured a member of the crew and forced him to go with them. After marching several miles, the Indians stopped, made a fire, and burned their prisoner to death. Though Tecumseh did not do anything to save that man, he decided that he would never again allow a prisoner to be killed if he could do anything to prevent it. He became known to the settlers as a man who showed compassion to captives. He persuaded many other Indians to follow his example.

When Tecumseh was about twenty years old, Chiksika led an attack on Buchanan's Station in Tennessee. During the fighting, Chiksika was wounded so badly that he soon died. Tecumseh took over leadership of the small raiding party, and when the warriors returned to Ohio two years later, Tecumseh was a war chief.

In the colonies, the American Revolution was over and the Americans had won their freedom from Great Britain. However, British soldiers remained in Canada and gave supplies and gifts to tribes who continued to fight the westward-moving Americans. The Shawnees saw the Americans as a continued threat to their homes, but they thought that the British would not take any more of their hunting lands. Tecumseh helped the British fight the Americans.

In August 1794, an American force of more than 3,000 men prepared to attack an Indian army of about twelve hundred warriors who came from many different tribes. The Indians had taken a stand at a place near present-day Toledo, Ohio. A storm had blown over many trees along the river, and the Indians hid among the fallen trees. There they waited for the British to join them. However, three things happened to turn the battle into a disaster for the Indians. The British stopped to build a small fort and did not arrive when they were expected. The Americans began to march sooner than the Indians had thought they would. Finally, a severe thunderstorm with heavy rain struck in the night and many of the Indians left their positions to take shelter in a nearby Indian village. When the Americans attacked, there were fewer than 400 Indian warriors and no British soldiers. The greatly outnumbered Indians were soon defeated. Tecumseh and his companions escaped, but one of Tecumseh's brothers was killed. This battle, the Battle of Fallen Timbers, was a turning point for Tecumseh and for all of the Indian tribes.

Tecumseh refused to acknowledge the Treaty of Greenville, which some of the tribes agreed to after the Battle of Fallen Timbers. In the Treaty of Greenville, the Indians agreed to give up some of their land. Tecumseh believed that no tribe had the right to give up land.

No tribe owned the land. The Shawnees believed that the land, like the air, was for all people to use.

At twenty-seven, Tecumseh had little power in the politics of the tribes, but his influence as a war chief was growing. Many of the young warriors followed his example. He continued to practice compassion toward captives, and people knew that he always spoke the truth. He was a powerful speaker and could sway people to believe as he did.

Following the Battle of Fallen Timbers, Tecumseh and a small band of warriors went to live in the Indiana Territory. Tecumseh's younger brother lived with the small band. He was not popular, and he was often drunk. He tried to be a medicine man, but no one had any confidence in his medicine. Then one night in 1805, he fell into a trance so deep that he appeared to be dead. After several hours he awakened to find his wife preparing to bury him. He claimed that he had been taken to the spirit world. There the Master of Life told him that if the Shawnees were to regain their land, they must give up drinking whiskey and return to the way of life they had lived before the white settlers came. He became known as Tenskwatawa (Tehns KWAHT uh wuh), which means "Open Door," and was commonly called "the Shawnee Prophet."

Tecumseh and the Shawnee Prophet moved back to Indiana Territory and built a new town, Prophetstown, on the Wabash River near the Tippecanoe River. Here, there was still game in the forest and fish in the river. It was easier to feed the people who came to hear the Shawnee Prophet. The people came—and they kept coming. Tecumseh had a plan to unite the Indian tribes into a single nation much as the United States had formed a nation from a group of colonies. He realized that this was the only hope the Indians had of keeping their land.

In 1811, while Tecumseh was visiting tribes in the south, William Henry Harrison, then the governor of the Indiana Territory, marched against Prophetstown with an army of about one thousand men. Though Tecumseh had told Tenskwatawa not to fight, the Shawnee Prophet decided to attack. He assured the warriors that the American bullets would turn to water and not harm them. The Indians attacked at about 4:00 A.M. on November 7. Two hours later, Tecumseh's plans and his careful work of twenty years lay in ruins.

As Tecumseh turned homeward, the earth shook as if in sorrow. The earthquakes continued for several days. Rivers changed their courses and entire forests fell. It was one of the worst earthquakes ever recorded. In Prophetstown, Tecumseh found that the tribes had scattered and the town and supplies had been burned. He turned on Tenskwatawa, grabbed him by the hair, and shook him until the Shawnee Prophet fell screaming to his knees.

Tecumseh set to work to rebuild his confederacy. Those who joined him fought with the British in the War of 1812 between Great Britain and the United States. The United States finally defeated the British and the Indians on October 5, 1813. Tecumseh was killed near Ontario, Canada, as he fought in the final battle of that war, the Battle of the Thames. He was forty-four years old. The Indians east of the Mississippi had been defeated.

Tecumseh's plan to unite the Indian tribes and prevent the loss of their homes and hunting lands had failed. Twice, however, he came very close to establishing his dream of a united Indian nation. Each time, he failed largely due to factors beyond his control. He lives in American history as a brave and honest man, one who was trusted by the white settlers as well as by the Indians. His memory flames as brightly today as the meteor that glowed in the sky on the night of his birth.

Directions: On a separate sheet of paper, answer the following questions about Tecumseh.

1. Why do you think Tecumseh and his tribe sided with European countries and against the United States both in the American Revolution and in the War of 1812? Explain your answer.

2. How might American history have been different if Tecumseh had been able to make his dream come true?

DANIEL BOONE

Explorer, settler, hunter, trapper, and militiaman; born in 1734 in Pennsylvania and died in Missouri in 1820

On November 2, 1734, when Daniel Boone was born, the United States did not exist. Daniel was born near Reading, Pennsylvania. Pennsylvania was one of thirteen American colonies that belonged to Great Britain. To the west were strange lands where few English-speaking white people had ever journeyed. These areas were controlled by tribes of American Indians. The British and their American colonists often fought the Indians on whose land they were settling.

Eastern Pennsylvania, where Daniel spent his childhood, had been settled years before by the Quakers. Daniel's family, like all Quakers, believed in being peaceful and friendly to all people. Squire Boone, Daniel's father, was a farmer and a blacksmith. Although Daniel helped him plant crops and shoe horses, it was at hunting that Daniel excelled. The time he spent in the woods was the most enjoyable for the young boy. Often, he would leave his chores undone or be late for dinner. Normally, his parents did not get angry at him for this, because Daniel usually returned from his hunting trips with plenty of fresh meat.

When Daniel was sixteen years old, his family left Pennsylvania and headed south for the Yadkin Valley of North Carolina. Squire Boone had tired of eastern Pennsylvania because more and more people were settling in the area. As a result, the amount of game had dwindled. This dislike of living in an overpopulated area was shared by both father and son. Years later, whenever Daniel moved from a settlement to the wilderness, he did so because he wanted more "elbow room."

Soon after settling in his new home, Daniel joined the North Carolina militia to fight in the French and Indian War. These volunteer soldiers became part of a much larger army under the command of the British general, Edward Braddock. Braddock's mission was to capture the French Ft. Duquesne (now Pittsburgh) in western Pennsylvania.

Not far from Ft. Duquesne, Braddock's army was ambushed by a force of French soldiers and Indians. As the battle developed, it became clear that the British and colonial troops were losing badly. General Braddock had been killed. His men knew that if they surrendered, they would be tortured and killed by their enemies. As a result, most of the survivors ran for their lives. Daniel, whose job it was to drive a wagon, was in the rear, away from the fighting. When it became clear that the battle was lost, he unhitched a horse from the wagon. He mounted the horse and rode away to safety.

Upon his return to the Yadkin Valley, Daniel married seventeen-year-old Rebecca Bryan. For fourteen years, he, Rebecca, and their children lived in the valley in peace. Then, one day, John Finley appeared at their door.

Finley was a hunter and trapper whom Daniel had met during the war. On their way to Ft. Duquesne, Finley had told Daniel stories about Kentucky. The land there was largely unpopulated. Herds of wild animals roamed freely over the green mountains, through the dense forests, and in the fertile valleys. Daniel was entranced. Now that the war was over and France defeated, Kentucky was even more appealing to Boone. He decided that he would lead a hunting party there in the spring.

On May 1, 1769, Boone and five others set out for Kentucky. They crossed the Appalachian Mountains at Cumberland Gap and found themselves in Kentucky. When they arrived, they built a cabin.

For seven months, Daniel and his company hunted and trapped. Kentucky was everything Finley had said it would be. Not only was it beautiful, but it contained the greatest amount and variety of game Daniel had ever seen.

Unfortunately for Daniel, this paradise had long ago been discovered by two Indian tribes: the Shawnees and the Cherokees. On December 22, 1769, Shawnee tribesmen captured Daniel and his brother-in-law, John Stuart. They stole the white men's valuables and warned them never to come back. Most of Boone's party returned to North Carolina, but Stuart and Daniel remained. Not long after, Stuart disappeared, never to be found again. Boone remained for a full year more before going back to the Yadkin Valley.

Four years later, Daniel returned to Kentucky. This time his family and other families from the Yadkin Valley were with him. They were going to make Kentucky their permanent home. Not long into the journey, however, Daniel realized that they were short of some supplies. He sent his sixteen-year-old son James and three others back to North Carolina to get more supplies. On their return trip, the group was ambushed and slaughtered by a band of Cherokees. Frightened by this incident, many of the families returned to the Yadkin Valley.

Over the next few years, Daniel and a large company of men worked on building the Wilderness Trail. This would make the journey from the states east of Kentucky less difficult for settlers. The work was very hard. Thousands of trees had to be cut down. Underbrush needed to be cleared. In addition, the men had to be constantly on their guard for any sign that Indians were nearby. In the spring of 1775, the Wilderness Trail was completed.

That same year, the American Revolution began. The British enlisted the Indians to help fight against the Colonists. Fear of their enemies did not stop settlers from journeying to Kentucky, however. By 1776, the settlement of Boonesborough had been established. Daniel's family and many others lived in Boonesborough.

On Sunday, July 7, Boone's daughter Jemima and two of her friends were canoeing in a nearby river. Without warning, five Shawnee warriors appeared beside their craft. The girls were pulled from the canoe and taken prisoner. On the first day, the Shawnees marched the girls thirty-five miles. Along the way, Jemima and her friends left markers for their rescuers to follow. They dug their heels into the ground, broke twigs, and dropped bits of their dresses as signs. As a result, it was not difficult for Daniel and his search party to follow their trail.

On the second evening, Boone's men discovered the Shawnees' camp. The rescuers knew that if they were heard, the Shawnees would kill the girls immediately. They raised their muskets, took careful aim, and fired. Two of the Indians were killed, and the others fled into the woods. The girls were unharmed.

Two years later, the Shawnees captured Daniel. One snowy day, while Daniel was checking his beaver traps, a band of Shawnees surprised him. The Indians immediately recognized their captive. Bringing such a famous prisoner back to their tribe would make them heroes to their people. Daniel pretended he was happy to see them. He found out from them that their tribe was about to attack Boonesborough.

In return for his life, Daniel had to tell the Shawnees where the rest of his men were. He said he would do so only if the Indians promised not to kill or torture them. If the Shawnees kept their promise, in the spring, Daniel would help them capture Boonesborough. He convinced them that they would have a better chance of success once the snow had melted. The Shawnees agreed.

Daniel had no intention of betraying his people. He was trying to stall for time. In the spring, Boonesborough would be prepared better to withstand an enemy attack. Also, Boone was smart enough to realize that he must appear friendly and agreeable. Otherwise, the Shawnees would kill him and his men.

The braves led the white men out of Kentucky and into Ohio. There Boone was adopted by Chief Blackfish. For four months, Daniel lived happily (or so it seemed) among the Shawnee. He now looked, dressed, and even acted like a member of the tribe. All this time, Boone waited for his chance to escape.

It came on June 16, 1778. That day, Daniel and a number of braves were at a salt spring making salt. As usual, Daniel was being watched by at least one member of the tribe. Without warning, a flock of wild turkeys flew into the sky above the Shawnees. This drew the guard's attention away from Daniel, giving him just enough time to make his getaway.

For the next four days, the 44-year-old Daniel Boone ran as fast as he could. He raced through forests, over hills, and across streams. Daniel had to warn the people of Boonesborough of the coming attack. The settlement would need as much time as possible to prepare for it. By the end of the fourth day, Boone had covered 160 miles. When he arrived at the gates of the settlement, he was exhausted, but he had made it.

When the attack came, Boonesborough was ready. Heavily outnumbered, the defenders fought bravely and successfully for ten days. On the eleventh day, the Shawnees left. Boonesborough was saved.

Other encounters with hostile Indians did not end so happily for Daniel. On a hunting trip with his brother Edward, Boone shot a bear. Leaving Edward alone, Daniel chased the animal into the woods. While he was making sure the bear was dead, Boone heard gunshots. He guessed that his brother was being attacked by a band of warriors. There was nothing he could do. He returned the next day and discovered his brother's body.

After the American Revolution ended in 1783, raids by the Shawnee Indians and other tribes lessened. It was not until many years later, however, that Kentucky was completely safe from attack.

During the revolution, Boone had grown tired of Boonesborough. Not only had it become crowded, but something had happened which had further disillusioned Daniel with the community. After his escape from the Shawnees and the siege of Boonesborough, Daniel had been put on trial. Some of his neighbors believed that he had betrayed his people by becoming a Shawnee. Even though he was found innocent, his neighbors' lack of trust in him hurt deeply. As a result, in 1779, he found the settlement of Boone's Station, Kentucky. Before long, his family and many others were living there.

As more and more settlers came to Kentucky, Daniel became more and more discontented. Also, he never had filed a legal claim for any of his property. Other settlers came along, filed the necessary papers, and took Boone's land from him. Angered and hurt, Daniel decided to leave Kentucky. In 1799, with his family and some friends, he set off for Missouri.

When he arrived at St. Louis that fall, he was greeted by the Spanish governor. Daniel's fame had spread west, so the Spanish treated him with great respect. They also gave him a large tract of land on which to settle. Boone even became a Spanish official. His duties included being judge, financial and land administrator, and military leader for his district. However, all of that ended when the Spanish left Missouri, and the land became the property of the United States. Once again, Daniel did not have legal claim to his property. Again he lost it.

During the War of 1812, Daniel tried to enlist in the militia. Why he was rejected due to age—he was only seventy-eight—Boone could not understand. He knew that he was still stronger and swifter than many men half his age.

Rebecca Boone died in 1813. After that, Daniel moved in with one of his children. He spent the last seven years of his life hunting, trapping, and exploring. It is known that he traveled as far as Kansas City. Some people said that he even reached the Rocky Mountains.

On September 26, 1820, Daniel Boone died. He was eighty-six years old. Twenty-five years later, his and Rebecca's bodies were returned to Kentucky for honorary burial. The country had finally begun to appreciate one of its greatest heroes.

Directions: On a separate sheet of paper, answer the following questions about Daniel Boone.

1. Daniel Boone was captured by the Shawnees a number of times. Why did they consider it an honor to capture Boone?

2. Daniel Boone made great sacrifices to be able to live on the frontier. How did his sacrifices contribute to the westward expansion of the United States?

NOAH WEBSTER

Author of an American dictionary, the *Blue-Backed Speller,* and high school textbooks; born in Connecticut in 1758 and died there in 1843

It was an evening in the 1840s in the Indiana countryside. The members of a whole farming community, young and old, were gathered in the schoolhouse for a social evening. Mothers were setting out pies and cakes. Young couples were holding hands in the corners. There was no fiddler tuning up for square dancing, however. Every one was getting ready for another kind of social evening—a spelling bee. Two teams lined up on opposite sides of the room. The county judge prepared to give out the words and decide the points for each side. In his hand he held a copy of Webster's *Blue-Backed Speller*. This famous spelling book had been used in that Indiana county for two generations. The grandparents had used it back in New England before they came to Indiana as pioneers.

The spelling bee began. At first, only a few were eliminated on either side. Then the judge came to the long, hard words at the back of Webster's speller. People from both teams dropped out as they tried to spell words such as atrocious, theodolite, and incomprehensibility. Finally, only two people remained: the new young schoolmaster and an intelligent young woman named Hannah. She was an excellent speller and had proved to be quite a match for the schoolmaster. The judge gave the schoolmaster the next word: daguerrotype. After thinking a moment, the schoolmaster began to spell the word. Unfortunately for him, he misspelled it. Hannah was declared the winner, and refreshments were served. This spelling bee was described in a famous novel, *The Hoosier Schoolmaster,* by Edward Eggleston. Many of the people who read this novel learned to spell from the *Blue-Backed Speller* compiled by Noah Webster in 1782.

Noah Webster was a farm boy from West Hartford, Connecticut. He did very well in the country school he attended, and his father borrowed money to send him to college. Noah attended Yale College in New Haven, Connecticut. The Revolutionary War broke out when he was still a freshman, and Noah and other students at Yale College enlisted as soldiers.

In 1777, Noah returned to college. He graduated in 1778 and then studied law for a year. Before he could practice law, however, he needed to rent an office and buy law books. Times were so hard after the Revolution that Noah's father could only give him eight Continental dollars. Noah could not set up a law practice with this. Instead, he devoted his talents to teaching.

There were children of all ages in the school where Webster taught. The only textbooks he had were the Bible, a booklet published in England containing lists of very hard spelling words and names of English kings and cities, and the *New England Primer* for teaching the alphabet. The primer taught the alphabet by using rhymes. Unfortunately, the rhymes were uninteresting to young children. For example, for the letter A, the primer said "In Adam's Fall We sinned all." Webster wrote a happier primer for his students. It began "A was an Apple-pie made by the cook, B was a Boy that was fond of his book." Webster was sure that his students would learn the alphabet better from apple pie than from Adam.

Noah Webster did not like the booklet of English spelling words either. It was so expensive that there was only one copy for the entire school. The United States was now independent, and Webster thought that his students should learn to spell the names of American leaders and American places. He decided to write a spelling book of words most commonly used in the United States.

Webster worked hard and finally produced three books. The first book was the new speller with rules for pronunciation. He included sentences that showed how the words were used. These sentences mentioned events from America's recent history, as well as things that children knew about from their own lives. The second was a new grammar book, and the third book was a reader. Noah arranged with a printer to prepare several thousand copies of the three little books. He arranged to sell each book for fourteen cents—so cheaply that every child could have one. Then each child could study alone. Webster would receive a payment, or royalty, of one cent for each copy sold. When the books went on sale, so many people bought them that Webster thought he could soon quit teaching and live on the royalties. Unfortunately, the idea of the speller was so good that other printers began to copy the book and sell it under another name. This happened before there was a federal copyright law to keep people from copying an author's work and selling it. Noah Webster went from state to state asking each legislature to pass a law protecting his right to the royalties on his spelling book.

While traveling in Philadelphia, Pennsylvania, Webster visited Benjamin Franklin. This wise old man had just returned after spending several years in England and was full of ideas on how to make the United States completely independent of England. English was a very difficult language to spell. Why shouldn't the United States have a new, easier way to spell English? Franklin and Webster became good friends and decided to work together on a new alphabet. The letters C and Q would be abolished, and the letters S and K would be used instead. For example, *quick* would be spelled *kwik*. In this new method of spelling, the two reformers dropped the silent E at the end of words such as *give, have, live,* and *shone*. These words would be spelled simply *giv, hav, liv,* and *shon*. They drew up many other rules, and finally they wrote an article using the new spelling. When the article appeared in a Philadelphia newspaper, readers thought it was a joke. Benjamin Franklin must have brought this back from Europe to amuse us, they said.

Noah Webster went on to make other attempts to simplify English spelling, but most of them were unsuccessful. However, he was able to change words such as *publick, musick, traffick,* and *centre* to *public, music, traffic,* and *center*.

On a trip to Philadelphia, Noah met a beautiful young girl named Rebecca Greenleaf. She lived in Boston and was visiting friends in Philadelphia. At first, Webster referred to her as "the agreeable Miss Greenleaf." Then he wrote of her as "the sweet Miss Greenleaf." Later, he called her "the lovely Becca." Noah Webster married Rebecca Greenleaf in 1789 and took her to Hartford, Connecticut, near the village of his birth. There he planned to practice law. His wife bought fine furniture and linens, draperies, and rugs such as her family had in Boston, while Noah struggled to pay for them.

The United States had a strong government by this time. The new Congress passed laws protecting authors' copyrights. People could no longer print and sell illegal copies of Webster's speller. Noah revised it and added many more words. He filled his example sentences with facts about the Revolutionary War and the new government. Webster's spellers had heavy cardboard bindings covered with blue paper. The *Blue-Backed Speller* soon became famous. Other teachers wrote grammars and alphabet books that were as good as Webster's, but no one produced an easier and more complete method of learning spelling. The time finally came when Noah Webster could settle down and live on the royalties from his speller. He began to write about other things that interested him, such as the history of America.

Webster and his wife had six daughters and one son. During an epidemic of scarlet fever, all the Webster children fell ill. Although the children recovered, Webster was amazed that doctors knew so little about the disease. For a period of four years, he gave up his historical and patriotic writings and studied the cause of disease.

No one knew what caused the terrible scourge of yellow fever that killed one-tenth of the population in Philadelphia in 1793. Webster went to Philadelphia and talked to doctors and survivors. He searched through libraries in New York, Boston, and Philadelphia, reading anything that described epidemics. Of course, he did not find the cause since no one knew about the existence of bacteria. However, Webster did realize that epidemics were not caused by wickedness, the wrath of God, thunderstorms, or eclipses. He thought epidemics were caused by things such as filth, rotting garbage, and open sewers. Webster wrote a book about his theories on the causes of epidemics. No better book on the subject appeared for sixty years.

When the oldest Webster girl finished elementary school, there was no academy or high school that she could attend. Webster decided to start one, called the Union School. He found that there were no high school textbooks except Latin grammars, so he wrote a set of four textbooks. These were the first science and history textbooks ever written for high school students in America. The first two textbooks told the history of the United States, from the founding of Jamestown through the year 1789. The third book described the history and geography of Europe, Asia, and Africa. The fourth book was a simple biology textbook.

At about this time, Webster had a new idea. He would write a dictionary of the words of the English Language as they were used in the United States. A distinguished English scholar, Dr. Samuel Johnson, had written an enormous dictionary in London some fifty years earlier. Most educated people assumed that no new one would ever be necessary. Webster used Dr. Johnson's dictionary all the time in his own writing. However, he was not satisfied with it, because Dr. Johnson listed thousands of words that Americans never used. The words were marked for pronunciation according to the way people spoke in England. The people in the United States pronounced many of the words in quite a different way. What the new nation needed was its own dictionary.

Webster wanted to give the history of every word in his dictionary. He knew that the English language contained words from Latin, Greek, French, and German, as well as from the languages spoken by the ancient people of England, Scotland, and Ireland. Many English words came from other languages, too. He planned to trace every English word back to its origin.

With the help of his son and his unmarried daughters, Noah Webster began to collect the words of the English language. Each word went on a separate sheet of paper. Webster checked the spelling of each word, explained its pronunciation and history, and listed all the possible meanings. He gave examples of the uses of many of the words. These examples were taken from famous writings, preferably by American patriots.

Noah worked on the words for the dictionary for twenty years, from 1804 to 1824. In 1806, he published a short dictionary, but continued his work on the longer, complete dictionary. His final manuscript, written in longhand, contained 70,000 sheets of paper. Webster read through the manuscript and decided that he must improve the histories of the words. He went to libraries in France and Great Britain for more information. Webster finished the last history of the last word in the dictionary while he was in Europe. He later wrote that when he came to the last word he was trembling so much that he could hardly keep his pen steady on the page.

Noah Webster lived many more years. He saw his dictionary received with enthusiasm by scholars and teachers everywhere. The first edition of the dictionary came from the printer in two volumes in 1828. Webster did not earn very much money from the sale of his dictionary, but the praise it received pleased him. In his old age, he worked on an improved version of the dictionary. He finished this in 1841. He died two years later, surrounded by his wife, his six surviving children, and his sixteen grandchildren.

Noah Webster wrote the first truly American dictionary. It standardized American spelling and distinguished American usage from British usage. Revised editions of his dictionary still set the standards of American English and are used in schools and libraries all over the United States.

Directions: On a separate sheet of paper, answer the following questions about Noah Webster.

1. Noah Webster was a Federalist. Federalists believed that the United States needed a strong federal government. What reasons might Noah Webster have had for supporting the Federalists? Explain your answer.

2. Why did Webster's grammars and readers not become as popular as his speller? Explain your answer.

PART II: EXPANSION AND TURMOIL

During the late 1700s and early 1800s, Americans showed a great interest in expanding their new nation. The wilderness to the west of the states beckoned to the adventuresome spirits of daring men and women. They endured great hardships to tame the wild country, yet a feeling of excitment filled them. This was their land to conquer, and conquer it they would.

The joyfulness that accompanied expansion did not extend to all peoples, however. The American Indians, who once called the eastern United States home, were slowly being pushed westward. The Cherokee Indians were forced to travel the sorrowful "Trail of Tears" from their homes in the Southeast to the newly established Indian Territory west of the Mississippi River. Other American Indians suffered a similar fate.

At the same time, two totally different economies were arising in the United States. In the South, where the climate and soil were right for growing crops, huge plantations arose. Slaves imported from Africa worked on these plantations. In the North, industry began springing up everywhere. The industrial North had no use for slaves, and many Northerners thought that slavery was wrong and immoral. Thus arose the controversy that led to the Civil War.

The Civil War was one of the bloodiest wars in United States history. Part of the tragedy was that, in many cases, families had divided loyalties. When at last the war was through, the North had won and slavery was abolished in the United States.

The freedom won at so great a cost, however, did not assure black Americans the same rights that white Americans enjoyed. The long, hard battle for civil rights had only just begun.

The United States continued to expand. Immigrants began to arrive in great numbers, settling in many of the industrial towns in the North. Gold was discovered in California in 1848. The citizens of the United States kept up their quest for more knowledge of their ever-expanding nation.

SEQUOYAH

Inventor of a system of Cherokee writing; born in Tennessee about 1770 and died somewhere in northern Mexico in 1843

Sequoyah (sih KWOY uh) sat on a low boulder, his crippled leg stretched straight out in front of him. Around him in a circle sat men, women, and children. In a soft voice, Sequoyah told an old story about how the Great Spirit had given the book to the red people, the first race of people he had created. The Great Spirit then gave the bow and arrow to the second race he created—the white people. The red people, said Sequoyah, were slow to use the book, so the white people took it away from them. The red people were left with no choice except to take the bow and arrow and live by hunting. The people wanted to hear more, but Sequoyah had something else to do, and he sent them away.

The people gone, Sequoyah lit a knot of pine at the dying fire and went inside the small windowless house built of logs. He set the pine torch in an iron holder that he had crafted at his forge, picked up a stack of papers, and began to work. Sequoyah did not believe the old legend he had just told the people. He thought writing was something white people had learned to do and that red people could also learn to do. For almost twelve years, he had been working on a system that would enable the Cherokees to write in their own language. He had even worked on it throughout the long trip to Arkansas and back. Soon his people would not have to depend on the memory of storytellers to remember their history. Red people, like white people, would be able to turn to "talking leaves," which was what the Cherokees called any paper with writing on it. Then they could know what people in faraway places had said. They could even know what people who no longer lived had said. Sequoyah thought that it was the white people's ability to write that gave them so much power over the Indians. White people did not have to keep everything they knew in their memories. Perhaps, once the red people could catch words and hold them on paper, white settlers would not find it so easy to take away their lands.

The storyteller was about fifty years old. He had been born sometime around 1770, but exactly when is not known, since the Cherokees did not keep close track of the years. Sequoyah's mother was a Cherokee. His father was a white man, but it is not certain who he was. There is reason to believe that he was Nathaniel Gist, a friend of George Washington. Gist lived many years among the Cherokees as a hunter and explorer, and the Cherokee liked and respected him. Sequoyah's English name was George Guess, which may have been the way *Gist* sounded to the Cherokees. Little is known about Sequoyah's youth, other than that he was born and grew up near the Tennessee River, about five miles from Echota, the old sacred town of the Cherokees.

As a young man, he learned blacksmithing by watching a white settler working at a forge. He learned to work with silver and became famous for the beautiful pieces he crafted. He taught himself to draw and paint, creating brushes from the hair of wild animals. Then, about 1809, Sequoyah began to work at capturing Cherokee words. Cherokee is a difficult language to write in English letters because its sounds are very different from English sounds. Sequoyah had never learned to speak English and did not know how to read or write. That made his task all the more difficult. He did not know how the white people's "talking leaves" spoke.

In 1813, Sequoyah volunteered to fight with Andrew Jackson against the Creek Indians. He fought in the Battle of Horseshoe Bend in Alabama, during which Jackson's army defeated the Creeks. It is possible that this is when Sequoyah's leg was injured. The war over, Sequoyah returned to his work of capturing words.

It was not an easy task. Some of his neighbors thought he was practicing magic that would cause the Cherokees great harm. His wife often had to tend the farm, and she bitterly resented the time Sequoyah spent on the writing. Once, in anger, she threw all of his papers and pieces of bark into the fire. Sequoyah went into the woods and built a cabin so that he could work in peace on the writing. A group of villagers found the cabin and burned it, again destroying all he had done, but Sequoyah did not give up.

He thought about the Cherokee words. First, he made a picture for every word he could think of, but soon he had several thousand pictures. He knew that no one could keep all those pictures in memory. There had to be a better way.

He tried several other systems, but none seemed to work. Then he began to think about the sounds, or syllables, that make up Cherokee words. He wrote down a symbol for each syllable he could hear. His six-year-old daughter helped him listen for the sounds because her hearing was sharper than his. Eventually, he had eighty-six symbols. Sequoyah used some symbols that look like the letters in English words, but the symbols do not represent the same sounds that they represent in English. This is because Sequoyah did not know the sounds given to the letters in English. Sequoyah may have decided to use those particular symbols when he found a newspaper someone had thrown away. He may have seen a child's spelling book. Missionaries, hearing about his work, may have shown him books they had.

In 1818, Sequoyah left the Cherokee Nation in the East and went to Arkansas to join a part of the tribe who had emigrated. He continued to develop the Cherokee alphabet. Sometime before 1821, he returned to the eastern part of the Cherokee Nation. He brought messages that tribe members in Arkansas had written to their relatives and friends in the East. They used the new Cherokee writing, which Sequoyah had almost finished. The people in Tennessee thought that Sequoyah was trying to trick them for some reason. They did not believe he could read the marks on the paper. They simply thought he had a very good memory. He continued his work and soon finished the alphabet.

Sequoyah's great work was only half done, however; now he had to convince his people that the writing was real and useful and not something that could harm them. In 1821, he called a meeting of important Cherokee leaders. He explained his writing to them as well as he could. To prove that he had captured words on paper, he sent his young daughter out of hearing. One person told Sequoyah a sentence to write. Sequoyah then called to his daughter, and she came and read what he had written. Next, she wrote a phrase someone told her out of Sequoyah's hearing, and he read what she had written. However, the Cherokees were still not convinced that it was not a trick. At Sequoyah's suggestion, the tribe's leaders selected several young men to learn the writing system. In a few days, Sequoyah had taught all of the young men to read and write the Cherokee language. At last, the Cherokees were convinced that the writing was real, and they held a great feast in Sequoyah's honor.

Anyone who spoke the Cherokee language well could learn to use the Cherokee writing in just a few days. There were no schools to teach the writing. People exchanged the information as they walked or as they worked in the fields. They carved words on tree trunks, drew and painted them on rocks, and even wrote them on the ground. The writing spread from village to village.

In 1822, Sequoyah returned to his home in Arkansas. He could see that life for his people was changing. White settlers were crowding in and all of the tribes were losing their homes and their hunting lands. Sequoyah knew that the Cherokees would have to adjust to a new way of life.

In 1828, a group of missionaries helped the Cherokees establish a printing press in New Echota, Georgia, the new capital city of the Cherokee Nation. In February 1828, the Cherokees published the first issue of the *Cherokee Phoenix*. The *Cherokee Phoenix* was a newspaper printed partly in English and partly in the Cherokee writing of Sequoyah. During its short life, the *Cherokee Phoenix* carried news of special interest to Cherokees, articles on laws affecting the Cherokees, and articles about Cherokee history. The newspaper helped keep the scattered tribes in touch with each other. In 1832, however, the paper was seized by the state of Georgia. The state began printing articles in the *Cherokee Phoenix* in favor of Cherokee emigration to Oklahoma.

At the time the first issue of the *Cherokee Phoenix* came out, Sequoyah was in Washington, D.C., among the Cherokees negotiating for the tribal land in Oklahoma. In 1829, Sequoyah moved to Oklahoma, and in 1835, a missionary board established a printing press there. During the next twenty-five years, this press printed more than fourteen million pages of literature for the tribes, much of it in Sequoyah's Cherokee writing.

In December 1835, the Cherokees gave up all of their lands east of the Mississippi River. In the spring of 1838, the tribe set out on the "Trail of Tears" to its new home in Oklahoma. Thirteen thousand Cherokees began the journey; more than four thousand died on the way. The Cherokees found life difficult in their new home, but information printed in Cherokee writing made the transition a little easier.

In the summer of 1842, Sequoyah, then more than seventy years old, set out to search for Cherokee tribes that had long ago gone West. The next year, he located a small group of Cherokees in northern Mexico and, while visiting them, he died.

Sequoyah, a man who never gave up, devised a complete system of writing for the Cherokee Indians. It is in his honor that the largest trees in the world are named: the Sequoias, which are found only in California.

Directions: On a separate sheet of paper, answer the following questions about Sequoyah.

1. What did Sequoyah hope to accomplish by inventing a writing system in the Cherokee language?

2. The Cherokee writing system was a tool that helped Cherokees communicate with each other over long distances. It also helped them begin to understand the ways of white people. Why do you think the Cherokees resisted Sequoyah's system of writing at first?

JOHN JAMES AUDUBON

American birdlife painter; born in Haiti in 1785 and died in New York in 1851

John James Audubon led a life that was as colorful and exciting as the paintings of birds that would one day make him famous. He was born to a wealthy sea-captain father and a Creole mother in the small Caribbean country now known as Haiti. However, John James's mother died shortly after his birth. His father, wanting only the best opportunities for his son, sent the boy to the family home in Nantes, France, to be raised. There John James was provided with the best tutoring available, but he soon began developing other interests.

As John James was growing up, he preferred to spend his days wandering the woods and parks outside of Nantes. He liked making drawings of birds and small animals. For John James, watching the birth and growth of birds was like viewing the unfolding of a beautiful flower. By the time John James was fifteen, he had already begun a collection of original drawings of French birds.

Captain Audubon encouraged his son's interest in nature and art. He even sent his son to study with the famous artist Jacques Louis David. However, he considered his son's interest to be only a hobby and hoped the boy would someday become a sea captain.

John James never showed any interest in becoming a sea captain. He preferred to continue making drawings and paintings of birds. The captain could not understand his son. When John James refused to take his studies seriously, his father sent him to the United States to manage a farm near Philadelphia.

In 1803, John James landed in Philadelphia. He knew very little English, but he knew all the popular dances and could play the violin and flute well. He was very popular in the community.

John James was soon spending much of his time painting scenes from nature around him. In the woods and meadows near Philadelphia, he found more birds than he could ever hope to find near Nantes. He painted kingfishers and the great blue heron. He drew phoebes and redwings building nests and caring for their young.

The many young people in the community were as delighted with John James as he was with his life in the New World. One of his neighbors was a pretty sixteen-year-old Quaker girl named Lucy Bakewell. Lucy helped John James with his English, and he taught her to draw. Before long the couple became engaged. They planned to marry and set up a store farther southwest, where they would seek their fortune.

After a four-year engagement, the young couple married and moved to Louisville, Kentucky. A close friend named Ferdinand Rozier helped the Audubons open a store there. While Rozier ran the store much of the time, John James was out in the woods drawing and painting. Snowy egrets, whooping cranes, and passenger pigeons were present in large numbers. He learned to imitate bird calls to bring the birds near enough so that he could sketch them. He painted wild turkeys, swifts, blue-winged teal ducks—all birds that he had never seen in France. He also hunted some of the birds so that he could examine them in detail and draw them accurately.

After a few years passed, John James moved his family to Henderson, Kentucky and opened another store. Again, his friend ran the store while Audubon painted.

In the meantime, Lucy had given birth to two sons, Victor and John. John James tamed wild birds as pets for the children. Many of the wild birds in the neighborhood came at John James's call and ate grain at a feed tray. From them, he learned to sketch lifelike pictures of birds in flight.

Then came the War of 1812, followed by an economic depression. Times were hard for storekeepers in Kentucky. The Audubons borrowed money to buy goods and then found they could not sell the goods. They tried to make money by running a mill, but that too failed. John James was arrested for unpaid debts and found himself in debtors' prison. He declared himself bankrupt and was finally released. At that point, the family had nothing left. Everything they owned, including John James's art supplies, had been sold.

To help out, Lucy Audubon went to work as a governess for a wealthy family. She took their two little boys with her, for the Audubons no longer had a home of their own. Audubon took a job stuffing animals for a new nature-study museum in Cincinnati, Ohio. He made a little extra money painting watercolor portraits and managed to send a few dollars to help his wife.

Then came an idea. If farmers' portraits could bring money, why not bird portraits, which he could do so much better? He could make a book with colored drawings of every type of bird in America. Surely many Americans would buy such a book, and maybe many Europeans as well. John James's first thought was for his wife and the little boys. How would they live while he was working on the book? Lucy Audubon insisted that she could support herself and the children with her earnings. Then he worried because he had not seen all the different birds there were in North America. In the warm climates of New Orleans and on the coast of the Gulf of Mexico, there would be many more. His wife answered this objection, too. He could work his way down the Mississippi to New Orleans, then go along the Gulf coast to the tropical islands off the tip of Florida. Everywhere that he saw a new type of bird, he could make sketches. Then he could use the sketches to paint large watercolors, in which most of the birds would be shown full size.

Thus John James Audubon started downriver, working his way on a flatboat. All the way down the river he made drawings of birds living along the Mississippi. He stayed more than a year in New Orleans, trying to earn enough money to get to Florida. New Orleans was a colorful port, with muddy streets filled with Yankee trappers, Spanish smugglers, French plantation owners, and wandering Indians. John James went from door to door in the rich French quarter, offering to paint portraits in return for food and lodging. He also continued sketching and painting birds. He filled a whole portfolio with pictures of birds of the New Orleans area.

John James Audubon at last had enough money to send for his wife and the boys. Lucy Audubon again worked as a governess, while Audubon earned money giving drawing lessons. These lessons took place in the mornings. In the afternoons, John James went off in the woods to draw yellow-winged warblers, ivory-billed woodpeckers, and red-winged blackbirds. He worked steadily on his book.

At last, in 1822, John James Audubon started out for Philadelphia with a portfolio of hundreds of bird pictures. He took his fourteen-year-old son Victor with him. They went up the Mississippi by steamboat and then saved money by walking to Louisville, 250 miles away. Victor afterward wrote that this three weeks' hike through the woods with his father was one of the happiest times of his life.

In Philadelphia, many people were pleased with the beautiful, lifelike pictures. No one, however, thought John James would be able to sell the pictures in book form in America. A few artists encouraged him to persist in his project. Perhaps wealthy English nobles would buy books full of engraved pictures of birds.

Discouraged, John James and his son went back to Louisiana. Audubon worked four more years there, painting 200 new bird pictures. He also did portraits to earn enough money to go to Europe. He finally could afford to buy passage on a ship sailing from New Orleans to Liverpool, England. When he sailed, he took along four hundred finished pictures in perfect color. The pictures showed more than 300 different species of birds.

Friends of both Lucy and John James Audubon welcomed him in England. They helped him give an exhibition of his drawings. Many visitors to the exhibition ordered copies of the pictures.

John James also made new friends at the exhibition, and some of them put him in touch with an engraver named Robert Havell, Jr. Havell agreed to help Audubon. Havell's employees, using engraving tools, copied the bird pictures, line for line, on copper plates. When John James was satisfied with the black-and-white prints made from these copper plates, Havell's color copyists went to work. They colored each print by hand, following the colors of the original paintings. John James took ten prints each of five of the bird pictures and used them as samples to show to wealthy English people. Would

300 of these people each agree to buy a bound volume of such drawings? The bound volumes would contain more than 400 pictures of North American birds. If John James could get enough subscribers, Havell would make copper plates for all the drawings and color the prints of each one.

For the next two years, John James lived in Europe. To earn money, he lectured and sold paintings of birds. He showed people his samples and tried to get subscriptions. Then he decided that he needed more paintings, so he returned to the United States.

He traveled about the country, finding more birds to paint. He went to Florida and northeastern Canada. All the while he painted steadily, adding new pictures to his collection. Finally, he returned to London with his paintings, and there *The Birds of America* was at last published. It was soon a very famous book.

John James Audubon lived out much of the rest of his life near New York City, painting nature-study pictures, playing the violin, and teaching his grandchildren old French dances. Today, copies of the hand-colored first editions of *The Birds of America* are quite valuable and are usually seen only in libraries or museums. John James Audubon's pictures awakened many Americans to the beauty of their country's birdlife. Thousands of Americans now belong to clubs named after Audubon. Members of the Audubon Society are dedicated to the enjoyment and protection of the birds John James Audubon loved so well.

Directions: On a separate sheet of paper, answer the following questions about John James Audubon.

1. Audubon, who was born into a wealthy family, made two attempts at running a store but failed. Why do you think he tried to run a business even though he was interested only in painting birds? Explain your answer.

2. Audubon faced poverty and danger as he traveled in search of new birds. Why do you think he never gave up his search for new birds? Explain your answer.

SAM HOUSTON

Frontiersman, general, and governor of two states; born in Virginia in 1793 and died in Texas in 1863

Sam Houston and his brothers and sisters piled the family belongings into the wagons. They loaded bedding, clothing, cooking utensils, and food supplies. Sam took his books, his rifle, and his whittling knives. Finally, everything was packed. They were ready to go. Elizabeth Paxton Houston and her nine children were moving from Virginia to Tennessee. Their caravan included two wagons—one pulled by five horses, the other by four. As he rode, Sam thought about life on the frontier. He imagined what it would be like to live near Indians. While he rode, he whittled away.

Sam Houston was born on March 2, 1793, in a log cabin near Lexington, Virginia. He was the fifth son born to Samuel and Elizabeth Houston. Another son and three daughters followed. Meanwhile, Major Samuel Houston, a veteran of the American Revolution, had lost a lot of money. He hoped to do better out West. He sold his Virginia farm and bought a 419-acre farm in Tennessee. Just before the move, tragedy struck. Major Houston died. The family had no alternative but to move. The Virginia farm now belonged to someone else.

After three weeks, the family crossed into Tennessee and reached Blount County. The Tennessee hills were turning bright green in time for summer. The Houstons found their farm near the town of Maryville. They were just a few miles from the river that bordered Cherokee Indian land.

As soon as the family was settled, the older Houston boys began to farm. They had a long list of chores for Sam. Sam did not like taking orders, and farming bored him. In addition, Sam's brothers found him a job in Maryville, working as a clerk in a general store. Now Sam had to take orders from his brothers, customers, and from the store owner.

While he was working at the store, Sam made friends with a Cherokee youth named John Rogers. At fifteen, Sam ran away from home. He went to live with John Rogers and the 200 Cherokee Indians who lived across the river. He stayed with them for three years. The chief, Oo-loo-te-ka, also known as John Jolly, adopted Sam as his son. The Indians called Sam *Co-lon-neh,* meaning "raven" and "military leader." From then on, Sam considered ravens a sign of luck. Sam began to dress in the Indian fashion. He wore a leather shirt and beads. Sam learned the Cherokee language and became familiar with their customs and medicines. He learned the ways of the forests. He also learned to appreciate the peace-loving Cherokee people and their culture. He made several trips back to the store at Maryville to buy presents for his Cherokee friends.

Sam knew he could not stay with the Indians forever. He had gone into debt at the Maryville store to buy presents for his friends. He had to repay his debts. In 1812, he returned to Maryville to make some money. He opened a school and charged $8 per student for the term. After one term, Sam paid off his debts.

One day, in 1813, an army recruiter marched into Maryville. He attracted a crowd. He asked for volunteers to fight the British in the war that became known as the War of 1812. The recruiter threw silver dollars on a drumhead. There was a silver dollar for anyone who would join the army. Sam Houston stepped forward and picked up a silver dollar. He would become an army private.

Sam wanted the blessing of his mother. She told him to be brave, and she gave him a gold ring. Inside the ring was the word *honor*. He promised her that he would always act with honor.

Within a few months, Sam was promoted to lieutenant. He wanted to fight the British, but he was assigned to serve under General Andrew Jackson against the Creek Indians. The Creeks, as warlike as the Cherokees were peaceful, were allied with the British.

On March 28, 1814, Sam Houston was with Jackson's troops at the Horseshoe Bend of the Tallapoosa River in Alabama. There was fierce fighting, and a Creek Indian shot a barbed arrow into Sam's thigh. Sam tried to remove it but couldn't. He yelled at a fellow officer to pull it out. The more the officer pulled, the more Sam bled. Finally, the officer pulled it out of Sam's thigh. General Jackson ordered Sam out of battle. However, in a few hours, when there was a call for someone to lead a charge, Sam was the only volunteer. He and his men ran down a slope. They shot fire arrows into the brush where the enemy was hiding. The Creeks were defeated. Moments before the Indians surrendered, Sam was hit by two bullets, one in his arm and another in his shoulder. An army surgeon removed only one bullet; he thought Houston was going to die, anyway.

Sam slowly recovered. General Jackson never forgot Sam's bravery. While Sam waited for his next military assignment, he often visited Jackson. The United States government, under the Department of War, was moving Indians from the Southeast to Indian reservations in the West. In 1817, when Sam was twenty-four, he was appointed an agent to help move the Cherokee Indians from east Tennessee to a reservation in what is now Arkansas.

As the Indian agent, Sam now heard Cherokee complaints and doubts about the intentions of the United States government. Houston decided to lead an Indian delegation to Washington to confront the War Department. To make his Indian friends feel comfortable, he wore his Indian beads and buckskin clothes. In Washington, the delegation met with John C. Calhoun, the Secretary of War. Calhoun spoke politely to the Indians. Then he turned angrily to Sam. What, he wanted to know, was a member of the United States Army doing dressed up like an Indian? Sam tried to explain. Calhoun yelled at Sam and charged him with dishonesty.

Now Sam was angry. Calhoun had offended his honor. Sam resigned from the army and moved to Nashville, Tennessee. He opened a law practice and entered politics. He began working to elect Andrew Jackson to the Presidency of the United States. Within one year, Houston himself was elected District Attorney for the district of Nashville. He soon found that politics was a reckless game. Once someone challenged Houston to a duel. Houston tried to dissuade the man. "No, General," he replied, "Pick your weapon!" Sam chose pistols at fifteen feet. He was so inexperienced that he went to Jackson for advice. Jackson told Sam to bite a bullet if he wanted to keep the pistol steady. Sam shot his opponent and won the duel. He thanked God when the man recovered.

Between 1823 and 1827, Houston represented Tennessee in the Congress of the United States. He was gallant and popular; an eloquent speaker, but tough. In 1827, the people of Tennessee elected Houston to be their governor.

Then, one day, Sam Houston fell hopelessly in love. Eliza Allen was the eighteen-year-old daughter of a wealthy Tennessee family. Houston was twice her age. On January 22, 1829, they were married. He later said that on his way to his wedding, he saw a dead raven fall from the sky. Three months after the wedding, Eliza left Sam and returned to her parents. Everyone knew that Sam loved Eliza very much. No one knew why she left him, and he never told.

On April 16, 1829, the heartbroken Houston resigned as governor. He left Tennessee and went west in search of his Cherokee friends. He found them living on the Arkansas River. Sam decided to become an Indian trader. He opened up a trading post and called his post *The Wigwam*. Sam put on his Indian clothing again. The Cherokees formally adopted Sam as a member of the Cherokee nation.

Sam became acquainted with Diana Rogers. She was a beautiful Cherokee widow and the half sister of Houston's old friend, John Rogers. One of her relatives was Sequoyah, the creator of the Cherokee alphabet. She also was a distant aunt of Will Rogers, the cowboy-humorist. Sam and Diana were soon married.

Then Sam's attention turned to Texas. He bought land on the Trinity River and moved to Texas. Diana decided to stay behind. She remained with the Cherokees until her death in 1838.

In Texas, Sam Houston took a law course. He finished the course in six months and began to practice law. In 1832, Texas was part of Mexico. Only 25,000 people lived there—not many compared to the 8 million people in the rest of Mexico. Some Texans wanted independence from Mexico. Houston told them that independence meant war. The Texans were not yet strong enough to win a war. He cautioned them to wait.

Then a villainous tyrant, Antonio Lopez de Santa Anna, seized power in Mexico. He tore up the constitution and marched throughout Mexico, crushing all of his opposition. As Santa Anna spread terror closer and closer to Texas, more Texans talked about independence. Still Sam was cautious.

Early in 1836, Santa Anna crossed the Rio Grande and entered Texas. In February, he reached San Antonio and stormed the Alamo. Nearly all the Texans at the Alamo were killed. Sam Houston, miles away, remembered the lessons of his Cherokee friends and put his ear to the ground. When he heard no rumble from the firing of cannons, he knew what had happened. The Alamo had fallen.

A group of Texans met in a tiny wooden building in a place called Washington-on-the-Brazos. There they drew up the Texas declaration of independence. On March 2, 1836, the delegates signed the document. It was Sam Houston's forty-third birthday. He was named commander of the Texas army. Houston managed to gather about 900 men—not much of a match against Santa Anna's 4,500 trained soldiers. Houston's first strategy was retreat.

Houston kept retreating until April 21. On that day, he decided that the time had come to fight Santa Anna. Houston's troops hid on the banks of the San Jacinto River. Santa Anna's soldiers were camped nearby. Late in the day, while the Mexicans took a siesta, Houston attacked. The cavalry charged. Houston, with only two cannons, sent volleys into the enemy camp. Within twenty minutes the battle was over. The Texans, far outnumbered, surprised and defeated the Mexicans. Santa Anna surrendered.

The Texans announced their independence from Mexico. Sam Houston became the first president of the Republic of Texas. He served from 1836 to 1838 and from 1841 to 1844. During his first term, he saw a new city named in his honor. During his last term, he worked for the annexation of Texas by the United States. In 1845, Texas became the twenty-eighth state of the Union. The next year, Sam Houston was elected United States Senator.

In 1840, at the age of forty-seven, Houston married once again. His bride, Margaret Lea, was only twenty-one years old. They had eight children. Their marriage lasted for the rest of his life.

In 1859, Houston became governor of Texas, but his days in public office were numbered. There was talk of Civil War and seceding from the Union. Abraham Lincoln was elected President of the United States. The movement in Texas to secede gained strength. Houston strongly opposed this. He believed that secession would bring on war between the North and South—and that the North would win. Some Texans listened, but most did not. The Texas legislature voted overwhelmingly to secede from the Union and join the Confederacy.

Houston refused to swear allegiance to the Confederacy. He would stand by his honor. The Texas legislature demanded that he resign. They declared he was no longer governor of Texas. He was powerless, but he was right about one thing. Civil War soon followed. It began one month later.

Houston lived out his last years at his home in Huntsville, Texas. He died there on July 26, 1863, before the North defeated the Confederacy. Sam Houston lived and died by his principles. As the hero of the Battle of San Jacinto, champion of Indian rights, governor of Tennessee and later of Texas, and opponent of secession, he remained steadfastly loyal to the United States. To the end, he never abandoned his pledge of honor to his mother.

Directions: On a separate sheet of paper, answer the following questions about Sam Houston.

1. There are a lot of legends about Sam Houston. Why do you think this is so? Explain your answer.

2. Sam Houston was known for his bravery, independence, sense of honor, honesty, and sympathy for American Indians. How did these traits help shape his life and his contributions to society? Explain your answer.

DOROTHEA DIX

Social reformer who worked for better conditions for the mentally ill; born in 1802 in Maine and died in New Jersey in 1887

Day after day, the woman wrote the shocking details of what she had seen. As she walked through the places where the mentally ill people were kept, she saw humans confined in cages, cellars, and closets. She witnessed horrible scenes of cruelty. Her hand often shook when she wrote down her notes. She was outraged by this inhumanity. Dorothea Dix became a spokesperson and social reformer for the mentally ill.

Today, there are many new drugs, treatments, hospitals, and trained doctors to help the mentally ill. Most of the hospitals are supported by state governments and are paid for by taxes. These hospitals are monitored to ensure that mentally ill patients get proper treatment. Those who suffer from mental diseases should be treated with kindness and given help and attention. However, this was not always the way the mentally ill were treated.

In the 1800s, few people understood that some people had diseases of the brain in the same way that other people had diseases of the body. Almost everyone was suspicious and frightened of mentally ill people. Few people treated them with kindness, and no one considered them ordinary human beings. Some people even thought they were possessed by evil spirits. Instead of putting mentally ill people into hospitals where doctors could treat them, officials often locked them up in jails.

By the early 1800s, a few states had begun to establish facilities for mentally ill people, but these places were more like prisons than hospitals. People were left untreated. By 1841, however, one woman was beginning to think about these unfortunate people.

Dorothea Dix was living in Boston, Massachusetts. She had been a schoolteacher, but her health was poor and she had to stop teaching. One day a young man studying to be a minister visited her. The student knew that Dorothea had been a teacher, and he asked her to recommend someone to teach Bible classes to women prisoners in the East Cambridge House of Correction.

Dorothea Dix replied that she would go herself, ignoring her poor health. She went to the jail, taking a hymn book and a Bible with her, and led a class for the women. After the class, Dorothea walked around the jail and talked with the prisoners. Among the prisoners, she found a number of mentally ill people. Then she asked the jailer to show her the cells where the mentally ill were kept. She was taken down to see them. They had rags for clothes, and no bedding. They huddled together to keep warm. Dorothea Dix felt compassion for them as they looked up at her with pleading eyes.

The cell was terribly cold. Dorothea wanted to know why there was no stove in it. The criminals in the upper part of the jail had stoves to warm their cells in the cold winter. The jailer told Dorothea Dix that the "lunatics" did not feel the cold as others did.

As a little girl, Dorothea Dix had known what it was to be cold. She had also known what it was to be lonely, forgotten, and unhappy. Her father, Joseph Dix, was a traveling preacher. Joseph Dix was better educated than the average minister of the time, and he spoke with great conviction. He became known as a preacher of great ability. However, this work did not pay much, and Dorothea's parents had little money. The house was often cold. Dorothea's father was away much of the time, and her mother was unhappy and ill.

Dorothea felt neglected, and she craved attention. Finally, when she was twelve years old, she was sent to live with her grandmother in Boston. When the shy, lonely girl from the Maine woods arrived at the beautiful red brick house in Boston, she felt a surge of enthusiasm. The home contained many wonderful things: beautiful furniture, carpets, paintings, and books. She looked forward to the opportunities that awaited her. Dorothea did well in school and decided that she wanted to become a teacher. However, conflicts arose between Dorothea and her grandmother. Dorothea was sent to live with a great-aunt in Worcester, Massachusetts.

Dorothea was much happier living in her great-aunt's home. Her great-aunt Sarah gave Dorothea the kindness and understanding she needed. Dorothea recognized that there were not many educational opportunities for young children, and she asked to be allowed to start a school for little children. Dorothea was fourteen years old when she began teaching lessons to her younger cousins and the neighborhood children. She ran the school for almost three years. In 1819, she returned to Boston to live with her grandmother and to study.

After Dorothea had received the best instruction in Boston, she was ready to start another school. She persuaded her grandmother to let her teach children in her home. Dorothea's private school was successful. However, she longed to give instruction to poor children. Dorothea was afraid that her grandmother would object to having poor children in the house. So, Dorothea wrote her grandmother a letter and told her of her desire to help the poor and unfortunate. She begged her to let her turn part of the barn into a school. Dorothea's grandmother could not refuse such a sincere plea. Dorothea invited poor children to attend classes in the remodeled barn. Meanwhile, she continued to teach private classes in the house. Dorothea Dix enjoyed teaching both classes. She also began work on a science textbook for her students, entitled *Conversations on Common Things*. It was published in 1824.

Overworked and tired, Dorothea came down with tuberculosis. She was advised to stop teaching for two or three years. She did stop teaching, but she continued to write books. Finally, she felt strong enough to return to teaching. She started a day and boarding school in her grandmother's home and at the same time continued her work with poor children. However, she worked too hard and had to return to bed for rest. In 1836, Dorothea Dix had a complete physical collapse. Her doctor realized that as long as Dorothea stayed in

Boston, she would not rest. He advised her to take a trip to Great Britain.

In Great Britain her health improved slowly. While there, she met many social reformers, especially among the Quakers. These people worked to improve the sanitary conditions in jails and the nursing treatment in hospitals. During Dorothea Dix's stay in Great Britain, she received news of her grandmother's death. Dorothea Dix had been left money that she would eventually use in her work.

Dorothea returned to the United States. She was not well enough to teach school every day, but she felt that she could do some type of social work. She traveled for several years, thinking about what she should do. Then, in 1841, she paid a visit to the East Cambridge House of Correction and saw the mistreatment of the mentally ill. She knew then that she had found a cause to work for. Dorothea Dix decided to help the mentally ill.

Dorothea knew from her experience in Great Britain that it would first be necessary to get the support of government officials. She went to see other reformers and philanthropists in Boston. She talked to Dr. Samuel G. Howe, who had founded schools for the blind. He advised her to publicize the sufferings of the mentally ill. Dr. Howe and other supporters investigated the Cambridge jail. He wrote an article about the inhumane conditions he had seen. People read the newspaper article but believed that it was untrue or exaggerated.

Dorothea Dix felt that laws were needed to protect the mentally ill. She wanted the state of Massachusetts to pass such laws and enforce them. She also wanted the state to build special hospitals for the mentally ill. She needed facts to present to the legislature. So, Dorothea began a survey of every place in Massachusetts where mentally ill people were housed. They were kept in jails, hospitals, or homes. She often found living conditions that shocked her terribly. Animals were often better treated than the mentally ill. She noted all the examples of mistreatment she saw. In January 1843, she submitted her findings to the Massachusetts legislature.

Dorothea Dix anxiously awaited word from the legislature. The press called her a busybody and a slanderer. The public could not believe that such mistreatment existed. Others felt that it was improper for a woman to go into these places. Various newspapers printed articles from some of the jails and hospitals she had visited;

they denied her findings. Dorothea was very upset by these responses. Her friends defended her, however, and stirred up interest in Dorothea's report. Dr. Howe addressed the senate and reminded them that Dorothea Dix was not accusing individuals, but the system that had made no provisions for the care of the mentally ill. Without these provisions, there was no hope that the mentally ill would receive the treatment they needed. The senate committee verified Dorothea's report and recommended that the hospital at Worcester be made larger to accommodate more patients. When the public learned of the senate's response, people began to withdraw their objections and to acknowledge that perhaps Dorothea Dix's report was true. Late one night, someone knocked on her door. The Massachusetts Hospital bill had been passed.

Dorothea Dix realized that other states needed to pass laws and build hospitals. She went to Rhode Island and inspected conditions there. When she described what she found in Providence, Rhode Island, a millionaire gave her most of the money needed to build a hospital for the mentally ill. She then appeared before the legislature to obtain the rest of the money for the proposed hospital. The next time she visited Rhode Island, the hospital fund was overflowing.

Dorothea Dix began to gain a reputation as a reformer. She went to New Jersey and collected facts to prove that conditions were bad. When her information was presented to the New Jersey legislature, the members were impressed. They offered Dorothea their support, and New Jersey built a state hospital for the mentally ill.

Everywhere she went, Dorothea Dix's reputation went ahead of her. Her method was always the same. First she visited the places where the mentally ill were kept. Then she wrote reports about the bad conditions she found and sent letters to the state officials. She made appeals through the newspapers and in person before state legislatures. In fifteen states during the next ten years, Dorothea Dix succeeded in getting legislatures to build thirty-two state hospitals for the mentally ill.

She could not, however, stay in these places to see that the new hospitals were properly staffed or that the patients were warm and well fed. Dorothea Dix wanted a plan that would take care of the mentally ill not only during her lifetime but also in the future. She decided that only the federal government could pass standard humanitarian laws that all states would have to obey. Dorothea thought about the vast stretches of unused land that the federal government owned. Why not get the government to sell twelve and one-half million acres of that land at one dollar an acre? The money raised would be enough to give proper care to every mentally ill person in America.

Dorothea Dix went to Washington, D.C. She wrote letters and interviewed members of congress every day. For six years, Dorothea Dix appealed to Congress to make provisions for the mentally ill. Finally, in 1854, her suggestions were written into a bill that was approved by both houses of Congress. However, President Franklin Pierce was afraid to interfere in the matter, which he felt belonged to the states. He refused to sign the bill.

Dorothea was bitterly disappointed, but she continued her efforts for the poor and mentally ill. She continued to travel across the country and urged reforms and the passing of bills. While Dorothea traveled across the country, she heard rumors of political unrest. Dorothea also heard that if the South could not prevent Lincoln's inauguration by seizing Washington and all of its records, then his life would be sacrificed. Dorothea immediately shared this information with the president of the Philadelphia and Baltimore Railroad. He listened to her story and hired detectives to investigate. As a result, Lincoln was safely smuggled into Washington.

After the Civil War broke out, she traveled to Washington and offered her services to the government. On June 10, 1861, she was appointed Superintendent of United States Army Nurses. While Dorothea Dix worked to set up hospitals, Dr. Elizabeth Blackwell trained nurses. Clara Barton went out to the battlefields to take supplies to and nurse the wounded.

Dorothea Dix tried to get generals and politicians to support her ideas for military hospital improvements. However, this was not easy. She often criticized doctors, and they began to dislike her very much. Dorothea felt that she knew much more than the military doctors did. Her hospitals did save many lives during the war, but the war was nearly ended before the hospitals were organized as she wanted them to be.

For the rest of her life, Dorothea Dix continued her work to improve institutions for the mentally ill. She wanted to be sure that the patients in these hospitals always had proper treatment, clean, cheerful surroundings, exercise, and nutritious food. In her last years, Dorothea Dix established permanent living quarters for herself in the Trenton Hospital in New Jersey. In her last illness she could look out at the Delaware River and think about the victory she had won. She had won a victory over a strong enemy. Dorothea Dix had helped break down a nation's ignorance about its mentally ill citizens.

Directions: On a separate sheet of paper, answer the following questions about Dorothea Dix.

1. Why do you think the mentally ill were mistreated before Dorothea Dix pushed for reforms? Explain your answer.
2. Why did Dorothea Dix enlist the help of other reformers before beginning her campaign in the United States? Explain your answer.

HARRIET TUBMAN

"Conductor" on the Underground Railroad, born about 1821 in Maryland and died in New York in 1913

There was a great celebration at Edward Brodas's big plantation house near Bucktown, Maryland. Neighbors came from miles around, riding in shiny carriages and on prancing horses. The sun shone on the smooth green lawns and on the bright dresses of the women. The air was full of the scents of flowers and good food. Edward Brodas smiled at his young son, who was showing off a new horse. The boy gave an order to a slave, and Brodas nodded with approval. The boy had just the right touch of authority in his manner. He would need that authority when he took over the plantation with its many slaves in just a few years.

Down in the slave quarters, Old Rit gave birth to her sixth child. The baby girl was strong and healthy, but Ben and Old Rit did not rejoice. They knew that their daughter would live the hard life of a slave. They could give her nothing but love. Sometime during that year, probably 1821, Edward Brodas wrote in a record book that the baby increased the number of his slaves by one. Other than that, no written record was made of the birth of the baby who would become known to history as Harriet Tubman, the Moses of her people.

Harriet's first years were spent in the cabin with her parents and her brothers and sisters. The cabin was one tiny room with a dirt floor. Meals were cooked at a fireplace, and the family slept on piles of straw and rags on the floor. There were no windows and no furniture. There was plenty of love, however.

Harriet was five or six years old when she began to work. Edward Brodas was not a cruel master, but his slaves were his property and he could do what he wished with them. Sometimes he would "hire out" his slaves to work for other people. People would give money to Brodas, and the slaves would work for the people who had "hired" them. People who hired slaves were often cruel to them. Several times Harriet was hired out to people who mistreated her.

When Harriet was about six or seven, she was hired out to Mr. and Mrs. Cook. Mrs. Cook planned to teach her to weave cloth. However, by the time Harriet finished all the housework for Mrs. Cook, she was too tired to learn to work the loom. After a few days, Mrs. Cook decided the little girl was too stupid to learn weaving, so Mr. Cook sent Harriet to check his muskrat traps. For days, Harriet waded the icy streams and swamps where Mr. Cook had set the traps. She got measles, but she still had to go into the swamp to check the traps. When she became so ill she could not walk, she was sent home. Old Rit gave her medicine made from herbs. Her father risked getting punished to catch rabbits to make broth for her. Slowly, slowly, the little girl got well.

After that, Edward Brodas put her to work in the fields. That was the hardest work of all, but Harriet was happy. She was with her parents, and that made the work seem lighter. Sometimes, she was allowed to work in the woods with her father. He was a good woodsman, and he taught her many things about finding her way in the woods.

Harriet wanted more than anything to be free. She heard whispered stories about slaves who ran away. She knew that when runaway slaves were caught they were badly beaten and sometimes even killed. One day, she was at the little store in the village when she saw a slave named Jim try to escape. A man named Barrett yelled at Harriet to stop Jim. Instead, Harriet stepped into the doorway so that Barrett could not leave the store. Barrett picked up a heavy piece of iron from a table and threw it at Jim. The piece of iron hit

Harriet in the forehead. She was taken to Old Rit's cabin. For a long time, it seemed as if Harriet would die, but at last she began to recover. For weeks she did not know what had happened. It was months before she learned that Jim had escaped and was living free in the North, where slavery was against the law. Harriet had struck her first blow at slavery.

Harriet never completely recovered from the blow to her forehead. For the rest of her life, she suffered from severe headaches, and she would often fall asleep in the middle of whatever she was doing. Sometimes she would fall asleep in the middle of a sentence, sleep a while, then wake up and pick up the sentence with the next word, just as if she hadn't been asleep. Edward Brodas decided to sell Harriet, but whenever a buyer came to look at her, she would pretend to fall into one of her strange sleeping spells. The buyer would decide not to buy her, and Harriet could remain on the plantation.

Edward Brodas died, and his son took charge of the plantation. Harriet and her father were hired out to a man named John Stewart to work in the woods. By this time Harriet was so strong that she could lift logs most men could not lift. She said that her strength came from working in the fields. John Stewart liked Harriet, and after a while, he let her "hire her time." This meant that she could work for other people for pay. She had to give John Stewart half of her pay, but she could do whatever she wanted with the rest. She began to save money so she could buy her freedom.

When Harriet was about twenty-four years old, she married a free black man named John Tubman. John's parents had been slaves, but their owner had given them their freedom. It was hard for a free black man to find a job and earn money. John was unable to find a job, so Harriet shared her money with him. John spent Harriet's money freely. Soon the money was gone, and with it, Harriet's hope of buying her freedom.

In 1849, young Brodas died and the plantation was sold. The new owner decided to sell off many of the slaves. Two of Harriet's sisters were sold South. Life was even harder for slaves who lived on the southern cotton and rice plantations than it was for slaves in the tobacco lands of Maryland. Harriet feared she was about to be sold as well and begged John to run away with her. He refused to go with her, so she decided to escape to freedom without him.

Harriet had heard that slaves could reach free states in the North by following the Underground Railroad. The Underground Railroad was a network of people who helped slaves escape. People who made their homes available were called "stationmasters" and the houses were called "stations." People who led groups of slaves from one place to another were called "conductors." It was very dangerous to be a part of the Underground Railroad.

One Sunday, Harriet went to a house in Bucktown where she had heard she could get help. There, a woman encouraged Harriet and told her how to reach people who would help her escape. First, Harriet had to make her way across the state line into Pennsylvania. Harriet left that night with no guide except the North Star. She traveled at night, taking care to avoid people, who might be slave catchers, or who might report her. It was hard to find her way through unfamiliar woods in the dark, but she did not give up. Her father's training helped her find the right paths to take. Quakers gave her directions to find her way out of Maryland and through Delaware. A week after she left, Harriet walked into Pennsylvania and freedom.

Harriet enjoyed her freedom less than a year. Then she heard that her sister Mary and Mary's two children were to be sold South. She made the dangerous trip to Maryland and brought Mary and her children into freedom. Harriet was now a "conductor" on the Underground Railroad. By that time, the Fugitive Slave Act had become law. Under that act any slave found in a free state had to be returned to his or her owner. Because escaped slaves were no longer safe in the free states, Harriet led them on to Canada. She helped so many slaves escape that the government offered a $40,000 reward for her capture. In all, she made nineteen trips back into Maryland, and she led out more than three hundred slaves. People knew she was coming when they heard her singing a song they had sung often, "Go Down, Moses." Then the people knew that, just as the Moses of the Bible had led his people out of slavery, their "Moses" would lead them out of slavery.

She made her last trip in December 1860, just before the Civil War broke out. During the war, Harriet continued her work for the cause of freedom. She worked for the Union forces as a nurse, a scout, and a spy. She led the way on one Union raid in South Carolina that freed 756 slaves. She worked in hospitals set up in South Carolina, caring for slaves who now had no masters, and for wounded Union and Confederate soldiers. She encouraged the slaves to help the Union forces.

After the Civil War ended in 1865, Harriet Tubman lived in Auburn, New York. She took people into her home and cared for them when they were sick or unable to care for themselves. One day she received a package from Victoria, Queen of the British Empire. In the package were a black silk shawl, a silver medal, and an invitation to visit the Queen in London. Unfortunately, Harriet did not have enough money to make the trip to London.

Harriet lived until she was about ninety-three years old. At her death in 1913, she was given a full military service. The baby born with no hope had made a mark on the world that will not go away.

Directions: On a separate sheet of paper, answer the following questions about Harriet Tubman.

1. Harriet Tubman was one of many conductors on the Underground Railroad. Why was this work dangerous?
2. When Harriet Tubman escaped to the North, she was free. Why do you think she risked her freedom to go back again and again to bring more slaves to the North?

CLARA BARTON

Founder of the American Red Cross; born in Massachusetts in 1821 and died in Maryland in 1912

Hundreds of soldiers lay wounded around the cornfield that concealed the house. The surgeons in this makeshift hospital had nothing but their medical instruments. They had torn up all the sheets in the house to use as bandages. More bandages were needed to keep the men from bleeding to death. Clara Barton traveled many miles through the battlefield before she arrived at the house. When she arrived, she saw that the surgeons were using green corn leaves for bandages. Men unloaded her wagon and she distributed bandages, medical supplies, and food. This woman, courageous, independent, generous, and kind, spent her life helping others.

Clara Barton was the fifth and youngest child in her family. Every member of the family contributed to her education which she initially received at home. She did math problems with her brother Stephen and rode horses with her other brother David. Her mother taught her how to sew, cook, and how to take care of her dog, Button, and her cat, Tommy.

Captain Stephen Barton, Clara's father, was a farmer and local politician. He was also a soldier who had fought against the Indians.

Clara grew up hearing her father's war stories rather than fairy tales. She loved to sit with him in front of the fire, hear his stories, and ask him questions. As a result, young Clara was interested in the military and felt comfortable discussing military tactics as well as working around soldiers.

When Clara was eight years old, her father sold his land to his sons and moved with Clara and her mother to a large farm. There, Clara had the companionship of her cousins. Together they explored the forests and hills and played with the farm animals. She learned to help the family with whatever work was being done. When the family repaired the farmhouse, for example, she learned to use a hammer and saw and how to use paint and putty.

One day Clara's brother David was badly injured during a barn raising. Eleven-year-old Clara became a nurse to her brother. For almost two years, she waited on him and nursed him. Since all of her time was spent with David, she had no time to participate in other activities. Finally, a new doctor was called in to treat David. Under his care, David's health improved enough that he was able to go back to work on the farm. Being a nurse to David left a lasting impression on Clara.

After David's recovery, Clara's family realized that her education had been neglected. They arranged for her to attend classes at a nearby school. After Clara had attended school for several years, her teacher told Clara's family that she would make a good schoolteacher. Soon, teenage Clara was teaching her first class. She joined in her pupils' games, and they liked her immediately. Clara Barton was so successful in this first school that she was asked to teach in many other schools throughout the local school system.

After teaching for ten years, Clara decided that she wanted to attend a school where she could learn more about subjects in which she was interested. She attended the Liberal Institute of Clinton, New York, and signed up for every available course. In 1852, after completing the courses, Clara Barton went to Bordentown, New Jersey and set up a free public school. At that time, free public schools were rare. The students in Bordentown had to pay money to attend school. Their money helped pay the teacher's salary. Clara was disturbed by the number of children on the streets who could not afford to go to school. She offered to teach without salary for three months if these children could attend her school. Her idea was so successful that she again received wages, a larger schoolhouse had to be built, and another teacher had to be employed. Then, that spring, the damp dust from the newly built brick school affected Clara's vocal chords. She did regain the use of her voice, but it was no longer strong enough for her to teach.

Clara moved to Washington, D.C., to recover her health. A representative from her home district helped her get a job in the United States Patent Office (now the Patent and Trademark Office). She was the first female clerk in the United States Patent Office. In the years that followed, Washington, D.C., was the scene of more and more political debates between Northerners and Southerners. People began to talk of war.

On April 12, 1861, the Civil War began. Many Northerners predicted that the war would not last more than three months. However, the war did not end until 1865, and many thousand American lives were lost in the Civil War. After the First Battle of Bull Run, the Northerners realized the seriousness of the war. This battle occurred on July 21, 1861, and the tired, defeated Union soldiers were forced to retreat to Washington, D.C.

The people in Washington were horrified to see so many wounded men. The hospitals could not even hold them all. The wounded soldiers lay on blankets on the floors of government buildings and warehouses. Those who were able came into the city on foot; others were carried by their fellow soldiers. There was no organization to care for them.

Clara was anxious to help the wounded men. She learned that much of the suffering on the battlefield was due to a lack of supplies. She began to advertise for supplies for the wounded. The food, clothing, and other supplies came pouring in, and Clara established a distribution agency. She also wrote letters home for the wounded soldiers in Washington, D.C., and tried to ease their homesickness.

In August of 1862, the Second Battle of Bull Run was fought. Clara Barton had collected food, clothing, and bandages. She was prepared to load these supplies on a wagon and take them onto the battlefield to help the soldiers who were wounded. She knew that many of the soldiers would die if their wounds were not cared for and if they did not have food.

Before she could go out on the battlefield, however, she had to obtain official permission. She finally obtained the necessary passes from various government departments and was able to take her supplies and wagon onto the battlefield. Clara arrived at the battlefield hospital just as the hospital was about to run out of bandages. Clara Barton walked among the wounded, giving them chunks of bread and drinks of water or coffee. She tried to keep the suffering men dry and warm. She comforted and encouraged them, using all of the knowledge she had gained during her two years of caring for her brother David.

Fifty men were assigned to help Clara. Under her supervision, they distributed soup and loaded the wounded into mule wagons, taking them to the railroad, which carried them back to Washington, D.C. The soldiers and surgeons admired Clara and her ability to assist in any type of emergency. She was able to make meals for soldiers out of any kind or amount of food, and she often held a candle while surgeons performed operations.

After the Second Battle of Bull Run came the Battle of Antietam Creek in September 1862. Again, Clara Barton went out onto the battlefield to help the wounded. She was often under fire as she treated the wounded. On the third day of the battle, regular army supplies arrived. Clara Barton was completely exhausted and slept on the trip back to Washington.

After the Battle of Antietam Creek, the fighting moved farther away from Washington, D.C. Clara Barton again put herself in charge of gathering bandages, clothing, and medical supplies, this time from all the northern states. In 1863, she took her supplies and carried on with her work in the area of Charleston, South Carolina.

Clara Barton moved back to Washington, D.C., and continued to offer assistance whenever she could. She spent more and more of her time trying to create an organization to help the wounded. The government, she realized, should take responsibility for soldiers wounded in battle.

After the war ended, Clara Barton received permission from President Lincoln to head a voluntary bureau to find missing Union soldiers. She organized a group of assistants, and in May 1865, she put together her first lists of missing men. Information came in from many places. Soldiers who had seen other soldiers die gave her names and dates. Families that had sheltered wounded soldiers also volunteered information. One soldier in particular helped Clara identify missing men. He had been a prisoner in the Andersonville Prison in Georgia. While he was there, he was the clerk assigned to keep a list of soldiers who died there. When he heard of Clara's work, he offered his list to her. He had a list of approximately 13,000 soldiers who had died at Andersonville. No private printer in Washington had sufficient resources to print her lists. Consequently, she asked the President (now Andrew Johnson) to allow the Government Printing Office to print the list. Soon the names of the missing men were published.

Clara Barton was a pioneer in the organization of care for American soldiers wounded in battle. She was also one of the first people to attempt a large-scale gathering of medical supplies when the United States was at war. After the war ended, she found that she was famous. She was able to earn her living by writing for newspapers and magazines. She also gave lectures about her experiences, though these lectures often resulted in physical exhaustion.

In 1869, Clara went to Europe to rest. There she met Jean Henri Dunant, the Swiss citizen who had organized the International Red Cross. The purpose of this organization was to give aid to soldiers wounded on the battlefields of Europe. Dunant urged Clara to start such an organization in the United States. While Clara was still in Europe, the Franco-Prussian War broke out between France and Germany.

Many people suffered in this war, and thousands lost their homes and possessions. When the war ended, homeless civilian refugees were everywhere. Clara used her war experience to help organize relief for these people. She realized that the civilians who were caught in a war or some other disaster needed help just as much as wounded soldiers did.

After she had done all she could in Europe, Clara came home to the United States to spread the idea of an international society that would provide emergency help in any kind of disaster. She was determined, and she worked night and day to make her idea known. Some members of Congress opposed her plan, not wanting America to sign any kind of international treaty. Clara did not give up, however, and in 1881, Congress agreed to a treaty that brought the United States into the International Red Cross system. On May 21, 1881, a meeting was held at which The American Association of the Red Cross was organized. Clara Barton became the honorary president of the American Red Cross, as it became known, and she held that position from 1882 to 1904.

When natural catastrophes struck, the American Red Cross was able to provide quick relief. It worked to help victims of the terrible flood at Johnstown, Pennsylvania in 1869 and those of the hurricane that hit Georgia and South Carolina in 1893. Wherever people suffered from disasters, Red Cross workers were ready to help with food, clothing, and shelter. Clara Barton supervised these relief efforts whenever possible, and she often appeared on the scene of the disasters.

After her resignation from the American Red Cross in 1904, Clara went to live in Glen Echo, Maryland. Clara Barton had great initiative, and she was devoted to human welfare. When she saw a need, she did everything possible to respond to it. Today, Clara Barton's spirit lives wherever the American Red Cross saves lives in wartime or brings relief to victims of disaster.

Directions: On a separate sheet of paper, answer the following questions about Clara Barton.

1. How did Clara Barton's childhood education and experiences help prepare her for the work she did on the battlefield? Explain your answer.
2. Clara Barton is sometimes referred to as "Angel of the Battlefield." Why do you think she is called this? Explain your answer.

ULYSSES S. GRANT

Military leader and 18th President of the United States; born in Ohio in 1822 and died in New York in 1885

Ulysses Simpson Grant was one of the greatest generals in United States history. As a president, however, he was not as successful as he had been as a general. Grant was a man of contradictions. His 1,200-page autobiography was one of the best-written and most successful life stories ever published. However, as a businessman, Grant was a dismal failure. Seeing an animal mistreated or in pain upset him deeply, but sending men into battle did not appear to bother him at all.

Part of this may have been due to the dramatic differences in his parents' personalities. Hannah Simpson, his mother, was a farmer's daughter who rarely spoke and never smiled. His father, Jesse Grant, was an emotional know-it-all who ran a number of successful small businesses. Ulysses was more like his mother, keeping his thoughts and emotions to himself.

He was born in a two-room house in Point Pleasant, Ohio, on April 27, 1922. From the very beginning, there was confusion as to who exactly Ulysses S. Grant was. For the first six weeks of his life, the baby had no name. One day his family gathered, wrote names on pieces of paper, and placed them in a hat. The name picked was Ulysses. His grandfather was unhappy with that. He wanted the boy to be called Hiram. It was decided that he would be Hiram Ulysses. His mother called him Lyss.

Lyss's family moved to Georgetown, Ohio, when he was two. There Jesse Grant opened a tannery. A tannery is a shop where people convert animal skins into leather. As a boy, Lyss worked for his father. He hated the tannery because of the smells and the sight of blood. Fortunately, Jesse Grant also owned a stable. He let Lyss work there, tending the horses and performing other chores.

Lyss became an expert rider and horse trainer. When a circus came to town, five dollars was offered to anyone who could ride a particular horse. There was no bridle or saddle, and the animal's bare back was covered with grease to make it slippery. Although the horse looked tame, it had been trained to throw its rider. After watching a number of other people fail to stay on the animal, Lyss decided to give it a try. The horse kicked and bucked and did everything it could to throw the boy. Lyss held on tightly, and after awhile, the horse gave up. Lyss had won the five dollars.

Grant was successful with horses; however, the only school subject he excelled at was mathematics. In addition, he was shy and quiet, and in no way shrewd like his father. That made his neighbors think he was stupid and not good at anything but riding horses. They began calling him "Useless" Grant.

At seventeen, Grant was accepted into the U.S. Military Academy at West Point. By then, he had already changed his name from Hiram Ulysses to Ulysses Hiram. Being called "Useless" had been bad enough. As Hiram Ulysses Grant, his initials were H.U.G. To be called "Hug" was equally unacceptable.

Upon arriving at West Point, Grant experienced still another name change. The congressman who had recommended him for the academy had not known his middle name. Since he knew that Mrs. Grant's maiden name was Simpson, he had assumed that this was the boy's middle name. At West Point, Ulysses Simpson Grant was the name under which the new cadet was registered. Rather than complicate things further, Ulysses kept this name. Afterward, he became known as "United States" Grant, "Uncle Sam" Grant, and simply "Sam" Grant.

Grant was only an average student at West Point. He graduated twenty-first in a class of thirty-nine. After graduating in 1843, Lieutenant Grant was sent to Jefferson Barracks in St. Louis, Missouri. There he met Julia Dent, a pleasant, athletic girl from a well-to-do southern family. He and Julia often went horseback riding together. Ulysses could talk to Julia. She made him feel comfortable. Before long, they were engaged to be married. In 1846, the Mexican War began. Grant's position was that of quartermaster for his regiment. His duties included buying supplies and transporting them on mules. During an attack on the Mexican city of Monterey, part of the American army was pinned down by enemy fire. The captain asked for a volunteer to ride back to the rear to get more ammunition. Riding on the side of his horse, Grant dodged bullets fired from buildings. When his horse leaped over a four-foot wall, he was safely away from the firing. Grant was a hero.

After the war, Ulysses and Julia married and began to raise their family of four children. Quite often, Grant would be stationed in parts of the country where Julia and the children could not go. Long periods of separation from his family made him lonely and unhappy. It came as no surprise then, when Grant resigned from the military in 1854.

The seven years that followed were mostly unhappy ones for the Grants. Their family was together, but Ulysses failed at everything he attempted. First, he managed his father-in-law's farm unsuccessfully. Then he tried to sell real estate. Finally, he ended up in Galena, Illinois, working as a clerk in his father's leather goods store. The family was so poor that Grant began believing that maybe he was useless after all.

In 1861, when the Civil War began, Grant spent months training the young men of Galena to be soldiers. When a captain was chosen for their company, it was not Ulysses Grant. Although he had trained the men well, no one believed that this failure in life could be successful in battle.

As time went by, Grant believed that he never would get his own command. Nevertheless, he kept trying. Finally, in the summer of 1861, he was appointed colonel of the 21st Illinois Regiment. At the time, Grant was so poor that he could not afford to buy his own uniform. A businessman from Galena purchased it for him.

The troops Grant commanded were a disorganized, rowdy bunch of soldiers. Their commander knew that they would have to be disciplined if they were going to be effective. His strict disciplinary tactics soon had their effects. Even though he never raised his voice, cursed, or threatened his men, Colonel Grant gained their respect. Soon they were ready for battle.

In the months that followed, Ulysses S. Grant proved that he could, indeed, be successful on the battlefield. He was soon promoted to Brigadier General. On November 7, 1861, more than 3,000 of Grant's troops sailed down the Mississippi to attack the town of Belmont, Missouri. At first, the Confederates retreated, but later they were reinforced. Outnumbered, the Union troops returned to their boats. The last soldier aboard was Brigadier General Ulysses S. Grant. He had waited to make sure that all of the survivors of the battle were safe.

In February of 1862, General Grant won one of his greatest victories. On a bitter cold February 13, his troops attacked Fort Donelson, Tennessee. Three days later, a force of approximately 12,000 Confederates surrendered. The Southern commander asked what the terms of the surrender would be. General Grant replied that no terms but an unconditional and immediate surrender would be accepted. The southern commander consented to the unconditional surrender. As a result of his victory, Grant was promoted to major general. He also received another nickname—U.S. ("Unconditional Surrender") Grant.

On April 6, 1862, an army of 41,000 Confederates launched a surprise attack against Grant's forces at Shiloh. For hours, his men were beaten back. Casualties were high, and morale was low. As the afternoon wore on, Grant gathered his troops for one last stand. Wave after wave of the enemy attacked, and wave after wave was defeated. Finally night came, and the crisis was over. Union reinforcements arrived soon after. On the following day, Grant's troops drove the Confederates off.

Although the North won the Battle of Shiloh, the cost had been terrible. More than 13,000 of Grant's men had been killed, wounded, or captured. The people who had so recently praised the hero of Fort Donelson were shocked. Their hero had allowed his army to be surprised and almost had lost a major battle.

The next few months were discouraging for Ulysses Grant. He was reduced to second-in-command of his army. His duties were few, and rarely was he asked for advice. In the middle of the summer of 1862, however, the United States Army decided once again that General Grant was needed to lead his troops. He spent the next few months securing the important railroad town of Corinth, Mississippi. His ultimate goal, however, was the Mississippi fortress of Vicksburg.

To defeat the Confederacy, the North needed to control the Mississippi River. That could happen only when the last major fort on the river—Vicksburg—was captured. From Grant's position on the northwestern bank of the river, the fort seemed impossible to take. On every side was an overwhelming obstacle. In addition, deep, well-fortified trenches completely surrounded Vicksburg.

From December 1862 until April of the following year, Grant made every attempt he could to take the fort. Everything failed. Finally he tried something extremely daring. One dark night, he sent his gunboats silently past Vicksburg. Meanwhile, Grant marched his men down the west bank of the river. If the two movements succeeded, his men could board the ships and be transported to the south side of Vicksburg. If they failed, Grant's boats would be destroyed and his army captured.

The gamble paid off. By April 30, Grant's men were safely ashore on the south side of Vicksburg. During the next seventeen days, Union forces won five battles, defeated two Confederate armies, and completely surrounded Vicksburg. On July 4, 1863, the city surrendered. More than 30,000 prisoners were taken. More importantly, Union forces now controlled the entire Mississippi River. The South was split in half, and Ulysses S. Grant had been responsible for the victory.

The Lincoln administration rewarded Grant by making him commander of the armies in the West. After capturing Chattanooga, Tennessee, in November, Grant was appointed general-in-chief of all Union armies. His rank was that of lieutenant general. Only George Washington had ever been so honored.

For the remainder of the war, Ulysses Grant's principal opponent was Confederate General Robert E. Lee. For nine months, their armies fought some of the bloodiest battles of the war. Although Lee sometimes defeated the Union commander, Grant refused to retreat. By June of 1864, Grant had surrounded Lee's outnumbered army in Petersburg, Virginia. Eight months later, the city fell.

Lee retreated toward Appomattox, Virginia. There, on April 9, 1865, the Confederate commander surrendered his army to Grant and the war was over. Grant continued on as general-in-chief of the United States army. Before long, he was promoted to the rank of full general. But Ulysses S. Grant was not to stay a soldier for long. His country had a higher office in mind for him.

In May of 1868, the 46-year-old general received the Republican Party nomination for President. Ten months later he was sworn in as the eighteenth President of the United States. The mild-mannered, humble ex-soldier had risen from poverty to the Presidency in less than eight years.

During Grant's two terms as President, he achieved some success. He was responsible for the Fifteenth Amendment to the Constitution, which gave black males the right to vote. He also prevented his rival in battle, Confederate General Robert E. Lee, from being tried for treason. Ultimately, however, Grant's Presidency was considered a failure. An honest man himself, Grant never realized that many of his associates were cheating the government. Even the Vice President, the Secretary of War, and Grant's private secretary committed illegal actions. Because Grant failed to notice and correct the corruption in top government positions, the people assumed that Grant, too, was dishonest. His presidency became known as one of the most corrupt in United States history.

When his second term of office ended, Grant and his family traveled around the world. At every stop along the route, he was welcomed by enormous crowds of cheering people. Rulers of nations from Germany to Japan entertained him as an equal. Depressed from his lack of success as President, Grant's two-year trip abroad revived his spirits.

In 1881, the 59-year-old ex-general and former President again became a businessman. He accepted a position in Grant and Ward, an investment firm owned by his son and a friend. During the next three years, Grant put his entire fortune into Grant and Ward. Little did he or his son know that Ward was swindling them. In May 1884, Ulysses S. Grant discovered that he had been cheated out of every penny he owned. To make matters worse, soon after, doctors discovered that Grant was suffering from an incurable throat cancer.

Partly out of pity, but mostly out of great respect, the author Samuel Clemens approached Grant with an offer. He would pay Grant a large sum of money to write his life story. When the book was completed, Clemens's company would publish it. Grant agreed.

From February to July, 1885, the dying man wrote of his life. At times, the pain caused by his disease seemed unbearable, and yet he continued. Finally, *The Personal Memoirs of U.S. Grant* was finished. Four days after completing the book, Ulysses Grant died. He was sixty-three years old.

Grant's refusal to give in to death until he had completed his work made him a hero once more. The profits from his autobiography kept Julia Grant financially secure for the rest of her life. Considered one of the finest autobiographies ever written, the book was Ulysses S. Grant's last success.

Directions: On a separate sheet of paper, answer the following questions about Ulysses S. Grant.

1. Among all of Ulysses S. Grant's victories in life, which would you say was the greatest? Explain your answer.

2. Ulysses S. Grant was a consistent failure at business undertakings, yet he was stubborn enough to fight until he won the Civil War and to finish his book before he died. Given this "never-give-up" attitude, why do you think Grant was unsuccessful in running his business affairs? Explain your answer.

ROBERT E. LEE

Military leader, college president, and engineer; born in Virginia in 1807 and died there in 1870

Robert E. Lee was born to a historically impressive and influential family. His father, Henry ("Light Horse Harry") Lee, was a famous Revolutionary War commander and the first American governor of Virginia. Two of his uncles were signers of the Declaration of Independence. Among the family's dearest friends were Presidents Washington, Madison, and Monroe. The Lee estate at Stratford was one of the finest in the country.

Despite all that, the Lee family did not live happily. "Light Horse Harry" was a gambler and a poor investor. By 1810, he had lost the family fortune and was serving a sentence in debtor's prison. His wife and five children were evicted from Stratford and forced to live in a small house in Alexandria, Virginia. Robert Edward, who had been born on January 19, 1807, had no memory of when his family had been wealthy.

When Robert was eleven years old, his father died. With his two older brothers away from home, he became the leading family member. By then, his mother, Ann Carter Lee, had become quite ill. Robert took charge of the daily running of the house. He shopped for the food, saw to its preparation, and made sure the house was kept clean and tidy. In addition, he took care of his ailing mother.

As busy as his life was, Robert had time for recreation and for school. Among his favorite sports were swimming, skating, and rowing. In school, Robert was a very good student. Although he dreamed of becoming a doctor, there was no money for him to attend medical school. Instead, he applied to the Military Academy at West Point, which was free.

During his time at the Military Academy, Lee was the perfect image of a West Point cadet. An excellent student, Lee graduated second in his class. Always hard working, well disciplined, and popular, he soon rose in rank among his fellow cadets. In his senior year, he received a great honor. He served as the highest officer of the cadet corps.

After graduating in 1829, Lieutenant Lee was assigned to the Army corps of engineers, the elite of the military. Over the next several years, he was stationed in many different parts of the country. In Missouri, he built sea walls to keep the St. Louis harbor from being eroded. He also was in charge of constructing a fort off the cost of Georgia. At Fort Hamilton, New York, he saw to it that cannons were properly assembled and positioned. These and many other assignments kept Lee constantly occupied.

Life was not all work, however. In 1831, Lee married Mary Custis, the wealthy daughter of George Washington's stepson. Through the years, the couple had seven children. Although Mary's family owned a number of large homes, the main one was at Arlington, Virginia. This mansion still stands, perched on a hill across the Potomac River from Washington, D.C.

Robert was a devoted husband and a loving father. Tall, handsome, strong, and cheerful, Lee was as popular with his children as he was with other people. However, duty called Robert E. Lee away from Arlington quite often.

In 1846, the United States invaded Mexico. The victories of the American armies and the capture of Mexico City were in large part due to Lee's efforts. The route to Mexico's capital crossed through mountains and ravines. Atop these heights were enemy troops with cannons. If the American forces made frontal attacks, the higher ground would give the Mexicans a great advantage. It was Captain

Lee's job to find ways for the Americans, their horses, and their cannons to come around behind the enemy.

This was extremely dangerous work. Once, while searching for a path, Lee heard Spanish being spoken nearby. Quickly, he crouched behind a log. Moments later a squad of Mexican infantry appeared. Some of the soldiers sat on the log, smoking and joking with each other. Little did they know that an American officer was hiding just inches away from them. Finally, the soldiers moved on. Lee waited until nightfall. Later, he found the path. On the following day, the American forces won another great victory.

The years following the Mexican War were quite successful for Robert E. Lee. He was appointed superintendent of West Point in 1852. His three years at the academy were both enjoyable and productive. Lee loved guiding the cadets. By being fair, firm, and friendly, he won their love and their respect.

In 1855, he was made second-in-command of a regiment of cavalry stationed at Camp Cooper, Texas. Keeping the area safe from bandits and warring parties of American Indians were among his duties. Two years later, at the age of fifty, Lee became the regimental commander.

Soon after, his wife became ill. To take care of her and to run their estate, Colonel Lee returned to Virginia. Two years passed before Lee again saw active duty.

On October 17, 1859, he received orders from the War Department. John Brown, a violent anti-slavery leader, had captured the Federal arsenal at Harpers Ferry, Virginia. He had come to Virginia to arm the slaves so that they could fight against their owners. Brown's mission had failed. Now, he and his seventeen men and their hostages were barricaded in one of the buildings. Lee, commanding a force of marines, was assigned the job of recapturing the arsenal.

Arriving on the scene, Lee's forces surrounded the building. When Brown refused to surrender, Lee ordered a bayonet assault. He was afraid that some of the hostages might be hurt if he allowed his soldiers to fire their weapons. In very short time, the marines had broken down the door and were inside. Within a matter of minutes, all of Brown's men were killed or captured. None of the hostages were hurt, and only two of the marines lost their lives.

In the South, Colonel Lee became a hero. Not only had John Brown tried to free slaves, but he had murdered many white slave owners over the years. A number of Northerners, however, felt that the old man had been right. To them, slavery was wrong, and it had to be stopped at all costs. Robert E. Lee hated slavery, but he also hated violence. Unfortunately, the men who started the Civil War did not agree with him. On April 12, 1861, in Charleston, South Carolina, Confederate guns fired on Union troops inside Fort Sumter. The Civil War had begun.

The Lincoln Administration offered Lee the command of all northern armies. Although he did not think the southern states should leave the Union, Lee could not bring himself to fight against Virginia. When that state seceded a few days later, he resigned from the U.S. Army. He then accepted a generalship in the army of the Confederate States of America.

For Lee, the first year of the war was somewhat frustrating. He was largely unsuccessful in trying to defeat Union forces in western Virginia. Later, he organized the defenses of Richmond, Virginia, the Confederate capital. He also served as chief military advisor to the President of the Confederacy, Jefferson Davis. Although General Lee was a good administrator, his greatness would come as a battlefield commander.

Lee's chance came quite unexpectedly. In April 1862, a large force of Union troops landed on the Virginia Peninsula east of Richmond. By late May, this army was threatening Richmond, the Confederate capital. A great battle was fought with neither side actually winning. During the battle, the Confederate commander was wounded. President Davis appointed Robert E. Lee to take his place.

For the next three years, Lee led the Army of Northern Virginia through battle after battle. The men grew to love this gray-haired, gallant man as if he were their father. They fought for him gladly. From the very beginning, Lee proved that he was worthy of their devotion. Rather than wait for his enemy to attack, Lee ordered his outnumbered troops to take the offensive. In a series of engagements known as the Seven Days Battles, the Confederates drove the Union forces away from Richmond.

With the capital safe, Lee marched his men north. During the last days of August, he battled another Union army near the town of

Manassas, Virginia. Totally outwitting his opponent, Lee led his forces to victory in the Second Battle of Bull Run. Fresh from the Bull Run victory, Lee decided to invade the North. He felt that by winning a battle on Union soil, he would discourage Northerners from continuing the war. On September 5, he crossed the Potomac River into Maryland.

Lee's plan was to split his army into two parts. One wing, lead by General Thomas "Stonewall" Jackson, would attempt to capture Harpers Ferry, where 10,000 Union troops were located. The second would hide behind South Mountain so that the commander of the main Union army would not know its whereabouts. After Harpers Ferry fell, the two parts would come together. Then Lee would be able to destroy the main Union force.

The plan was daring and brilliant. Unfortunately, General McClellan, the Union commander, found out about it too soon. Two of his soldiers, while searching a deserted Confederate campsite, discovered a copy of Lee's plans wrapped around three cigars.

When Lee realized what had happened, he knew that McClellan would attack. While waiting for the second part of his army to return from Harpers Ferry, Lee tried to hold McClellan off at South Mountain. That proved to be impossible for Lee's forces. By the time Jackson arrived, Lee had retreated to the town of Sharpsburg, Maryland. Near Sharpsburg, at Antietam Creek, the Confederates made their stand.

The Battle of Antietam, fought on September 17, 1862, was a victory for neither side. On the bloodiest day of the Civil War, more than 12,000 Confederate men were killed, wounded, or missing. Enemy losses were similar, but Union troops greatly outnumbered the Confederates. As a result, Lee was forced to retreat to Virginia.

Antietam was a setback for Robert E. Lee. However, two great victories awaited him in the near future. At Fredericksburg, Virginia, on December 13, the Army of Northern Virginia was positioned on the heights overlooking the town. The Union Army of the Potomac, under General Burnside, attacked. Wave after wave of Union infantry marched toward the Confederate guns. When Lee's men opened fire, thousands of Union troops fell. Finally, Burnside was forced to retreat.

Burnside was replaced by General Joseph Hooker. Hooker was convinced that he could defeat Robert E. Lee. In May of 1863, the two armies met at the Battle of Chancellorsville. Although Lee was outnumbered two-to-one, he once again divided his forces. He would hold off the enemy while "Stonewall" Jackson's corps circled around Hooker's army and launched a surprise attack. The plan worked perfectly, and Lee won one of his greatest victories. That night, General Jackson was shot accidentally by one of his own men. Losing his best general saddened Robert E. Lee. He would never be able to replace the great "Stonewall."

Once more, Lee decided to invade the North. On July 1, 1863, his army attacked Union forces under General Meade at Gettysburg, Pennsylvania. Beaten back, Meade's men formed a defensive line on high ground south of the town.

Over the next two days, Lee's men failed to break through either the left or right flanks of the enemy. On the afternoon of July 3, he sent 15,000 of his best troops against the center of the Union line. The attack failed. On the following day, the Army of Northern Virginia retreated. At Gettysburg, Lee lost more than 20,000 troops. After this defeat, he would never again invade the North.

In March 1864, Ulysses S. Grant was appointed general in chief of the Union armies. Two months later, Grant led the Army of the Potomac against Lee. For the first time, the Confederate general was fighting against an equally talented military leader. Grant, however, had more soldiers and better supplies.

Their first battle was fought in a thick woods called the Wilderness. At one point, it looked as if Grant's army would win a victory. General Lee rode into the front lines to gather his men for a charge. The troops refused to obey Lee unless he went to the rear. They did not want their commander to risk his life. He did as they wished, and their attack was a success.

For eleven months, the two armies fought. Even though the Confederate forces won some battles, Grant's troops continued to attack. Finally, on April 9, 1865, at Appomattox Court House, Virginia, Lee was forced to surrender.

After the war, Lee showed no bitterness toward the North. He believed that the two sections of the country should reunite in a spirit of friendship. Lee accepted the position of president of a small college in a remote part of southwestern Virginia. At that time, Washington College only had forty-five students and four teachers. As president, Lee improved the quality of the school significantly. He raised money, increased enrollment, hired more teachers, and started elective courses. Thanks to him, Washington College was the first college in the United States to offer a course in journalism.

For recreation, the old general rode his horse Traveler over the hills and through the small towns nearby. He now had the time to spend with his family that he had not had while he was in the army. He also took what he thought would be a restful journey through the South. At one of his stops, he was recognized by a Confederate veteran. From then on, wherever Lee went, he was greeted with cheers and celebrations. The South had not forgotten its greatest hero. They would never forget Robert E. Lee.

Worn out after his years in the military, Lee did not live long after the close of the Civil War. In 1871, at the age of sixty-three, he died of heart failure.

Directions: On a separate sheet of paper, answer the following questions about Robert E. Lee.

1. Lee was loved and admired by his family, his students, and his soldiers. What qualities did he have that made people feel that way about him?

2. Robert E. Lee experienced much success in his life. What do you think was his greatest success? Explain your answer.

FREDERICK DOUGLASS

Black speaker, abolitionist, and crusader for the rights of blacks; born in Maryland in 1818 and died in Washington, D.C. in 1895

Frederick Douglass never knew his father and did not remember much about his mother. His mother, Harriet, was sent to work on another plantation when he was an infant, and he saw her only four or five times. She had to steal away at night to visit him. Harriet's workday began at sunrise and ended at sunset. She could not begin the twelve-mile walk to visit her son until after sunset. When she arrived, Harriet would lie down next to her son and talk to him until he fell asleep. When he woke up, she would be gone. He never saw her face in the daylight. Harriet had to be back to the field by sunrise, or she would be punished.

Frederick and his mother did not choose to be separated. They had no choice; they were slaves. The young boy lived for six years in the slave quarters with his grandmother, Betsey. He spent his early childhood taking care of cows, feeding chickens, and running errands for his master's children. Although Frederick was not treated harshly, he seldom had enough food to eat.

When Frederick was about eight years old, his owner, Captain Aaron Anthony, decided to send him to Baltimore, Maryland, to work.

He worked as a houseboy in the home of Hugh and Sophia Auld, relatives of Captain Anthony. At first he ran errands for Mrs. Auld. Later, he performed small jobs in Mr. Auld's shipyard. When Frederick arrived at the Baltimore home, Mrs. Auld taught him the alphabet and a few simple words. When Mr. Auld discovered that his wife was teaching a slave to read, he became very angry. Mr. Auld felt that educating slaves would spoil them and make them unmanageable. Mrs. Auld had never owned a slave, and she was not aware of how to treat one "properly." The lessons were discontinued.

Frederick did not want to stop learning, and he soon thought of a plan to continue. He decided to make friends with the poor white boys in the streets and have them become his teachers. Before Frederick left the house to run an errand, he made sure that he had a book and plenty of freshly baked bread. He would complete the errand as swiftly as possible. Then Frederick would approach a boy and ask him to teach him how to read, offering the bread as payment. Gradually, during the seven years he worked in Baltimore, Frederick learned how to read and write.

With the small amount of money he was allowed to have, Frederick bought a collection of essays that discussed slavery. He also began to read the newspapers. Frederick learned that people had different opinions about slavery and that some men and women, known as abolitionists, were trying to end slavery in the United States. He became interested in the work of the abolitionists.

Unfortunately, Frederick was forced to leave Baltimore. Anthony had died and left Frederick to Thomas Auld. Now Auld demanded that Frederick be returned to him. In 1833, fifteen-year-old Frederick Douglass began work as a field hand on Auld's farm. Life on the farm was hard for Frederick. There was not enough food for the slaves, and they often had to steal food from other farms. Thomas Auld was a cruel master, and the sullen Frederick received many beatings. Eventually, Mr. Auld grew tired of trying to control Frederick. He decided to send him to Edward Covey for one year. Mr. Covey was a "slave breaker"—he punished strong-willed slaves until they lost the will to rebel.

During his first six months on Covey's farm, Frederick was beaten nearly every day. Then, one hot summer day, after he had been working in the fields for many hours, Frederick staggered and fell down. Covey ordered Frederick to get up and get back to his work, but the young man could not move. Covey kicked him repeatedly while he lay helpless on the ground. When Frederick was able to get up, he walked to Auld's farm and pleaded with his master to take him back. Auld, however, was not sympathetic and sent Frederick back to Covey.

Frederick walked back to Covey's. He was tired, bruised, and angry. He knew that he would be severely punished for leaving the farm. Covey took Frederick to a whipping post. He intended to "break" this slave. However, Frederick Douglass refused to suffer more abuse, and he defended himself. The two men fought for about two hours. Eventually, Edward Covey gave up. Frederick Douglass was never abused again by the "slave breaker." Frederick was sold to another man who was kinder to his slaves. By now, however, a kind owner, good food, and a reasonable amount of food were not enough. Frederick Douglass wanted to be free.

After working for his new master for a year, Frederick decided to run away to the North. He and five other slaves began to make escape plans. Before they had a chance to escape, one of the slaves exposed the plan. Frederick Douglass was put in prison. He expected to be sold into the deep South, far from the North. To Frederick's surprise, his former master, Thomas Auld, arranged for his release. Auld sent Frederick back to work for his brother Hugh in Baltimore.

Eighteen-year-old Frederick Douglass started work in the shipyards as a caulker—a person who puts sealing material in the seams of a boat to make it watertight. Within a year, he was earning the highest wages possible for a person at his level. Frederick had to turn his wages over to his master. Although his master sometimes let Frederick keep a little of the money, Frederick felt that the arrangement was unfair.

While working in Baltimore, Frederick met a free Negro named Anna Murray. The two became good friends, and soon were engaged to be married. Frederick did not want to marry Anna while he was a slave. He decided that he would escape to the North.

At that time, every free black person had to carry identification papers to prove that he or she was not a slave. Frederick borrowed identification papers from a friend. He knew that he was taking a great risk. If he were caught, he would never see Anna again, and he would probably be killed or sold to slave traders. Frederick Douglass said goodbye to his fiancee and boarded a northbound train.

Frederick held his breath when the conductor asked to see his identification papers. He knew that the description on the papers did not match his appearance. Fortunately, the conductor merely glanced at the papers and handed them back to him. The escape was successful. On September 4, 1838, Frederick Douglass was in New York, a free man.

Despite his joy at being free, Frederick found that his cares were not over. He heard that there were slave catchers in the city looking for escaped slaves. Frederick did not dare trust anyone, black or white. He knew no one, and he needed food and shelter. A kind man noticed Frederick and put him in touch with a group that assisted runaway slaves. Secure in one of their homes, he sent for Anna. She joined him in New York, and on September 15, 1838, they were married. After the wedding, they were advised to move to New Bedford, Massachusetts. There, the Douglasses would be safe from slave catchers, and Frederick could find work as a ship caulker.

Frederick was not able to get a job in the New Bedford shipyard because white shipyard employees did not allow black tradesmen to work beside them. Instead, he took any job that he could find. Frederick sawed wood, cleaned chimneys, and shoveled coal. He barely earned enough to feed his family, which soon included two children, Rosetta and Lewis. Anna Douglass took care of the children and worked as a household servant.

One day, Frederick Douglass was approached by a man who wanted to know if he would like to subscribe to the antislavery newspaper, the *Liberator*. Frederick learned that the *Liberator* was edited by the white leader of the American Anti-Slavery Society, William Lloyd Garrison. The American Anti-Slavery Society was a part of the abolition movement to end slavery. Frederick wanted to learn more about the abolition movement. He began to read the newspaper and attend antislavery meetings. In 1841, at one of the meetings, Frederick Douglass was asked to speak about his own experiences as a slave. Ill at ease and shy, he stood up and began to talk. At first he spoke with hesitation, but soon the emotion of describing what he had lived through made him forget his shyness. Frederick spoke with such deep feeling about his slave days that when he had finished speaking, the audience was stunned. After the meeting, William Lloyd Garrison asked Frederick to become a lecturer for the society. This was the beginning of Frederick Douglass's public career.

For many years, he traveled from town to town giving speeches about his life as a slave. Although Frederick enjoyed his work, he was often separated from his family and his life was sometimes threatened by proslavery groups. However, he continued to give lectures and his speaking abilities improved. They improved so much that some people began to doubt that Douglass had ever really been a slave. To protect his reputation, Frederick decided to write a book about his life. In 1845, the *Narrative of the Life of Frederick Douglass, an American Slave, Written by Himself* was published. In the book, he listed specific names, dates, and places. The facts were verified. There was no doubt that Frederick Douglass had indeed been a slave. The book became very popular and his fame spread.

Frederick Douglass now began to fear that he would lose his freedom. In his book, he had disclosed his identity and location. He decided to go to Great Britain to protect his freedom. After lecturing in Europe for two years, Frederick wanted to go home. However, he was afraid that as soon as he returned to the United Sates, he would be captured and returned to his master. Two British friends decided they would raise enough money to buy Frederick's freedom. The required amount of money was sent to Frederick's master. On December 5, 1846, 28-year-old Frederick Douglass received his papers and was legally a free man.

Safely home, he again made lecture tours. Frederick Douglass had gained an international reputation and a new independence. He decided that he wanted to start a new antislavery newspaper. Frederick believed that a newspaper written and edited by a black person would be a useful weapon against slavery and discrimination. He decided not to publish his newspaper in the same town where the *Liberator* was published. He moved his wife and children to Rochester, New York. In December 1847, the first issue of his newspaper, the *North Star*, was published. Subscriptions to the *North Star* gradually increased. Despite many ups and downs, the newspaper succeeded and was published until 1863.

Frederick was not only a speaker, writer, and editor; he was also a "conductor" for the underground railroad. He welcomed and hid the "passengers" that arrived at his home. The underground railroad was neither underground nor a railroad. It was a number of people who passed escaped slaves from one safe place along the route to another. They used railroad terms as code words. The Douglass home was near the Canadian border, and during the 1850s it was an important part of the underground railroad.

During the years that Frederick had been lecturing about slavery, the North and the South had been arguing in Congress and elsewhere about many problems, including the subject of slavery. In April 1861, the Civil War began. On January 1, 1863, the President issued the Emancipation Proclamation, declaring that all slaves under Confederate control were free. Although this proclamation did not actually free the slaves, it lead to the ratification of the Thirteenth Amendment to the Constitution, which officially abolished slavery in all parts of the United States. This amendment became law on December 18, 1865. Frederick Douglass then helped to organize the Massachusetts 54th Regiment, the first black fighting unit. He served as a recruiting agent for the regiment. His sons, Lewis and Charles, were the first to enlist.

At last the war was over. Slavery had been abolished, and Frederick considered buying a farm and retiring. He soon found, however, that there was still much work to be done. Southerners were not willing to give their ex-slaves the same rights and privileges that Southern whites enjoyed. Frederick discovered that the newly freed slaves were not allowed to vote in elections. Once again, Frederick Douglass went to work. He argued forcefully that former slaves must be allowed to vote if they were to keep their newly won freedom. In 1870, the Fifteenth Amendment to the Constitution was adopted and blacks were granted the right to vote.

Frederick Douglass spent the rest of his life speaking and writing to end oppression and to advance racial equality. In 1889, President Benjamin Harrison appointed Frederick Douglass the American consul-general to Haiti, an island nation in the West Indies. He treated the Haitians with respect, and they got along very well. By 1891, however, Frederick's health began to suffer, and he decided to resign the counsulship and return to the United States. In a gesture of respect, the Haitains asked him to be their representative to the Columbian Exposition at the World's Fair in Chicago in 1893. He was the only black to have an official role at the exposition. The lack of black representation angered him. He wrote and published a pamphlet to point out that the country was ignoring its black citizens.

Frederick Douglass fought to get slavery abolished, and he fought for the right to vote. He saw both of these things happen, and he was proud of his achievements. Yet, he was saddened by the racial prejudice that continued. Until the day he died, he continued to share his ideas and dreams, that the United States could make a home for races of every color.

Directions: On a separate sheet of paper, answer the following questions about Frederick Douglass.

1. After Frederick Douglass became an accomplished speaker, why do you think some people doubted that he had ever been a slave? Explain your answer.
2. Frederick Douglass is considered by many to be the most outstanding of the black abolitionists. Explain his importance to the abolition movement.

SAMUEL L. CLEMENS

River pilot, author, lecturer, and humorist; born in Missouri in 1835 and died in Connecticut in 1910

Tom Sawyer and *Huckleberry Finn* have been enjoyed by people of all ages all over the world. The author of these books was an American named Samuel L. Clemens, although he wrote most of his stories under the name of Mark Twain. *Tom Sawyer* and *Huckleberry Finn* are filled with the adventures of two boys who lived in Hannibal, Missouri, a small town on the bank of the Mississippi River, during the 1850s.

Many of the adventures recorded in *Tom Sawyer* and *Huckleberry Finn* are based on true events in Sam's life. Once, for example, Sam's mother told him he could not go swimming because the weather was too cold. To be sure he obeyed, his mother sewed his collar together so he could not get it off without her knowing. Sam, however, was determined to go swimming. He took a needle and thread along, ripped open the stitches, and went in swimming anyway. Later he sewed the collar together again. When he got home, his younger brother Henry showed their mother the big white stitches that had replaced her fine black stitches. In *Tom Sawyer,* Tom's half-brother Sid tells on Tom in just the same way.

For punishment, Sam was sent out to paint the back fence with whitewash. When other boys came by to watch, he pretended that he enjoyed the job. They wanted him to let them try splashing the whitewash on the fence with the big brush. Sam agreed to let them do it, but only if they gave him something in return. By the end of the afternoon he had collected an apple, a kitten, a blue glass bottle, a brass doorknob, and twelve marbles. The fence was all painted. This is just the way that Tom Sawyer, in the story, gets his friends to whitewash a fence for him.

The happy days Sam Clemens described in *Tom Sawyer* and Huckleberry Finn took place in the first eleven years of his life. Sam's father died before Sam turned twelve, and Sam left school to go to work. His first job was an apprenticeship with the printer that put out Hannibal's weekly newspaper, the *Courier*. Later, he went to work for his brother Orion, who had bought out the *Courier*'s rival, the Hannibal *Journal*. By the time Sam Clemens was fourteen, he knew how to set type. He often took charge of the newspaper while the editor was away. At the age of seventeen, Sam left Hannibal and traveled by train to St. Louis, New York, and Philadelphia. He made money to support himself by working in print shops.

When he was twenty-two, Sam Clemens decided that he wanted to visit the Amazon River in South America. On the first leg of his journey, he took a paddle-wheel steamboat to New Orleans. As a boy, he had once stowed away on one of these steamboats. However, he was discovered and put off almost immediately. Now Clemens once again boarded a Mississippi River steamboat. This time he could afford a ticket, and he traveled on the steamboat all the way down to New Orleans.

When he arrived in New Orleans, Clemens discovered that no boats were heading for the Amazon and none were likely to for many years. He changed his mind and decided to become a river pilot. The big paddle-wheel steamboats that ran down the Mississippi River had always fascinated Clemens. They reminded him of large hotels floating on the water. He also admired the skill of the steamboat pilots. There were no maps or charts of the river for the pilots to follow. The safety of each boat depended on the pilot's knowledge. The pilots had to learn by heart every turn and twist of the river.

They had to know the depth of the main channel in every season of the year. The only way a new pilot could learn to steer a boat on the twisting Mississippi was to be taught, mile after mile, by another, more experienced, pilot.

One of the pilots on Clemens's trip to New Orleans had been the famous Horace Bixby. During the whole trip, Sam had watched Bixby and listened to his stories. After discovering that he could not go to the Amazon, Sam Clemens persuaded Bixby to give him lessons in piloting.

As part of his training, Clemens learned how the crew measured the depth of the water when the river channel changed. This was important during the spring floods or when the river became shallow in the low-water season. A man would drop a line with a lead weight at its end into the river. When the weight hit bottom, the crew would call the depth up to the pilot. They called it in fathoms. A fathom is six feet. A Mississippi paddle-wheel steamer could only travel safely in water that was deeper than one and a half fathoms—that is, nine feet. The danger point was two fathoms, or "twain," as the crew called it. The crew would call out the "mark," or measurement on the line, as the boat crept slowly into a strange channel. "Mark three!" they would call when the line showed a depth of three fathoms. Then, as the water became shallower, "Mark half twain! Mark quarter twain!" When the pilot heard the danger call, "Mark twain!," he would quickly order the engines reversed to pull the boat back to safety.

After a little more than a year of training, Sam Clemens became a river pilot. He spent two exciting years piloting steamboats on the Mississippi. Because of his excellent knowledge of the river, he earned very high pay. Then, in 1861, the Civil War broke out. Steamboat piloting became a dangerous occupation. Northerners suspected the pilots because they ventured into the South, and Southerners suspected them because of their northern contacts. Soon steamboat traffic on the Mississippi nearly came to a halt. All in all, it seemed safer to Clemens to find another occupation.

Clemens had saved some money, and he now decided that he wanted to see the mining country in the West. He learned that President Lincoln had appointed his brother Orion as Secretary to the new Nevada Territory. He offered his penniless brother both his company and the money for the stagecoach tickets. Together, they traveled to the Nevada Territory.

In Nevada, Clemens and his brother separated. Clemens prospected for silver in Nevada, but without much luck. His money was soon all gone. He began to write for the *Territorial Enterprise*, the first newspaper in the area. He sent funny letters and news items from the prospectors' camps to the newspaper. Soon the editor asked the 24-year-old Clemens to come to the newspaper office in Virginia City, the largest town in Nevada. Clemens's job was to write about the legislative sessions in Virginia City. His reports caused many arguments and complaints from legislators. To avoid direct attacks on himself, Clemens began to sign his articles "Mark Twain," after the danger call used on the Mississippi steamboats. In addition to the legislative reporting, Clemens soon began writing humorous stories about the silver miners and the lives they led.

Sam Clemens then spent some time traveling around California and writing for other newspapers. He also spent a little time in mining camps in the foothills. While he was in the foothills, Clemens heard a folk tale about a jumping frog contest in nearby Calaveras County. According to the tale, a miner trained a bullfrog to jump, and then bet all comers that his frog could jump farther than theirs. In a famous contest, the miner's opponents filled the frog with buckshot. They filled the frog's stomach with so much lead that it could not jump, and the miner lost all his bets.

Sam Clemens wrote a story about it called "The Celebrated Jumping Frog of Calaveras County" and signed it with the name Mark Twain. He sent the story to a magazine in New York City. His was not the only account of the frog tale, nor was it the first published. Clemens simply told the tale so vividly and colorfully that other versions paled in comparison. His story was published and became famous—so famous, in fact, that Calaveras County now holds a Jumping Frog Contest every year.

Then Sam Clemens returned to San Francisco with a new idea. One of the first steamships to travel from San Francisco to Honolulu was about to set out. Clemens was hired to go along and write articles for the *Sacramento Union*. He wrote about the beautiful things he saw in tropical Hawaii. The "Honolulu Letters from Mark Twain" were published in Eastern papers as well in as in the *Union*.

From Honolulu, Sam Clemens went to New York. By this time it was easy for Mark Twain, as Sam Clemens was known by then, to interest publishers in his travel stories. He traveled with one of the first organized tour groups throughout Europe and the Middle East. These early American tourists were unaccustomed to foreign travel, and many ridiculous things happened to them. Mark Twain wrote a funny book about it all. He called it *The Innocents Abroad*. It was a bestseller—Sam Clemens's first really successful book. The name Mark Twain became famous overnight.

Soon after his trip abroad, Clemens fell in love with Olivia Langdon, the sister of one of the tourists on the European cruise. Her wealthy father opposed the match at first because Clemens had a reputation of being a wanderer and an adventurer. Not wanting to marry with the ill wishes of Olivia's father, Clemens bought a respectable house in Boston and tried hard to show that he could be a responsible citizen. At last her father agreed, and the two were happily married.

Sam Clemens, as Mark Twain, now settled down to writing. He filled his books with his experiences. Because of this, Twain's writing can be viewed as a fairly accurate reflection of his times. *Tom Sawyer* and *Huckleberry Finn* are more than just children's books. Beneath the humor, readers can get a glimpse of the social views and prejudices of the people of southern Missouri in the years before the Civil War. *Life on the Mississippi* takes place a little later, while Clemens was a river pilot just before the war. His book *Roughing It* is staged during the Civil War. Clemens put not only his earlier stagecoach trip to Nevada, but also all the funny stories he had written about mining into this book. Because Clemens found humor in the attitudes and practices of people, *Roughing It* reveals much about life in the Western territories during the Civil War.

Not all of Clemens's books are based on his own experiences. He became interested in the story of a boy king who had lived in England in the 1500s. He wrote a book about him called *The Prince and the Pauper*. In a funny story called *A Connecticut Yankee at King Arthur's Court,* he told of the adventures of a modern American who suddenly finds himself in the England of King Arthur. For nearly forty years before his death, Clemens worked on an autobiography. He insisted, however, that the autobiography be published after he died. He said he felt freer to express his opinions and could give truer accounts of his experiences if he knew he would not be around to face the world's reaction. He also started a publishing company and published all his own works, as well as the famous memoirs of General Ulysses S. Grant.

With his wife and their three daughters, Clemens traveled widely in Europe. He made friends all over the world. In Rome, Paris, Cairo, Delhi, and many other places, thousands of people crowded to see "Mark Twain." Speaking through interpreters, Clemens read from many of his stories and also gave lectures.

Sam Clemens, alias Mark Twain, was one of the funniest writers and one of the most comical lecturers in the world. In a white linen suit, with his bushy white hair and long mustache blowing in the breeze, he made crowds around the world laugh. Unfortunately, his own last years were sad. Most of his family died, and he lived out his final days alone and unhappy. However, the stories of Mark Twain—of boys and bullfrogs, river pilots and rafts, stagecoaches and miners—are still remembered and read with laughter.

Directions: On a separate sheet of paper, answer the following questions about Samuel Clemens.

1. The writings of Samuel Clemens, or Mark Twain, are generally classified as humorous fiction. How can reading his "comedies" help people learn more about how people lived during the 1800s? Explain your answer.

2. Sam Clemens enjoyed his brief employment as a river pilot. Why do you think he never returned to river piloting, even after the war ended? Explain your answer.

PART III: INVENTION AND REFORM

The recent Industrial Revolution had brought forth many changes in American society—some good and some bad. The prevailing attitude was one of supreme ability: there was nothing the American people could not do! One outgrowth of this line of thinking was the "Age of Invention." Inventors such as Alexander Graham Bell and Thomas Edison worked to improve the lives of people by designing usable and affordable household items. The telephone, electric lights, the phonograph, and many other conveniences that people today take for granted were the result of these inventive minds.

Another change brought about by industry was a major shift in the American population. More and more people began crowding into the cities to work in the factories. The immigrants, still pouring into the United States, also settled in the cities. This increase in city populations had farflung results on American society. One positive result was the increased popularity of tall buildings and the birth of the "skyscraper."

However, the crowded cities had many negative effects, too. There was often not enough work in the cities to go around. In addition, the more recent immigrants provided cheap labor for the factories. Conditions in the factories began to get worse. Men, women, and children worked in the factories from dawn until dark—sometimes up to sixteen hours a day. Safety features were practically non-existant, and if a worker was injured on the job, there was no way for the worker to earn any money to feed the family.

The need for reform in the big cities was answered by a number of dedicated people. Through the work of these citizens, new labor laws were passed, forbidding the use of child labor and regulating the conditions and working hours of the men and women in factories. Labor unions were organized to fight for the rights of workers.

Reform was also taking place in other areas of society. Black Americans continued their fight for civil rights, and women began to realize that they, too, needed laws to protect their rights.

EMILY DICKENSON

One of America's best-known poets; born in 1830 in Massachusetts and died there in 1886

The people of Amherst, Massachusetts, thought Emily Dickinson was a very strange woman. Sometimes, they saw her white dress move quickly behind the windows of her brick house. Some people said she only wore white. Folks knew that she rarely left her house and that she hardly ever saw anyone besides her immediate family. They did not know that she kept to herself to write poetry, and that she would one day be considered one of the country's greatest poets.

Emily had reddish-brown hair and auburn eyes. Friends said her face was plain and her build was slight. She spoke with a high-pitched, breathless voice. She had a special fondness for flowers, and she filled her house with bouquets. Her rye and Indian breads were considered remarkable, and once she won a baking contest.

When Emily was young, she was lively and had many friends. She often said things that were very funny. She wrote humorous articles for her school magazine. She sent some comic valentines to her brother's school friends. One of the valentines was published in a newspaper. In spite of her friendships and good humor, Emily was terribly shy. When her parents had guests to dinner, Emily had to leave the room. At school, she feared the afternoons when she had to recite her compositions.

As years passed, Emily grew more and more shy. After her thirtieth birthday, she withdrew into the house. Rather than visit with friends, she preferred to write letters. There were a few exceptions. She sometimes invited boys and girls into her kitchen, where she served them cake. Sometimes she looked through her second-story window and saw children playing in the garden. Then she would lower a basket of bread down to them. Soon she disappeared behind the curtains.

Emily Dickinson was born in Amherst on December 10, 1830. She was named for her mother, Emily Norcross Dickinson. Her father, Edward Dickinson, was one of the leading lawyers of western Massachusetts. He served in the state legislature and the United States Congress. His ancestors were among the early Puritan settlers in New England.

The house where Emily was born is also the house where she died. Except for four years in another house and one year at college, Emily lived in that house all her life. The house was in the middle of town. Because there was a great deal of land, the house was called the Dickinson homestead. There were chickens and horses, and a barn and stable. The house had been built by Emily's grandfather, Samuel Fowler Dickinson. Grandfather Dickinson also founded Amherst Academy and Amherst College.

Emily was a middle child. Her brother, Austin, was two years older. Her sister, Lavinia, was two years younger. Lavinia, like Emily, never married and lived out her life at the homestead. Austin did get married—to a friend of Emily's. They lived in a house that Edward Dickinson built for them next door to the homestead. The father wanted all of his children near him. The closeness of the Dickinson family often seemed like a wall to outsiders.

Emily's father had a reputation for being very demanding, very strict, and never showing affection. He was not unkind, however. He and Emily were very attached to one another. When he worried because Emily took long walks all by herself, he bought her a dog to keep her company.

Emily's father believed that reading for pleasure was sinful. Emily hid her favorite books behind furniture or in the barn so her father would not take them. Edward Dickinson thought that girls should receive the same quality of education as boys. As a result, Emily's schooling was better than usual for girls of her time.

Emily learned reading, writing, and arithemetic in public schools. When she was nine years old, she entered the Amherst Academy. The Academy, founded by her grandfather, was a private school that prepared young people for college. Emily was very happy in school and made many friends. Her favorite subjects were botany and literature. When she was sixteen, she left home to attend the South Hadley Female Seminary (now Mount Holyoke College). She enjoyed some of her classes. However, there was a religious revival going on at the school—a revival that Emily did not feel she could join. This troubled her very much. Throughout her life, Emily wrestled with ideas of religion and God. Also, even though the college was only ten miles from home, Emily was very lonesome. At the end of the first year, Emily returned home for good.

At college, one of Emily's teachers had urged her to write. After returning home, she began to write poetry. Soon, she was taking her writing very seriously. In the years 1862 to 1866, during and immediately after the Civil War, she wrote 800 poems. Many of the young men she knew had joined the Union Army, and Emily worried about them.

Emily wrote about love and death, God and nature. She wrote about the deep feelings of loneliness and insecurity. During the Civil War period she wrote:

> I'm nobody! Who are you?
> Are you—Nobody—too?
> Then there's a pair of us?
> Don't tell! They'd advertise—you know!
>
> How dreary—to be—Somebody!
> How public—like a Frog—
> To tell one's name—the live long June
> To an admiring Bog!

One day in 1862, Emily read an issue of the *Atlantic Monthly* magazine. There was an article of advice to young writers. The author was Thomas Wentworth Higginson, a man who had given up the ministry to devote himself to literary causes. Higginson urged young writers to work hard at writing. He cautioned that they must not be satisfied until their words were full of life. Emily wanted to ask Higginson's advice about her own poetry.

She decided to write to him. "Mr. Higginson," her letter began. "Are you too deeply occupied to say if my Verse is alive?" With the letter, she mailed four of her poems. Higginson wrote back to Emily, urging her to continue writing. However, he criticized her writing. He told her to practice her rhythms and rhymes and to eliminate all the dashes and capital letters. He wrote that she should not publish her poetry until she learned more. Scholars now know that Higginson did not understand Emily's poetry. He was not able to see the importance of her work. He had never seen poetry like hers. He only knew that popular poetry had definite rhymes and exact rhythm.

Emily wrote back to Higginson. She asked for his advice and friendship. They exchanged many letters. Emily regarded Higginson as a good friend, even though she did not change her poetry to suit him. He never offered to publish her poetry. He asked how old she was. She did not reply. She hid her age from him, just as she hid the rest of her poetry. He had no idea that Emily was over thirty and that she had already written hundreds of poems.

One day, when Emily was over forty years old, Higginson decided to visit her. He was one of the few outsiders that she agreed to see. He waited in her drawing room. Emily appeared carrying a bouquet. She handed Higginson the flowers, as an introduction. He later wrote that she looked like an innocent child.

Without encouragement from Higginson, Emily became even more secretive about her writing. Her father was not supportive, either. If reading for pleasure was sinful, perhaps he felt writing for pleasure was also. Day by day, as Emily wrote, she placed her finished poems inside a locked box. As the numbers of poems grew, she sewed groups of poems together into little booklets.

Emily's father died in 1874 when Emily was forty-four years old. The next year, her mother had a stroke. During the next seven years, Emily took care of her invalid mother. Her poetry writing lessened, although she continued to write many letters. In 1882, Emily's mother died. The next year, Emily was again saddened. A beloved nephew, Gilbert, died at the age of eight. Emily herself became ill with a kidney disease.

During the next few years, Emily's condition became more serious. She grew weaker. During the last months of 1885 and the first of 1886, Emily spent more and more time in bed. She wrote letters, but almost no poetry. She refused to be examined by a doctor. Her condition worsened. On May 15, 1886, Emily died. She was fifty-five years old.

Emily was put to rest in a white casket covered with violets, ground pine, and apple blossoms. Thomas Higginson came to the funeral to read a poem. It was not one of Emily's poems.

After Emily's death, Lavinia climbed the stairs to Emily's room. As terrible as she felt, she knew she had to go through Emily's things. She opened the cherry-wood drawers. In the bottom drawer, she found the locked box. When she opened the box, Lavinia was astonished to find the poems. She knew that Emily had written poetry, but she had no idea that there would be so many poems. Lavinia eventually counted more than 1,700 poems.

Lavinia was stunned. What should she do with the poems? What could she do to save them? Emily had left instructions to destroy the poems because she thought people would not understand them. Lavinia's brother was too busy to help her. Her sister-in-law was not interested. Lavinia went to a family friend, Mabel Loomis Todd. Mable agreed to help. She would try to find a publisher for Emily's poems.

Mabel contacted Higginson. He was not interested in publishing Emily's poetry. After all, she had never taken his advice. People would be bewildered by the poetry. It would never sell. Mabel urged him to change his mind. She appealed to his sense of friendship for Emily. He finally agreed to publish a few poems, but only a few.

In 1890, a book of 114 poems by Emily Dickinson appeared. They were edited, and sometimes changed, by Mabel and Higginson. Higginson was soon surprised. People liked Emily's poetry. They were asking for more. The next year, Mabel and Higginson published a second volume of Emily's poems. Soon they, and others, published more. Eventually all of the poems and letters were published.

Through the years, there have been many questions about Emily Dickinson. Why did Emily live the way she did? How did Emily know so much about love? Did she have a secret romance? Why did she always wear white? How could one woman write so many wonderful poems? There are many other unanswered questions about Emily Dickinson, too. However, nearly everyone agrees, Emily Dickinson was one of the greatest American poets of all time.

Directions: On a separate sheet of paper, answer the following questions about Emily Dickinson.

1. What effect do you think Emily Dickinson's father had on her work? Explain your answer.
2. Why do you think Emily Dickinson wrote most of her poetry in secret? Explain your answer.

ANDREW CARNEGIE

Industrialist, pioneer of the steel industry in the United States; born in Scotland in 1835 and died in Massachusetts in 1919

Andrew Carnegie sat at his mother's side. He threaded needles for her while she mended shoes. Someday, he mused, he would make enough money so his mother could wear silk dresses and ride in a carriage. Someday they would no longer be poor. Andrew's father was out of work. William Carnegie was a skilled hand-weaver of beautiful linen. At one time, his business was good enough to feed his family of four, but no longer. Cheap, factory-made linen had ruined his livelihood.

Andrew was born in Dunfermline, Scotland, on November 25, 1835. Dunfermline was an old town that was rich in history. The city was also the center for Scotland's finest damask linen. The family occupied a two-room cottage—one room upstairs for living and another room downstairs for working. Andrew and his brother Tom, five years younger, attended primary school. Later, Andrew was tutored by an uncle who inspired in him a love for learning.

When Andrew was twelve years old, his mother borrowed money from a friend for the family's passage to America. Margaret and William Carnegie wanted to give their sons a better chance in life than Margaret and William had had. They crossed the ocean in the summer of 1848 and joined a settlement of Scottish immigrants in Allegheny (now part of Pittsburgh), Pennsylvania. Some of Margaret's family already lived there. Andrew and his father went to work in a cotton mill. For twelve hours a day, Andrew tended the bobbins, the spools that held the cotton. He was paid $1.20 a week. The family was so poor that even this little bit helped.

When Andrew was fourteen, he became a messenger for the Pittsburgh telegraph office. He was soon a familiar sight, dashing across town in his green uniform. Andrew, who was small for his age, ran swiftly. His favorite deliveries were to the theater. He saved the theater telegrams for evening delivery. He knew the theater schedule by heart. Just as the curtain rose, Andrew arrived with the telegrams. The manager generally allowed Andrew Carnegie to stay and watch the play.

In those days, there was no free lending library in Pittsburgh. One day, Andrew heard that a prominent citizen of Pittsburgh was lending books to working boys. Colonel James Anderson, an elderly man with a love for literature, invited working boys to come to his home on Saturday evenings. They could pick out books from his library and keep them until the next Saturday. Andrew was one of the first to borrow books. Andrew never forgot Colonel Anderson or his library.

When Andrew was sixteen, he taught himself to transcribe telegraph sounds by listening to them. Only a few people knew how to do that. Most telegraph companies had to use machines to transcribe the telegraph signals into words. Andrew could now bypass the machine. He showed off his skill to his employer. That is how Andrew became a telegraph-key operator. He wrote a cousin in Scotland about his new job. Imagine, his salary was now an incredible $4 a week!

One day, an important man from the Pennsylvania Railroad came into the telegraph office. Thomas A. Scott was superintendent of the railroad's Pittsburgh Division. He quickly noticed Andrew's skills. Scott hired Andrew as his private secretary and personal telegrapher. The pay was $35 a month to start. Andrew Carnegie, the son of a poor weaver, was on his way to becoming a successful man. Soon, he would be able to buy his mother the silk dresses and the carriage he had wanted for her as a young boy.

Scott traveled often, and he left Andrew in charge while he was away. Sometimes Andrew had to make major decisions while his employer was away. Scott grew more and more impressed with his young assistant. In 1859, when Andrew was twenty-four, Scott became president of the Pennsylvania Railroad. Scott appointed Andrew the new superintendent of the Pittsburgh Division. In the next few years, Andrew introduced sleeping cars to the railroad. He invested in the sleeping car company and in some other businesses that interested him.

Scott went on to other tasks and took Andrew along. In 1861, when the Civil War began, Scott was appointed Assistant Secretary of War. He sent for Andrew to help him. Andrew helped organize the telegraph services for the Union Army. He transported troops, and sometimes prisoners, across the country.

Andrew was a short man. Some say he was five-foot five; others say he was only five-foot two. He had a very fair complexion. His fine hair was so blond that it actually looked white. He could not tolerate much exposure to the sun. One hot summer day, when Andrew was working outdoors, he became ill from sunstroke. This affected him the rest of his life. He always had to spend his summers in a cool climate.

At the time of the Civil War, the iron industry in the United States was in its infancy. There were many wooden railroad bridges that were falling into disrepair. Andrew noticed that the wooden bridges were being replaced with iron bridges. He realized that iron had an important future in the United States. He decided to invest in the Keystone Bridge Works, a manufacturer of iron bridges. In 1865, at the end of the war, Andrew resigned from the railroad. From then on, he wanted to devote himself to his own businesses.

In the early 1870s, young Carnegie went to Great Britain on business. While he traveled in Great Britain, he saw the growth of the steel industry. He met Sir Henry Bessemer, the man who invented a way to manufacture steel. He foresaw the importance of steel in the United States and he wanted to be at the head of the industry. Carnegie decided to take absolutely everything he had and invest it in steel. His critics called him rash, a gambler, foolish!

Someone said, "You're putting all your eggs in one basket!" Carnegie agreed that he was putting all of his eggs in one basket, but said that he intended to watch the eggs closely.

Time proved Carnegie to be right. In 1873, Great Britain led the world in steel production. Sixteen years later, thanks to Carnegie, the United States was the leader.

What made Carnegie so successful? He hired extremely gifted men to run his business. He also made clever use of bad economic times—something his competition did not do. From 1873 to 1879, there was an economic slump in the United States. During economic slumps, prices are low. Carnegie took advantage of these times to expand his steel business. While others were waiting out the bad times, Carnegie made his steel mill the largest and most modern of the day. During the next economic slump, in the 1880s, Carnegie bought out his greatest competitor, the Homestead Steel Works. He also acquired his own iron ore mines and a coke company. Coke, a coal by-product, and iron ore are essential for the manufacture of steel.

In 1886, Carnegie suffered personal losses when both his mother and his brother Tom died. Since his father had died many years earlier, Carnegie was now completely alone. He decided to get married. In 1886, already past the age of fifty, Carnegie married Louise Whitfield of New York. They had one daughter. The Carnegies named her Margaret, after his mother. The Carnegie family spent six months of each year in Scotland.

In the summer of 1892, while Carnegie was vacationing in Scotland, trouble came to his steel company. The young Iron and Steel Workers Union decided to stage a strike at the Homestead plant. Carnegie was far away. He had left Henry Clay Frick in charge. Henry Clay Frick was a partner who had no sympathy for labor. The Union members were angry because the company was cutting their wages. As it was, they worked very long hours for very little money. Many skilled, long-time employees were fired so that the company could replace them with cheap, unskilled labor.

Frick reacted to the strike. When it had gone on for 140 days, Frick hired 200 Pinkerton detectives to protect his non-union labor. The day the Pinkerton guards arrived, there was a riot. Seven men were killed and many more were wounded. Frick asked the governor of Pennsylvania for help. The governor sent the entire state militia to Homestead. The Union was crushed. After the strike, the angered Frick punished the workers. He made the employees work twelve-hour days and drastically cut their wages.

Throughout the lengthy episode, there was no word from Carnegie. When Carnegie finally returned, he and Frick argued about many troublesome matters. Before the shouting died down, Frick resigned. The two men never spoke to one another again.

Carnegie had definite ideas about acquiring and distributing wealth. He had written about it many times. Three years before the Homestead strike, he published his most famous written work. His article, "Wealth," appeared in the June 1889 issue of the *North America Review* magazine. In the article, Carnegie explained his so-called "Gospel of Wealth." He said it was a disgrace for a rich person to die wealthy. The rich owed their good fortune to the community and should return most of their money to the people. He did not believe in customary charity or handouts. He believed in providing educational and cultural opportunities for workers so that they could improve themselves.

In 1901, Carnegie was ready to retire. He wanted to devote himself to what he liked best—distributing his wealth. He sold his company to a group headed by the banker, J. P. Morgan, for $400 million. The sale of his company made Carnegie's personal fortune worth an estimated $500 million. When he shook hands with Morgan, Carnegie became the richest man in the United States. Morgan and his partners combined Carnegie Steel with other companies to form the United States Steel Corporation. Very soon after the handshake, Carnegie established a pension fund for his former employees. Five years later, Carnegie founded another pension fund, this one for college professors. Carnegie spent the rest of his life giving away his money.

Some wealthy people wait until they are very old to give away their money. Others do it after their death through a will. Carnegie gave his money away throughout his lifetime. In the 1870s, he donated free baths to his hometown in Scotland. Remembering Colonel Anderson, he opened his first free library in 1881. Eventually there were 2,500 Carnegie libraries throughout the English-speaking world.

He supported dinosaur digs in Utah and Wyoming—and had two dinosaurs named after him and his wife. He funded the Mt. Wilson Observatory in Pasadena, California. Schools he established make up today's Carnegie-Mellon University in Pittsburgh. He was a major contributor to the Tuskegee Institute in Macon County, Alabama. He built Carnegie Hall, the famous concert hall in New York City. He pushed for world peace and built the Peace Palace at the Hague in the Netherlands.

When World War I broke out in 1914, Carnegie decided that his work for peace was a failure. He was more than eighty and very tired. On August 11, 1919, Carnegie died at his summer home in Lenox, Massachusetts. He was eighty-four years old. Today, through the institutions and foundations he established, Andrew Carnegie is still returning his wealth to the public.

Directions: On a separate sheet of paper, answer the following questions about Andrew Carnegie.

1. Carnegie was well known for his "Gospel of Wealth." What was this philosophy and how did it influence Carnegie's accomplishments?
2. Do you think Andrew Carnegie could be such a success today? Explain your answer.

SUSAN B. ANTHONY

Advocate for women's rights; born in 1820 in Massachusetts and died in New York in 1906

She died a failure—a splendid failure, some said—but in her failure she did more to change the lives of women all over the world than anyone else had in United States history.

Susan B. Anthony was born February 15, 1820, in the Quaker village of Adams in the Berkshire Hills of Massachusetts. She was the second daughter born to Daniel Anthony, a Quaker with a mind of his own, and his wife, Lucy Read Anthony.

Before she was five years old, Susan had learned to read and write. She had only just started to attend the village school when she insisted that the schoolmaster teach her how to do long division. He did not know how to teach such "higher mathematics," so Susan was forced to figure out the process for herself.

Susan was seventeen when she and her older sister, Guelma, went to a finishing school near Philadelphia to learn etiquette and self-confidence. Susan did not learn much at the school. When a student was not perfect in her lessons or behavior, she was forbidden to study or read, and Susan was often in trouble. Once she tried to mail a letter home without first presenting it to the schoolmistress to read.

The schoolmistress found the letter and made such a scene that it was a long time before Susan could recall the incident without crying. The worst scene, however, occurred when Susan was helping with the weekly housecleaning. She saw a spot of dust on the ceiling that she could not reach. She stepped up on the schoolmistress's desk to reach the dusty spot—and the desk broke!

Susan left the school after only a year. The economic panic of 1838 brought much of the business in the nation to a standstill, and Susan's father lost everything, including the family's home and all its contents, even his and Lucy's eyeglasses.

Susan wanted to work and support herself. The panic of 1838 that had cost Daniel his business had caused the same kind of problems for other families. For the first time in American history, thousands of educated young women were forced to work outside of their homes to help support their families. However, there were few jobs for these women.

Teaching was one field that was open to women, so Susan became a teacher. In one of her early jobs, she was in charge of a school near the old town of Hardscrabble, which had changed its name to Center Falls. She replaced a man who had earned $10 a week; Susan was paid $2.50 a week. In 1843, she became principal of the girls' part of Canajoharie (kan uh joh HAR ee) Academy. However, after nine years of teaching, she wanted a change. She wanted to help people, but she was uncertain of the best way to do it.

In July 1848, a group of women led by Elizabeth Cady Stanton and Lucretia Mott held a convention in Seneca Falls, New York. It was the first attempt to organize women into a group to obtain for women the same rights that men had. At that time, women could not vote. They could not own property, sign contracts, or witness a legal document. Women could not even claim the wages they had earned. If a married couple had children, the children belonged to the father. He could give them away if he wished. In case of divorce, the father or his family received custody of the children, and the mother lost all rights to them.

Susan did not attend the convention, but she read about it. Two weeks later, the second women's rights convention met in Rochester. Susan soon learned that her family had attended and had approved of the goals of the convention. The issue of women's rights was important, Susan agreed, but there were other social problems that were more pressing.

Two problems that Susan thought more important were slavery and the heavy drinking that was a habit among American men. Susan knew that the abolitionists, who were working to abolish slavery, were not paying their speakers and organizers. Although she thought that slavery was the more important issue, Susan had to be able to support herself. She thought she had a better chance of earning a living by working with the temperance societies.

Temperance societies worked to educate people to the dangers of drinking hard liquor. Most of the people involved in these societies were clergymen or men who were reformed drinkers. A society of women was active in the temperance movement, but the men's society refused to recognize the women. Susan attempted to unite the two groups, and in 1852 was invited to Albany as a delegate to the state convention of the New York Sons of Temperance. However, when she rose in the meeting to speak, she was told that the women delegates were there to listen and learn, not to speak. She stalked indignantly from the hall and called the other women delegates to a meeting the next evening at a nearby church hall. Despite a bad snowstorm, women crowded the hall. During the meeting, a chimney filled the room with smoke, and in the middle of a speech, a stove pipe fell down. In spite of everything, the State Temperance Society was born. The society accepted men as members, but did not allow them to hold office. Within a year, however, the men began to claim that their rights were being denied them, and the women voted to allow them to hold office. The men immediately took control of the meeting and forced out the president, Elizabeth Cady Stanton. Susan resigned. She had become involved hoping to improve the lives of the drinkers' wives and children. She could see, now, that before women could do anything to improve their lives, they needed to have laws on their side. Men were not going to give women legal rights. If women wanted freedom, they would have to fight for it.

By 1853, five years after the Seneca Falls Convention, Susan's father was able to offer financial support. He encouraged her to become involved in social reform. She and Elizabeth Cady Stanton began a friendship that would last for fifty years. During those fifty years, the two women would carry forward the battle that has changed the lives of women all over the world—the fight for women's rights.

The two women were very different; Elizabeth gave speeches that were long and flowery and much admired. Susan said what she had to say in as few words as possible, then sat down. To help Susan gain confidence in her speaking ability, Elizabeth wrote a long, two-part speech, which Susan memorized. Thereafter, when Susan had to give a speech, she gave one part or the other of the memorized speech, gradually adding touches of her own. Throughout their association, Susan usually provided the content for their speeches and Elizabeth provided the beauty. Elizabeth was wealthy and the mother of seven children; Susan, now thirty-three years old, was considered an "old maid." At the beginning of the friendship, Elizabeth was the leader and Susan the follower. In later years, however, as Susan gained experience and confidence, the roles reversed.

Elizabeth was responsible for one custom adopted by the women's movement that amused the men and embarrassed the women. Elizabeth's cousin designed a dress with a skirt that came below the knees and was worn over a pair of long trousers. Elizabeth thought the new dress looked much more practical than the full, ground-sweeping skirts that women wore over many starched, stiff underskirts. She insisted that her friends wear the new dress as a symbol of freedom. The dress became known as "bloomers" because Amelia Bloomer wrote about it in a small newspaper she published. By 1854, however, the women realized that people could not hear what was being said because the people were laughing at their bloomers, and the women returned to more traditional dresses.

In September 1853, Susan began to organize groups of women in southern New York. She soon discovered that women had no money of their own to support the organization. She realized that before women could have any freedom, they had to have control of some money. She found out which laws concerning women were the most unfair. Susan and Elizabeth set to work to get the worst of these laws changed in the state of New York. They organized the women and went from door to door getting signatures on petitions.

In ten weeks, they gathered 6,000 signatures for the petition to grant married women the right to collect and control their own wages, and the right of joint guardianship of their children. They presented the petition to the Legislature; the men hardly knew what the women were asking. The petition was ignored.

Susan continued to work. On Christmas day of 1854, she went out into the worst winter in ten years to gather more signatures. In February 1855, she again presented petitions to the Legislature. When she could not get any bills introduced, she kept on collecting signatures. She could not get from town to town by train, so she traveled by stagecoach. A man began to follow her, bringing heated boards to warm her feet and cups of hot tea against the cold. He took her to his sister's house to rest. He began to drive her from town to town in his beautiful sleigh. He proposed marriage; he wanted to take her away from her difficult life. He went sadly away after her firm "no." Her feet, without the heated board to warm them, became frostbitten. Soon she could not walk. In Watertown, she decided to try the "water cure." She rented a tin tub and ordered two buckets of ice water. She sat in the tub while a chambermaid poured the ice water over her body. Then she wrapped herself in hot blankets, slept through the night, and woke up the next morning feeling well and ready to get back to work.

In 1856, Susan involved herself in the abolition movement. Her fame as an organizer had grown and the abolitionists were willing to pay her $10 a week. The movement was losing popularity, however, and there were constant problems. The speaking tour she agreed to do for the abolitionists was one of Susan's worst experiences, but from it she became a polished speaker and debater. During the next years, she used her skills for the cause of women's rights.

At last Susan gained a victory! On March 19, 1860, the New York Legislature passed laws giving women the right to own property, conduct business, sign contracts, be joint guardians of their children, and retain property rights at their husband's death. Other states soon passed similar laws.

When the Civil War broke out, the women's rights issue became of secondary importance. Now the battle cry was for emancipation of, or freedom for, the slaves. Many people did not want to hear that cry, however. Susan now saw angry faces at the meetings. Audiences yelled curses and howled so that abolitionist speakers could not be heard. They threw rotten eggs at the speakers and smashed benches. In Albany, the mayor sat on the platform as Susan spoke, a loaded revolver in his hand. The abolitionists gave up for the time being.

In 1863, Lincoln's Emancipation Proclamation was published, but it did not free the slaves. Slave owners in the border states were not affected, and slaves in the Confederate states would be free only if the Union won the war. Susan and her organization of women went to work to end slavery by an amendment to the Constitution. Susan declared that the war was to earn freedom for all—and "all" included women. This stand cost her the support of many people. Men wanted the slaves freed; they still did not consider women to be equal to men.

In 1865, the Confederate states surrendered. In December of that year, the Thirteenth Amendment, which abolished slavery, was passed. Now the effort to gain the right to vote for all races began—but only for men of all races.

Susan and Elizabeth went west collecting signatures on behalf of women's right to vote. They traveled in all sorts of vehicles and slept in all kinds of places. Each night they lost sleep fighting bedbugs, and every morning they picked thousands of the creatures out of the ruffles of their dresses. In Kansas, they met George Frances Train, who gave Susan the money to start her own newspaper, the *Revolution*. The first issue appeared January 8, 1868. The eccentric George Francis Train sailed that same day for England, where he became involved in a political problem. He was arrested and sentenced to life in prison. He sent money as long as he could, but in 1870 Susan lost the paper. She spent the next six years paying off her debtors.

In the Wyoming Territory, what began as a joke turned into a victory for women's rights. In 1869, the Legislature passed a law giving women the right to vote. The governor was expected to veto the bill. Instead, he signed it into law. In the Wyoming Territory, women were allowed to vote.

In 1872, Susan decided to put the Fourteenth Amendment to a test. Interpreting the word person to include women, she and fourteen other women marched into a barber shop in Rochester, New York, and registered as voters. The women were allowed to cast ballots, but a few days later Susan was arrested for voting illegally. At her trial, the judge ordered the jury to find her guilty. She was fined $100 and court costs, but she refused to pay. The women's rights movement had reached its climax.

Though Susan earned the respect of the nation and was honored worldwide, she did not live to see women voting all across the country. Women were able to vote in a few western states, but that was all. On January 26, 1886, she was present when Congress first voted on the amendment to give women the vote. Though the bill was defeated, Susan could see how far women had come. She died March 14, 1906. Not until 1920 was the Nineteenth Amendment ratified, giving women all over the nation the right to vote.

Directions: On a separate sheet of paper, answer the following questions about Susan B. Anthony.

1. Why was Susan B. Anthony unable to accomplish more toward her goal during her lifetime?
2. What do you think was Susan B. Anthony's greatest accomplishment? Explain your answer.

JOSEPH PULITZER

Newspaper editor and publisher; born in Hungary in 1847 and died off the coast of South Carolina in 1911

A shabbily dressed man, tall and thin as a scarecrow and wearing a tattered army uniform, entered fashionable French's Hotel in New York City. With just a few pennies in his pocket, the man wanted to have his shoes shined. It was 1865, soon after the end of the Civil War. Joseph Pulitzer, a Union army veteran and recent immigrant, spoke with a heavy German accent. The poor man looked and sounded terribly out of place. The porter kicked him out onto the street, telling him that his presence would surely offend the hotel's fine guests. Joseph Pulitzer never forgot that insult. Twenty-five years later, he bought the hotel and demolished it. On the site, he built a skyscraper with a golden dome. It was the tallest building in New York, and it was the headquarters for the New York *World*, one of the newspapers Pulitzer owned.

Joseph Pulitzer was born on April 10, 1847, in Hungary. His father was Philip Pulitzer, a Jew and a successful grain merchant. His mother was Louise Berger, an Austrian beauty from a prominent Catholic family. Joseph was their second child. When Joseph was seventeen, he decided to enlist in the army.

Joseph had poor eyesight and was very nervous. Although he was tall—over six feet, two inches in height—he was so thin that he looked like a weakling. The Austrian army rejected him. So did the French Foreign Legion and the British military. In the city of Hamburg, Germany, Pulitzer met a recruiter from the United States. This was the summer of 1864, the last year of the Civil War in America. The Union army was in desperate need of men. Pulitzer's recruiter did not care that a man had poor eyesight or was unusually thin. He told Joseph he could serve in the Union army. Joseph boarded a ship sailing to Boston. Soon he was a member of the First New York Cavalry. Joseph barely saw battle before the war ended.

Pulitzer tried to find work in New York, but without success. He heard that many German-speaking people lived in St. Louis. He sold his only valuable possession, a silk handkerchief, for seventy-five cents and purchased a ticket for St. Louis. After he reached St. Louis, he tried to find work. He took odd jobs, beginning as a mule tender. One or two days at that, and he decided to quit. Then, he became a waiter in a restaurant, and he became so fascinated by the conversation at one table that he dropped a tray of dishes. He lost that job. Then he clerked for some lawyers. This job worked out better. He used their library, studied law, and became a United States citizen one month before his twentieth birthday. Not long after, he knew enough about law to pass the local bar, or law licensing, examination. Perhaps he would become a lawyer. Still, he was unable to find work that pleased him.

That soon changed. One day, Joseph was hired as a reporter on a German-language daily newspaper, the *Westliche Post*. He had no training as a writer or reporter. That didn't matter. He threw himself into his work, often missing meals, pounding the pavements, searching for stories, writing from 10 A.M. to 2 A.M. He never gave up on a story, and his greatest pleasure was unearthing political corruption. His English-language competitors hired translators to read what Pulitzer was writing.

People often made fun of Pulitzer. They joked about his looks. Pranksters pointed to his nose and shouted, "Pull-it-sir!" They thought he looked odd. They laughed at his clothes. He wore workman's boots, trousers that were too short for his wiry legs, a cheap, soiled coat, and a hat that cost fifteen cents. Others may have laughed, but Pulitzer took himself very seriously. He had very little sense of humor. As he worked, however, he gained an increasing sense of politics.

Pulitzer was soon writing accurately and forcefully in English as well as German. He learned as much as he could about American history. Patriotism became his greatest passion. At the age of twenty-two, he ran for the Missouri House of Representatives and won. He was two years younger than the minimum age requirement, but no one stopped him. Now in the state legislature, he worked to enact laws to curb the same political corruption he had unearthed as a reporter. Back home in St. Louis, the joking stopped and people began to take Pulitzer seriously.

For some time, Pulitzer had admired the New York *Sun,* published by Charles A. Dana. Dana hired him to be the Washington, D.C., correspondent for the *Sun*. Pulitzer moved to the nation's capital. In 1877, he was admitted to the Washington bar and still thought that he might practice law.

One day, Pulitzer met a beautiful young woman, Kate Davis. Her father was a distant relative of Jefferson Davis, president of the recently defeated Confederacy. They fell in love and were married on June 19, 1878.

Visiting St. Louis after his honeymoon, Pulitzer bought two local newspapers. The first was the St. Louis *Dispatch*. Pulitzer found the sheriff auctioning off the bankrupt *Dispatch* on the courthouse steps. Joseph could not resist. He bought the daily paper for $2,500. The second newspaper, the *Evening Post,* had only recently been established. It did not yet have an Associated Press membership. Such a membership was costly, but a great advantage. The *Post* owner asked Pulitzer whether he would like to combine the newspapers. Pulitzer agreed and soon bought out his partner. He combined the newspapers into the St. Louis *Post Dispatch*. Immediately, he turned a profit and doubled circulation. He became excited by his growing influence. He now knew that he wanted to be the greatest, most influential newspaper publisher in the country.

Pulitzer hired imaginative editors and writers. His top editor was Colonel John A. Cockerill, who had a reputation for livening up dull newspapers. Cockerill used vivid details, colorful language, and dashing headlines. He wrote about crime, famous people, and scandals. Pulitzer could continue his crusade, or campaign, against corruption and people would enjoy reading the newspaper. Through the newspaper, Pulitzer became the champion of the average man and woman. He discredited unethical politicians. He fought against dishonesty in government and against tax breaks and special privileges for the rich. He fought for and got street repairs and a park system. By 1882, Joseph Pulitzer was becoming a very rich man. The fifteen-cent hat and soiled coat were gone. Now he wore felt hats and luxurious fur coats.

In 1883, Joseph and Kate Pulitzer left for New York with intentions of sailing for Europe. Instead, Pulitzer bought a New York newspaper and stayed on to run it. He rarely returned to St. Louis after that. The newspaper he bought was the New York *World*. It had very little circulation and was probably not worth the $346,000 that Pulitzer paid. However, Pulitzer reasoned, if he was going to be the country's greatest newspaper publisher, he had to own a New York newspaper. He began to change the *World* by imitating the style of the St. Louis *Post Dispatch*. He turned the *World* into a lively newspaper. For good measure, he brought Colonel Cockerill and others from his St. Louis staff to New York.

Within three months, the *World* circulation doubled. Within two years, it multiplied ten times. By 1886, the paper was earning $500,000 in profits. At first, Pulitzer used sensation and stunts to sell newspapers. He fought bitter battles and price wars against his newspaper competitors. Later, he gradually changed the *World* into one of the most distinguished newspapers in the country.

In March 1884, Joseph Pulitzer became involved with the Statue of Liberty. Twenty years earlier, a French sculptor named Frederic-Auguste Bartholdi decided to honor the American Revolution by creating the huge statue as a gift to the United States. For ten years, he worked on it. In 1876, a group in the United States hired a famous architect to design a pedestal, or base, for the statue. Before the pedestal was finished, the money ran out. Another $100,000 was needed.

Joseph Pulitzer came to the rescue. He asked his readers to send in whatever money they could afford. In return, he published the name of each contributor. Contributions flooded the newspaper office. School children sent in nickels. Every day more names appeared in the *World*. By August, there were more than 120,000 contributions, ranging from a nickel to $250. The collection passed the goal of $100,000. The pedestal could now be completed. What happened to the *World* during this time? Its circulation jumped to 170,000 a day—the largest in New York.

Not long after that, a young woman walked into Cockerill's office. Elizabeth Cochrane came from Pennsylvania and she wanted a job. Hire a woman? Cockerill was skeptical. Newspapers rarely hired women in those days. Elizabeth told Cockerill that if he hired her, she would pretend to "go insane," get into a hospital for the mentally ill, and write a story about her adventure. Cockerill agreed to let Elizabeth try. She was able to convince judges and doctors of her "insanity." They committed her to Blackwell's Island, a hospital known for its harsh treatment of mentally ill patients. A few days later, Elizabeth was rescued. She wrote a front-page story telling about how terribly the patients were treated. Elizabeth did not use her real name on the article. Instead, she used a pen name, Nellie Bly. Thanks to Nellie's story, there was an official investigation and the conditions at Blackwell's Island were corrected. Pulitzer was overjoyed with her work. Nellie Bly went on to become one of Pulitzer's greatest reporters. Using similar techniques, she exposed corruption in prisons and medical clinics. She also exposed corrupt state legislators. Because of Nellie Bly's good work, other women found it easier to get jobs on newspapers.

Nellie Bly's greatest stunt for the *World*—the one that sold the most newspapers—was her attempt to beat Phileas Fogg, the fictional hero of Jules Verne's novel *Around the World in 80 Days*. The *World* ran a contest for readers to guess exactly how long it would take Nellie to travel around the world. One million readers entered the contest. Every day, she filed a report from a different location. Every day, the *World* published her story. Nellie beat Fogg around the world. She made it in 72 days, 6 hours, and 11 minutes.

In 1887, Pulitzer's health began to fail. His already poor eyesight worsened. His nervous attacks increased. They affected his stomach and his ability to sleep. He began to travel all over the world in search of cures for his headaches. One sunny day in 1890, on board a ship outside of Turkey, Pulitzer mumbled to his secretary that it seemed strange that everything was turning dark. His secretary replied that it was not dark at all. Pulitzer was going blind. Besides blindness, Pulitzer also suffered a nervous breakdown and could not stand the slightest noise. When he stayed at hotels, all the rooms around his were kept vacant so he could have absolute quiet. At home, the doors of his mansion were padded and the floors corked. Still he sought more quiet.

He finally found quiet on his yacht. Pulitzer spent most of the last twenty years of his life on board his yacht. Even though he was blind and at sea, he directed both of his newspapers. Each day, his secretaries read his newspapers to him. He reviewed them page by page.

Joseph Pulitzer died aboard his yacht, off the coast of Charleston, South Carolina, on October 29, 1911. He was mourned by his wife and five surviving children. Before he died, Pulitzer laid out plans for a professional school of journalism at Columbia University in New York. He also planned annual prizes for outstanding accomplishments in the fields of journalism, music, drama, and literature. They were to be established after his death. Through the Pulitzer School of Journalism and the Pulitzer Prizes, Joseph Pulitzer is still contributing to his profession and to his country.

Directions: On a separate sheet of paper, answer the following questions about Joseph Pulitzer.

1. How did Joseph Pulitzer use his newspapers to show his patriotism and his belief in democracy? Explain your answer.

2. What do you think was Pulitzer's greatest accomplishment? Explain your answer.

THOMAS ALVA EDISON

Inventor and manufacturer; born in Ohio in 1847 and died in New Jersey in 1931

What would the world be like if Thomas Alva Edison had not been born? Would someone else have invented the electric light, or would we still be lighting our homes with gas or oil lamps? Without the phonograph, how would we play our records? If the movie projector did not exist, we could not watch movies.

The man responsible for these and many more inventions was born on February 11, 1847, in Milan, Ohio. Thomas Edison's father, Samuel Edison, Jr., owned a not-very-successful small business. His mother, Nancy Elliott Edison, was a former schoolteacher. Three of her first six children had died before Thomas was born.

As a child, Edison was called "Al" after his middle name of Alva. Al was a curious child, always asking people questions. One day he asked his mother how geese were born. After his mother explained, Al went off play. Later his father found the little boy in a neighbor's barn. He was sitting on a nest of goose eggs trying to get them to hatch. Unfortunately, thanks to Al, all of the eggs were cracked.

Sometimes Al's curiosity got him into even greater trouble. One day, when he was six, he tried to see what would happen if he burned some leaves. Al conducted his experiment in his father's barn. Before he knew what was happening, the flames had spread. Although Al escaped unharmed, the barn burned to the ground. This time, Al was punished for his curiosity.

When Al was seven, the family moved to Port Huron, Michigan. There, at the age of eight, young Edison attended school for the first time. Al found school boring because he was forced to memorize information. He preferred to ask questions, to experiment, and to analyze information. As a result, he and the head teacher did not get along.

The fact that Al was hard of hearing only added to his problems at school. He had been sick a good deal, often with ear infections. These illnesses had caused a hearing loss. As an adult, the condition worsened. By the time he was twenty years old, Edison was almost totally deaf.

Al's school days did not last very long. On one occasion, his teacher complained that the boy's brain was "addled." He meant that Al was always confused because he was not bright. When Mrs. Edison heard this, she was so angry at the teacher that she removed Al from school. Al's education continued at home, where he was taught by his mother.

Even as a young boy, Al's interests were mainly scientific. He began experimenting with chemicals. His mother allowed him to set up a small laboratory in the house. After Al accidentally dropped sulfuric acid on his family's furniture, the lab was moved to the basement.

At age twelve, Al took a job as a newsboy for the railroad. Every day at 7:15 A.M., he boarded the train in Port Huron. During the four-hour trip to Detroit, he sold papers, candy, and other items to the passengers. Al had about a five-hour layover before returning to Port Huron each night. In that time, he would purchase supplies. He also would visit the Detroit library and spend hours reading.

His work as a newsboy was very worthwhile. It gave Al not only the time to learn about science, but also the experience necessary to become successful in business. One of his first major business successes happened as a direct result of the Battle of Shiloh. News of this bloody Civil War conflict reached Detroit in early April of 1862. Al realized that it was a very important news story. Most of the passengers boarding the train between Detroit and Port Huron would be interested in reading about it. Instead of selling his usual 100 papers, he might be able to sell as many as 1,000.

From the newspaper publisher, Al obtained credit for 1,000 copies. Then he asked the telegraph operator in Detroit to do him a favor. The operator agreed. He wired news of Shiloh to every train station on the return route. By the time Al arrived at each station, the people waiting for the train were anxious for more details. At first, Al sold papers for five cents apiece. With each new station, the price went up. By the end of the day, papers were going for one dollar. All of the copies were sold, and Al had made a huge profit. From this experience, Edison learned how to judge what people wanted, how to get it, and what to charge.

The Shiloh incident had convinced Al of the importance of the telegraph. As a result, he desperately wanted to learn how to operate one skillfully. His opportunity to do so came quite by accident.

One hot summer day, fifteen-year-old Edison was waiting at a train station. The young son of the station manager was playing nearby. The boy was very close to the tracks. Suddenly, a boxcar entered the track on which the child was playing. Al, seeing this, dropped his newspapers. He ran to the boy and snatched him to safety just as the boxcar roared past. The boy's father was so grateful that he promised to teach Al how to operate a telegraph. For five months, the station master taught Al everything he knew. By the end of that time, Al had become a very good telegrapher.

Over the next few years, Tom (as he was now called) worked at one telegraph job after another. Sometimes he quit, but usually he was fired. Quite often, he took down messages which he forgot to deliver. At other times, without permission, he pulled apart the company's machinery and rewired it. Also, he had a habit of playing practical jokes on his employers. These jokes were not always appreciated.

He lost his first job because some chemicals he was mixing exploded, destroying part of the building. Working from 7 P.M. to 7 A.M. was the major challenge of his second position. Since the job was boring, Edison often worked on experiments or fell asleep. So that their employers could make sure that they were on the job, operators were required to send a signal every hour. Tom rigged up a device which would do this automatically. One night, a trainman sent a message across the wire. There was no reply. Shortly after, Tom's hourly signal came across loud and clear. The man investigated. He found Tom asleep.

Once Tom was fired because he dropped sulfuric acid. The acid ate out part of the floor in Tom's work area and went through the ceiling of his boss's office. Then it fell onto the boss's desk, ate through that, and landed all over his carpet.

From city to city Edison traveled. He lived simply, spending all of his spare money on his experiments. Because of his deafness, he did not make friends easily. One of the few friends Tom did have convinced Tom that he should move to Boston. There Edison found a job with Western Union, the largest telegraph company in America.

Edison quit that job in 1869 to become a full-time inventor. His first major invention was a vote recorder. This machine could add up the "Yes" and "No" votes for bills presented to Congress. To protect his invention from being copied, Tom registered his first patent with the United States Patent Office. A patent is an exclusive right to produce and to sell an invention. Between 1869 and 1910, Edison filed more than 1,000 patents.

Moving to New York, he took a well-paying job with a firm in the financial district. Then he quit to go into business with a friend. When he tired of that, he went to work for Western Union as an inventor.

Edison's next major invention, a stock ticker, helped correct a serious problem that Western Union was having. Tom thought he should be paid $5,000 for the invention. However, when his boss asked him how much he wanted, Edison said that he would take whatever his employer thought it was worth. Two days later he was handed a check for $40,000.

Tom had difficulty cashing his check. This was the first time he had been inside a bank in his life. When he handed the check to the teller, the man spoke to him. When Edison did not reply, the teller began shouting. Tom's deafness, however, made it impossible for him to hear. Upset, Edison took his check back and walked out of the bank. Now he believed that the check had been a fake, and that he had been cheated by Western Union. Later, the whole matter was cleared up, and Edison received his money. As strange as it may seem, at twenty-four, this great inventor had not known how to cash a check.

With his money, Edison set up a factory in Newark, New Jersey. His first order was for 1,200 of his stock tickers. After they were done, Tom and his workers began to fill other orders. Factory hours were not regular. If a job needed to be finished by a certain time, everyone would work until it was completed. On one occasion, Edison locked his employees in for more than two days to meet a deadline. When the task was accomplished, he threw a big party.

One of Edison's workers was a beautiful sixteen-year-old girl named Mary Stilwell. The two found themselves attracted to each other. Because of his deafness, Tom could not speak softly to Mary, nor she to him. Instead, Tom taught Mary the language of the telegraph—Morse code. To say something personal, he used a coin to tap the message onto the palm of her hand.

Tom and Mary were married on Christmas Day, 1871. They lived in a house in Newark until 1875. Then Tom purchased land in Menlo Park, New Jersey. Here he built a long, two-story, wooden building to serve as his laboratory. He bought a house nearby for his wife, his three children, and himself.

The invention that made Thomas Edison famous was the phonograph. His model, however, looked nothing like today's record players or tape recorders. To make the phonograph work, Edison had to turn the crank, which made a cylinder revolve. Then he spoke into the mouthpiece. For play-back, the cylinder was returned to its original position. A needle was put in place, and the machine was again cranked.

The phonograph provided an amazing side benefit for Edison—it enabled him to "hear," although by this time he was almost totally deaf. Edison found that when he bit into the wood cabinet of the phonograph, he could literally hear the words of music being played on the machine. The vibration of the cabinet was transferred to his teeth, then carried along his jawbone to his inner ear, allowing him to hear the words and music.

On February 19, 1878, he applied for a patent for his talking machine. By then, people everywhere had heard of this marvelous invention. Thousands came to Menlo Park to meet Edison and to see the new machine. The President invited Edison to Washington to give a demonstration. Kings and queens wanted to be the first to purchase a phonograph.

In time, Edison tired of the phonograph. He wanted to move on to another invention he had in mind. For centuries, people had been lighting their homes with candles and oil lamps. These lights were very weak. Recently, in cities, gas light had become popular. This form of lighting, however, was both dirty and dangerous. Edison's idea was to invent an electric light.

His greatest problem proved to be finding the right filament to burn inside the bulb. The filament is the fine wire through which the electric current passes. It is the part that glows. Edison needed a material that would burn for a long time. Otherwise, people would have to constantly be replacing bulbs.

In October 1879, Edison found the material he wanted—carbonized cardboard. After putting a tough strip of it inside the bulb, he pumped out the air inside the glass. Then he turned on a switch, and the lamp lit. It burned for 170 hours. Edison knew he had solved the problem.

At the age of thirty-four, Edison was now even more famous than he had been after inventing the phonograph. Crowds of people visited Menlo Park for demonstrations. World leaders wanted to meet him and to present him with honors. Businesses wanted to loan him money to continue his experiments.

The Edison family moved to New York City so that Tom could build a system to generate and distribute electrical power. Due to Edison's efforts over the next few years, New York became a city of electric lights. Unfortunately, Mary Edison did not live to see this. In 1884, at age twenty-nine, Mary caught typhoid fever and died.

Tom had loved Mary very much. When she died, he was crushed. Two years later he would marry again and later raise three more children. But for the rest of 1884, he relieved his sadness over Mary's death by working even harder than usual.

During the next few years, Edison became more and more interested in the idea of motion pictures. In 1889, he decided to do something about it. He began by inventing the movie camera, which he called a kinetograph. Then he created the vitascope, the first movie projector. Finally, he invented a peephole box through which people could see the movie. This he named a kinetoscope.

A movie studio was built in West Orange, New Jersey. Here, boxers were filmed fighting, dancers dancing, circus performers tumbling, and animals performing tricks. From these performances, one-minute films were put together. People could view the films by putting a coin into the Kinetoscope machine and then by looking through a peephole.

Thomas Edison lived for forty-two more years. In that time, he invented hundreds of other items. Some were successes; others were failures. Then, on October 18, 1931, Thomas Alva Edison died. He was eighty-four. That day, in his honor, lights were dimmed in cities and towns all over the country. That was the people's way of thanking Edison for all he had given them.

Directions: On a separate sheet of paper, answer the following questions about Thomas Edison.

1. As a boy, Thomas Edison was very much the same as he was as an adult. What traits in young Edison's personality helped make him the great inventor he later became?
2. Although Edison invented thousands of items, some were more important than others. Which of Edison's inventions do you think was the most significant? Why do you think so?

SAMUEL GOMPERS

Founder of the American Federation of Labor (A. F. of L.); born in Great Britain in 1850 and died in Texas in 1924

In many parts of the United States before the turn of the century, young children worked long, exhausting hours in factories. Men and women toiled in "sweatshops" that had poor lighting and ventilation. Workers who lost their jobs because of work-related injuries often ended up homeless. These are just a few of the many unfortunate scenes that occurred before workers organized to achieve better working conditions. At the forefront of the movement for better conditions was Samuel Gompers. His fight for workers' rights eventually led to the formation of a national labor union and better working conditions for all workers.

Samuel Gompers was born into a large family of six children in a poor section of London. He lived in a shabby tenement building that had no trees, grass, or flowers around it. His entire family lived in two crowded rooms. There was no running water in the tenement, and the children had to go for water to a public barrel that stood outside the building.

Samuel Gompers's father was a skilled maker of hand-wrapped cigars. Although his craft required special training, he could not make enough money at it to support his family. At the age of ten, Sam had to leave school and go to work to help support the family. Sam first took a job in the shoemaking trade. He worked from dawn to dusk, seven days a week, but earned the equivalent of only six cents a week. After eight weeks of this, Sam decided to give up shoemaking. He entered his father's trade instead, and by the time he was eleven he was able to earn two shillings, or twenty-four cents, a week making cigars.

Because their life in London was poor and offered little chance for improvement, the Gompers began to think more and more about moving to America. The skilled cigarmakers had a workers' club that collected small dues to help the members' families go to the United States during hard times. The year that Sam became thirteen his father could not find work, and the club gave Mr. Gompers money from this fund. He used the money to take the entire family to New York. They crossed the ocean in a sailing ship as steerage passengers. This meant that they slept on the floor of the cargo deck and had to provide all their own food.

In New York City, the Gompers were met by relatives and friends. Sam's father rented a four-room apartment in a slum tenement for the family. Mr. Gompers decided that the family would earn its living by making cigars at home. He bought a supply of dried tobacco leaves. His wife and the younger children "stripped" the tobacco, smoothing out the leaves and removing the stems. Then Sam, his father, and his oldest brother skillfully rolled the leaves into cigars. Sam's father took the finished cigars to a tobacco shop and sold them for two dollars a thousand. The whole family worked very hard, but Sam still found time to make friends and play games.

When Sam was sixteen he was able to get a job in a regular cigarmaker's shop. He brought his own bench and cutting tools and received pay at the end of each day according to the number of cigars he made. All the men worked at their benches in the shop from the earliest dawn hours until sunset. Sam tried to finish as many cigars as possible every day.

Always interested in improving his mind, Sam enrolled at Cooper Union, a school that had free evening classes for people who wanted an education but had to work during the day. He joined the young people's debating team. He had begun to resent the fact that he had so little education. He had an intense desire to learn. Every Saturday night for twenty years Samuel Gompers went to special lectures at Cooper Union.

Sam, who had joined a cigarmaker's union in 1864, began to study the working conditions at his job. All light in the shop had to come from daylight outside, and the only windows were small and high up in the walls. The men had to work swiftly, rolling and cutting the dark-colored tobacco in the poor light.

In 1866, the men decided to express their unhappiness over bad working conditions. They selected Sam as their representative to speak to the shop owner. The shop owner was rude and told Sam that he should be at home with his mother. However, Sam was persistent and told the shop owner that the men had the right to choose who they wanted to represent them.

In another case, Sam stood up to a foreman who was mistreating a worker. The men Sam worked with always allowed one of the workers who had very poor eyesight, but who had a large family to feed, to work nearest the window. When the foreman put a friend of his, new to the shop, into this good seat, Sam protested in the name of all the workers. The foreman told Sam to mind his own business. At this, Sam took up his tools and left, and all the other skilled workers left with him. In the face of this united action, or "strike," the foreman gave in. He knew he could not run the shop without the skilled cigarmakers. He moved the worker with poor eyesight back to the window, and Sam and the other men returned.

Another time, the owner brought his nephew, a thirteen-year-old boy from Austria, to work in the shop. When the boy made mistakes, the shop owner whipped and abused him. One day he thrashed the boy horribly until he was almost unconscious. Sam became outraged and told the owner that the boy was not his slave and that he had no right to punish him physically. Sam warned the owner that if he abused the boy again, Sam and all the other workers would strike.

Samuel Gompers could win strikes in his own job because his employer wanted to produce fine, expensive cigars and therefore needed to keep his skilled workers. In the tenements, however, women and children worked at making cheaper cigars by hand. Other workers were also making cheaper cigars on a new, small hand machine called a mold. These workers had little control over working hours and conditions. Sam organized one big union of all the cigarmakers, including skilled workers, tenement home workers, and workers who used the small mold machine. The union members went on strike for a ten-hour day and minimum price of six dollars a thousand for their cigars. This would enable the fastest workers to make from twelve to eighteen dollars a week.

Many of the families making cigars in the tenements lived in rooms owned by the tobacco buyers, above the tobacco shops. When these families went on strike, they were evicted from their tenements. Some of them had to beg on the streets. Other workers helped them as much as they could, and Samuel Gompers' union set up soup kitchens, but soon there was no money left. The strike was broken, and the families had to go back to work with no improvements. Even though this strike failed, Sam felt that it taught the cigarmakers a valuable lesson. It showed them that they must organize and get other workers to join them in the fight for better working conditions.

By the time Samuel Gompers was thirty years old, he was well known in New York for his speeches in favor of a shorter working day. A convention of many kinds of workers was called to meet at Pittsburgh, Pennsylvania, in 1881. Workers representing all trades attended. These representatives were all older than himself, and Sam felt very young. Sam urged the workers of all the different trades to form a federation of all their unions.

The workers made a list of the things for which the federation would strive. Children under fourteen years of age would be prohibited from working either in factories or at home. Instead of working, these children would be required to attend free public elementary schools, to be provided by the cities. Factories would be made more sanitary. Machinery would be made safer. The convention also asked for an eight-hour day for all skilled workers—something that was unheard of in those days.

The men at the convention decided that child labor had to be vigorously condemned. Samuel Gompers told of his experiences with child labor. He said he saw children as young as six, seven, and eight seated on the floor in the middle of a room, amidst dirt and dust, stripping tobacco. They worked from dawn until late evening. He would often see the children fall over in weariness onto a pile of tobacco. They would want to sleep but were not allowed to do so. Sam was outraged at the shame of these scenes. When the new federation was formed, the members voted unanimously for a resolution to prohibit child labor.

The Federation of Organized Trades and Labor Unions of the United States and Canada, as the new group called itself, began to work for the eight-hour day, the right to strike, and the abolition of child labor. In 1886, at another convention, the organization was modified and given a new name—the American Federation of Labor, or A. F. of L. Samuel Gompers became president. He was paid a salary of three hundred dollars a year.

The office of the American Federation of Labor was a little room. Packing boxes served as desks and chairs. Samuel Gompers' second son, Henry, helped in the office. Henry often had to run to a nearby school to borrow a little ink until the federation could afford a new bottle. Samuel and Henry Gompers issued a little newspaper called the *Trade Union Advocate*. They wrote it out every week in longhand. They folded it themselves, then took it down to the post office on a cart.

One by one, unions of skilled workers were able to reduce the workday, first to ten hours and then to nine. The strength of the united federation helped them. Sam moved the headquarters of the A. F. of L. to Washington, D.C., where he could talk to government leaders of both parties. He did not believe that the labor movement should form a separate political party. He told both Republicans and Democrats that working people would vote for whichever party gave them an eight-hour day and abolished child labor.

One of the things Samuel Gompers fought for was the protection of workers who were injured at their jobs. The A. F. of L. waged such a successful campaign over this issue that today most workers have some kind of insurance, commonly known as workers' compensation. This insurance, paid for by the employer, gives an injured worker his or her regular salary and pays medical bills. No longer do children go hungry or families sleep in the street because the main family wage earner has been injured in a mine or factory and can no longer work.

Another thing Sam wanted to accomplish in his lifetime was improvement in working conditions for workers all over the world.

After World War I, Samuel Gompers went with President Woodrow Wilson to the peace conference in Europe. Some of his ideas were incorporated into the Charter of the League of Nations.

One article of the charter held that all workers were entitled to form a union and to go on strike if they were underpaid or mistreated. They were entitled to a wage that permitted them and their children to live decently and have adequate food. Every worker should have one day of rest a week. Children should have the right to go to school and should not be allowed to work in mines or factories. Although there are many places in the world where these goals have not yet been attained, the workers of most countries are striving to achieve Samuel Gompers' ideals.

Samuel Gompers was also interested in the working conditions of the people in Latin America. He helped establish a Pan American Federation of Labor. He also helped organize the skilled craftspeople to get themselves better wages. In 1924, returning from a conference in Mexico, he fell ill at San Antonio, Texas. He died there at the age of seventy-four. The whole world honored Samuel Gompers for his life's work in the cause of the working person.

Directions: On a separate sheet of paper, answer the following questions about Samuel Gompers.

1. What experiences in Gompers' early life do you think encouraged him to stand up for workers' rights later in his life? Explain your answer.
2. Why do you think Gompers wanted children to attend school rather than work or just stay at home? Explain your answer.

FREDERIC REMINGTON

Painter of life in the Old West; born in Canton, New York, in 1861 and died in Ridgefield, Connecticut, in 1909

When most people talk of the Old West, they create images such as cowboys herding cattle, a wagon train rolling across the plains, or a stagecoach being chased by robbers or Indians. Many of these images come from scenes people have watched on television or at the movies. Nearly all of these scenes are based on sketches and drawings of the Old West, since photography had not yet come into wide use. Most of the sketches and drawings were the product of one man, Frederic Remington.

As a boy in school, Frederic Remington was always more interested in drawing than in anything else. His second love was horses. He made many sketches of the two teams of horses that were kept in the firehouse across the street from his house.

Remington's grandfather bought a set of paints for him, and Frederic set up a studio in his grandfather's barn during summer vacations. In school, the boy had learned about the ancient history of Rome. He read about the wars that Julius Caesar had fought in Gaul. During his summer vacation, he began to paint large pictures of Roman soldiers on horseback charging at the Gauls and the athletic-looking Gauls being marched off into slavery by the Roman horsemen.

Remington's pictures of the ancient Gauls and Romans were not very good. The men appeared to be all chunks of pink muscle. The horses, however, were fairly well done. Frederic decided to become an artist. He wanted to spend the rest of his life right there in his grandfather's barn, making up pictures of heroic scenes.

Frederic's father was anxious to send him to Yale. Frederic was willing to go when he learned that he could study in the new School of the Fine Arts at Yale. He entered Yale at seventeen. He was big and heavy for his age and, with a little instruction from the college coaches, made a fine football player. It was just as well that he enjoyed sports, for he was surely disappointed in the art classes. There was only one other art student, an older boy named Poultney Bigelow. The single art professor made them make exact pencil drawings of plaster casts of ancient Greek sculptures. Although Frederic needed the practice in drawing the human figure, he was angry about these exercises. What he wanted to do instead was draw live people and live animals. Unfortunately, the professor believed that there had been no true art since ancient times. He thought the young men could get all the training they needed by using his plaster models.

Frederic longed for the summer vacations so that he could return to his barn studio. Back home, however, he found that his summertime painting no longer seemed to go as well. Instead, he amused himself by riding horses and going on picnics with young people from the city who came to upstate New York for vacation. Frederic had never been too interested in girls; he even refused to paint portraits of his female cousins. Then, on one of these summer picnics, he met Eva Caten, who was known to her friends as Missie. She became his first and only love.

When Frederic was eighteen, his father died and left him a small inheritance. With the money in his pocket, he went directly to Missie's father to ask for her hand in marriage, without even mentioning it to Missie. Her father said no. Frederic was very young; he had had only two years of college and seemed to be interested in nothing but going on picnics, dabbling in art, and riding horses. How could such a young man think seriously about marriage?

Frederic decided to go West, make himself a wealthy man, and then return for the girl he loved. He spent part of his inheritance on a train ticket that would take him to Miles City, North Dakota—as far as the railroad went. Only six years earlier in this region, the United States Cavalry had been defeated at Custer's Last Stand. The thought of being at that very spot excited Remington's imagination. He watched eagerly out the train window for buffalo, only to be told by the conductor that the buffalo had been gone for more than ten years.

When he got off the train at the little military post of Miles City, Remington was again disappointed. He saw no Indians or cowboys. General Miles, for whom the post was named, was off fighting Apaches in the Southwest.

Searching for adventure, Remington decided to go on horseback into the Wyoming Territory. He bought a horse and plenty of cornmeal, beans, and bacon. He also bought a rifle for small game and fishing tackle to use in streams. He set out alone. In the first week out, before he crossed from Montana into Wyoming, he met a wagon driver. The old man told Remington of the days of the buffalo and of the warlike Sioux Indians, who had fought against Custer. His descriptions were so vivid that Remington could almost visualize each scene the old man described. After meeting this man, Remington decided to devote his artistic talents to recording scenes of the Old West.

Remington continued his journey and finally ended up in Kansas City, Kansas. He found real cowboys there and settled down happily among them. He sent a sketch to *Harper's Weekly,* one of the most popular illustrated magazines of that time. The editor bought the drawing. The editor thought that the drawing was a bit rough and had it done over by one of magazine's artists. Nevertheless, when the picture appeared in *Harper's Weekly,* Remington was given credit for the original sketch, and was quite happy at getting this recognition from the magazine.

Remington went on a trip to the Southwest, painting Indians and whatever else he could find that interested him. For months he roamed New Mexico and Texas, riding into Mexico as far south as Chihuahua, sketching everything as he went. When all the sketching supplies he had with him were gone, Remington returned to Kansas City. Although Kansas City was really only a large village at the time, there were other artists there, as well as a variety of writers and musicians. Railroad financiers and wealthy cattle ranchers were willing to pay well for big pictures of western scenes. Remington rented a little house in Kansas City and began to paint there. When he joined other artists at evening gatherings, everyone had a lady guest except Remington. His thoughts turned back to Missie. Remington had never even written her one letter telling of his adventures. He returned to New York to look for her.

Frederic and Missie had not seen each other for several years. Missie had refused to go out with other gentlemen and seemed headed for life as an old maid, all because Remington's first marriage request had been turned down. Now her father withdrew his objections and Frederic Remington and Eva Caten were married without further delay.

When he arrived back in Kansas City with his bride, Remington was almost penniless. However, his wife seemed delighted with the little house in Kansas City. It was full of big paintings. These paintings were of Blackfoot Indians, Mounties, General Custer and Sitting Bull, and stagecoaches being attacked by Indians. While Remington was in New York getting married, two of these paintings sold for nearly three hundred dollars. This convinced the Remingtons that Frederic was on his way to riches and fame. They quickly spent the money from the paintings, feeling sure that there would be more coming in soon.

Harper's took a few more of Remington's sketches. Although all the sketches were redrawn by magazine artists, the editors at least felt that Remington knew the frontier. Unfortunately, they did not pay much for the sketches, and Remington was able to earn very little money. After a year of poverty, the couple decided that as much as they loved each other, Eva had better return East. Remington then bought a gray mare and headed for the Southwest.

At this time, the United States Cavalry was in the New Mexico Territory trying to capture Geronimo, the Apache chief. Geronimo was causing trouble by raiding cattle ranches and settled Indian villages. Remington never saw Geronimo, but he did go to the San Carlos Indian Reservation on the Gila River in Arizona. There he made many sketches of Apache braves who were living on the reservation. He also went on desert trips with the Indian scouts who were working for the cavalry fighting Geronimo.

Remington took a group of sketches to New York City. He rejoined his wife there and tried to sell the sketches. The editors had some criticism of Remington's perspective drawing, and they were right. He had not had enough art training to show the correct size of distant figures in large group pictures. He also needed training in mixing colors and in working in watercolors as well as oils. He enrolled in the Art Students' League, a famous art school in New York City. Studying under all the best teachers, he worked on all his weak points. At the same time, he went to other magazine offices in New York.

Remington waited an hour to see the editor of a new sporting magazine called *Outing*. The editor finally appeared and turned out to be his fellow art student at Yale, Poultney Bigelow. Bigelow was delighted at the realism in Remington's sketches. The frontier was shown just as it really was—with lean horses on barren deserts and with bearded, dusty, tired cowboys. The editors at *Outing* bought every sketch that Remington had and commissioned him to do another entire set based on his experiences in Montana and Idaho.

By October, 1886, ten of Remington's full-page, pen-and-ink drawings had appeared in *Harper's Weekly*. One issue carried one of Remington's cowboy paintings called "In from the Night Herd." This painting sparked the enthusiasm for the first cowboy picture and cowboy stories. Fan mail began to pour in about these pictures and the ones in *Outing*. One of Remington's fans was Theodore Roosevelt, who had just written a series of magazine articles about his months on a ranch in South Dakota. Roosevelt told the publishers of *Century* that no one but that new artist Fred Remington should be asked to illustrate the series.

Remington was not merely a magazine illustrator. In 1887, the American Water Color Society gave a prize to his painting "Flag of Truce in the Indian Wars." The following year, an oil painting called "Arrest of a Blackfoot Murderer" was hung in the annual exhibition of the National Academy of Design. Remington was becoming famous.

When the Sioux revolted against their reservation life in 1890, Remington was sent to report on the war and to make illustrations of the life of soldiers in the bitter Dakota winter. All of Remington's winter scenes come from ideas he got during this adventure.

Remington always sought out new subjects and scenes to paint. He continued to make his horseback trips into the dry Southwest and northern Mexico every year. Then, suddenly, he died of a ruptured appendix in 1909.

It is from Frederic Remington's paintings and from his hundreds of pen drawings and watercolors that today we get our image of the Old West. Remington knew that the Old West would be gone before photographers could get to see it, so Remington kept the promise that he had made to himself—to record the facts of the vanishing West before it vanished from reality forever.

Directions: On a separate sheet of paper, answer the following questions about Frederic Remington.

1. Why do you think the horses in Frederic Remington's early drawings of the Roman battles in Gaul were drawn much better than the soldiers? Explain your answer.
2. Why were Frederic Remington's sketches and drawings important to magazines such as *Harper's Weekly* and *Outing*? Explain your answer.

BOOKER T. WASHINGTON

College president, educator, author; born in Virginia in 1858 and died in Alabama in 1915

Of all the success stories in American history, that of Booker Taliaferro Washington is among the greatest. At the age of seven, he was a slave. By the time he was twenty-three, he had become the founder and president of one of the finest colleges in America.

Booker's life began in 1858 on a Virginia plantation owned by James Burroughs. His mother, an older brother, a younger sister, and he lived in a one-room cabin on Burroughs's property. There was little furniture in the cabin. Everyone slept on the floor.

One of Booker's chores was to walk to school behind the plantation owner's daughter, carrying her books. When they arrived, the little girl would attend school with all the other white children. Booker and the other black children would peek in to see what was going on. They were not allowed to go to school. In fact, no slave was permitted to read. Booker swore that someday he would attend school and learn to read.

As he grew, Booker was given extremely hard jobs to do. One was to carry heavy buckets of water from the well to the slaves working in the fields. More difficult was bringing heavy loads of corn to be ground into meal. Booker was very small, and the sacks were heavy. If they fell off his horse, he could not lift them back on. He would have to wait for someone to ride by and help him. As a result, he was late returning home a number of times. Whenever this happened, he would be punished by the overseer, the plantation foreman.

Tom, Booker's stepfather, had run away from his owner. In 1863, President Lincoln's Emancipation Proclamation had declared all slaves in the South free. The North and South were still fighting the Civil War, however. If a slave in the South wanted to be free, after escaping, he had to find Union soldiers to protect him. Booker hoped that his stepfather was safe with the Union army.

The war ended two years later, when Booker was seven. His family and all of the plantation slaves shouted and sang with joy. They were free at last. After the first wave of happiness died down, however, the former slaves began to worry. When they had been slaves, at least they had homes and food. Now that they were free, how would they support themselves?

The problem was solved for Booker and his family one day soon after the war ended. A stranger brought word that Tom was safe in Malden, West Virginia. He wanted them to make the long journey there to live with him. After packing their belongings and hitching a mule to a cart, the family set off for West Virginia.

The difficult trip through the mountains took many days. When his family arrived, Tom was overjoyed to see them. His home, a simple cabin, was not much better than what they had lived in on the plantation. They loved it anyway, because it was theirs.

Because the family needed the money, Booker had to work in the local saltworks. His first day on the job came as quite a shock to him. Holding onto a rope, he had to climb into a deep salt well. After resting his feet on a crossbar, he slipped and fell to the bottom. The icy cold water broke his fall. Before he knew it, buckets and a shovel were thrown down on him from above. His job was to shovel the wet, salty earth into the buckets. These he would send up, while new buckets were lowered down to him. The work was tiring and monotonous, and Booker hated it.

His mother worked cleaning white people's homes. One day the woman Booker's mother was working for told her to throw out some of her son's old books. Instead of disposing of them, she kept the books for Booker so he could learn to read.

Although Booker studied the books very carefully, they were not enough. He would have to attend school. When a new one started up in Malden, Booker begged his parents to let him go. His stepfather allowed him to, as long as he continued working. From six to nine every morning, Booker would work at the salt mines. From nine to three, he would attend school, and from three to six he would be back at work.

Booker was embarrassed in school one day when the teacher asked him his last name. Like many former slaves, Booker did not have one. Among Booker's classmates, however, were many children who had been free longer and so already had last names. Booker thought for a moment, and then blurted out the name "Washington." From then on, he became Booker Washington.

In very little time, Booker Washington became the best student in the school. Unfortunately, the saltworks closed, and Booker was forced to take a job in the coal mines. This was much harder, more dangerous work. It tired Booker out so much that he started missing classes. He knew that if he stayed in the coal mines much longer, he never would get an education.

While working one day, he overheard two men discussing the Hampton Institute. This school had been started by white people to give vocational education to poor blacks. It was located about 500 miles away, in Virginia. As soon as he heard about Hampton, he knew he would have to go.

For many months, Booker worked to save enough money for his transportation. He was helped by his mother and brother, and by people in his town. When September came, Booker was ready to go. Before he left home, Booker's mother spoke to him. She told Booker that his real father's name had been Taliaferro. From then on, the boy became Booker Taliaferro Washington.

Although he left Malden on a stagecoach, Booker's money ran out long before he reached Richmond, Virginia's capital. He was forced to walk the rest of the way. Arriving in Richmond, Booker was hungry and tired. To add to his problems, he still had many miles to go before reaching Hampton. That night and many after, he slept under bridges. By day, he worked loading iron and other heavy items onto ships. In time, he had enough money saved to continue his journey.

The first adult he met at Hampton was the head teacher, Miss Mackie. For a penniless boy to be accepted at the school, she had to give her approval. Miss Mackie was a strict, stubborn, white New Englander. Booker was a dirty, poorly dressed, fifteen-year-old black. Convincing Miss Mackie was not going to be easy.

She led Booker into a nearby room, which was very large. Then she told him to clean it. When she was gone, Booker began. First, he swept the floor two or three times. Then he dusted all of the woodwork and cleaned the closet. Finally, he polished all of the doorknobs. Upon returning, Miss Mackie inspected everything very carefully. She even ran her handkerchief over the furniture to check for dust. There was no dust to be found.

Miss Mackie knew that Booker was right for Hampton. Anyone who would work that hard to get in would work just as hard to receive an education. That day she accepted him for the program and gave him a job as janitor.

Life at Hampton was not easy, but Booker enjoyed it. He rose before 5:30 each morning to light the fires in the fireplaces so the rooms would be warm. Afterward, students and teachers assembled in a large hall for prayer and breakfast. They were led in prayer by the school principal, General Samuel C. Armstrong. Armstrong was a handsome Northerner who had fought for the Union in the Civil War. After the war, he had dedicated his life to the education of blacks and other poor people. To do so, he had founded the Hampton Institute.

All of Hampton's teachers were white. Most were from wealthy Northern families. They were quite demanding, but they were also very kind. Booker liked all of his teachers. One of his favorites was Miss Lord, who taught him how to speak in public.

Although Booker was shy, Miss Lord thought he would make a good public speaker because he had a strong voice and a sincere manner. She taught him how to breathe properly, how to stand, and how to use his hands and body. Whenever Booker spoke, his hands would shake. Miss Lord made him hold a pencil whenever he gave a speech. That cleared up the problem. By the time he graduated in 1875, Booker had become an excellent public speaker. For the rest of his life, however, whenever he delivered a speech, he held a pencil.

After graduating, Washington returned to Malden to teach school. By then his mother had died, but the rest of his family was well. During the weekdays, Booker taught nearly eighty people of all ages. After an entire week's work, he also conducted two Sunday school sessions.

One day Booker received a letter from General Armstrong asking him to return to Hampton. The government was sending twenty-two American Indians to Hampton to be educated. Would Professor Washington consider becoming their teacher and leader? Booker accepted.

When the twenty-two men arrived, Booker was shocked to see how they looked. All were dressed in rags, dirty, and thin from lack of food. To make matters worse, none of them spoke English, nor were they happy to be there. Booker saw to it that they were well fed, bathed, and given new clothes. Through kindness and understanding, he won their trust and friendship.

The Indians lived with Booker in their own section of the campus, called the "Wigwam." He taught them English and many other things. In time, they were ready to live, work, and study with the other students. Booker's success with the Indians led the government to send more Indian students to Hampton. Later, thanks to Washington, schools were started for the education of all American Indians.

In 1881, General Armstrong gave Booker another job to do. He was to go to Tuskegee, Alabama, and start a college for black students. At this time, Booker was only twenty-three years old. Although the state of Alabama was funding Tuskegee, there were no school buildings on the grounds yet. There were no students, either. An old church on the property served as the original college building. Booker traveled from family to family to tell them about the new school. In that way, he managed to find enough students to begin the school year.

On July 4, 1881, Tuskegee Normal and Industrial School opened its doors for the first time. A normal school was one in which students were taught to be teachers. Booker believed that book learning was not enough, however. Pupils should be taught industry as well. They should be able to build, to farm, and to clear the land. As a result, there was much manual labor in a typical student's day.

The old church that Booker used as a classroom had a leaky roof. On rainy days, while Professor Washington lectured, students took turns holding an umbrella over his head. Later, Booker purchased an old plantation nearby. Over the years, numerous other buildings were added.

Booker wanted sturdy brick buildings constructed on the campus. This was a problem because there were no brickyards near the campus. There was plenty of clay in the soil, however. Washington had his students shape the clay into thousands of bricks. He made an oven, called a kiln, in which to bake them. Unfortunately, the kiln was poorly built, and the bricks fell apart. After trying and failing a number of times, Booker sent to Hampton for help. Students from Professor Washington's former school taught him how to construct a better kiln.

By then, money for the project had run out. To be able to continue, Booker pawned his gold watch. Finally, with the new kiln, the bricks that were baked came out perfectly. Not only did Booker have the bricks he needed, but he had taught his students a great lesson. With determination, hard work, sacrifice, and a willingness to ask for help when necessary, almost any task could be accomplished.

Enrollment at Tuskegee gradually increased. As time went by, more and more teachers were hired. With Tuskegee growing, additional money was needed. Booker traveled around the United States meeting with wealthy Americans and asking them for donations. Usually, he was successful.

Booker T. Washington married three times. Fannie Smith, his first wife, was a Malden girl who had been a Hampton student. She died shortly after giving birth to their daughter, Portia.

The second Mrs. Washington, Olivia Davidson, had been the first female teacher at Tuskegee. She and Booker had two sons. On a wintry evening in 1889, a fire destroyed the Washington house. As a result of a cold she caught that night, Olivia died. By the time he married his third wife, Margaret Murray, Booker was quite famous. Because of Tuskegee's success, he had been invited to speak at the Atlanta Exposition in 1895. In his speech, Washington called upon blacks to work hard, and upon whites to give blacks a chance to succeed. His address was praised throughout the country by members of both races.

Other honors followed. Booker was the first black in United States history to be awarded an honorary degree from Harvard. Later, Dartmouth College made him an honorary doctor of arts. President Theodore Roosevelt invited him to the White House. When he visited Europe, Queen Victoria invited him for tea and spoke of Tuskegee enthusiastically.

In 1900, Washington wrote his life story, entitled *Up from Slavery*. The book was very popular, selling over 100,000 copies in Booker's lifetime.

For the last fifteen years of his life, Dr. Washington continued helping Tuskegee grow. He also labored to improve the lives of his people. In 1915, at the age of fifty-seven, he died peacefully in his home.

Directions: On a separate sheet of paper, answer the following questions about Booker T. Washington.

1. To Booker T. Washington, education was extremely important. Why do you think slave owners did not allow their slaves to go to school, or to read or write?

2. General Armstrong offered Booker several difficult jobs to perform because he believed that Booker would succeed. What positive qualities did Armstrong see in Booker? What events in Booker's life demonstrated these qualities?

JANE ADDAMS

Social reformer, first American woman to be awarded the Nobel Prize for Peace; born in Illinois in 1860 and died there in 1935

When Jane Addams was a little girl, she was often sick. Her most serious illness was tuberculosis of the spine. This left her with a curved spine. Her crooked back forced her to walk with her toes pointed inward, and she had to hold her head tilted to one side. It would have been acceptable for Jane to remain in bed and let others pamper her. However, she did not allow her illness to be the focus of her life. There were days when she was in pain, but she seldom complained. Jane and her friends all attended the same one-room school. She was a good student and loved to read. Her childhood was much the same as that of her schoolmates, except that from an early age she had a sense of purpose and determination.

When Jane was about seven years old, her father asked her if she would like to accompany him on a short business trip. Jane enjoyed her father's company and looked forward to the trip. Her father was a wealthy businessman who had once been a state senator. Jane's father needed to visit one of the mills he owned. The mill was located close to a poor section of town. Jane had never seen such small, crowded houses or dirty streets. She and her family lived in a nice big house. It had never occurred to Jane that people might live in such miserable conditions. When she asked her father why people would want to live that way, he replied that the people were poor and were managing in the best way they could. Jane told her father that when she grew up, she would have a large house in the middle of the crowded houses and would invite children inside to play. Many years later, she carried out her childhood plan.

John Addams encouraged his daughter to read. After she read a book, he would ask her questions about it. Her favorite book, and one that she re-read many times, was *Little Women* by Louisa May Alcott. Jane also enjoyed reading many other types of literature, including philosophy and history. Her father believed that women should be educated, and he encouraged her to attend college in a nearby town.

In 1877, Jane Addams entered Rockford Female Seminary (now Rockford College) in Rockford, Illinois. She decided that she would become a doctor and treat poor people. Although her family wanted her to continue her education, they were against her decision to become a doctor. In the 1870s, many people thought that women should not attend college. In addition, many people thought that a young woman from a wealthy family should remain sheltered and protected from anything unpleasant, such as poverty. Nevertheless, Jane continued her college education and eventually received a bachelor's degree.

She continued her education and began to study medicine at the Women's Medical College in Philadelphia. Jane studied there for one year, but had to quit school after she became ill. A surgeon performed an operation on her spine, and after six months of bed rest, she was well enough to travel. Jane decided to take a trip to Europe.

During the next several years, Jane traveled to Europe many times. When she was in Europe, she saw greater poverty among the working people than she had ever seen before. In London, she saw poor people living in terrible conditions. It was not unusual to find people digging in garbage bins for decayed vegetables and fruit. This rotten food was all they could get to eat. Without this source of food, they would have gone hungry.

While Jane was in London, she had an opportunity to visit Toynbee Hall, a settlement house. A settlement house was an institution that provided many community services for people living in the city. At Toynbee Hall, educated people taught free classes for workers and children. Jane was inspired by what she saw at Toynbee Hall. For several years she had wanted to do something to help the poor people in America. She decided to go to the slums of a big American city and, using money she had inherited after her father's death, set up the large house she had dreamed of as a child. She persuaded a college friend who was traveling with her, Ellen Gates Starr, to accompany her to Chicago and help her find a suitable house.

Chicago was a large city near Jane Addams's own home town. It was then a growing factory city of one million people. A great many of those people had come to the United States recently from other countries. In the poor districts of the city lived people from Italy, Poland, Ireland, Greece, Germany, and France. These immigrants had little or no money. The streets were filthy and the living conditions were pitiful. Jane believed that a healthy environment was essential for all people. She thought that if decent housing, parks, playgrounds, and schools were provided, people would be happier and healthier.

Amid the slums in one of these districts stood an old mansion. The house had been built more than thirty years before by a man named Charles J. Hull. When Jane Addams and Ellen Gates Starr saw it, it was dilapidated and run-down. For a long time, it had been used as a factory. More recently, it had been used as a warehouse for storing furniture. The owner of the house agreed to let Jane and Ellen lease the second floor of the house as well as a large reception room on the first floor. On September 18, 1889, the two young women moved into the house they had decided to name "Hull House." The first thing they had to do was clean the rooms and make them more pleasant. Then, they brought in the furniture and pictures they had bought in Europe.

Before Jane and Ellen moved into the house, they talked with influential community leaders. They wanted people to know about the ideas they had for Hull House. Articles about the two women appeared in newspapers. They received many offers of support, mostly from people they did not even know. The purpose of their house was two-fold: they wanted to provide a place for college-educated people to use their talents, and they wanted to help those people who were trapped by poverty.

It was one thing to have dreams and ideas to help the unfortunate in the manner of Toynbee Hall in London, where all the tenement dwellers were British and spoke the English language. It was another thing to make friends among the many nationalities crowded into the slums of Chicago. Jane and Ellen had to begin by offering their help to people who did not even speak the same language. They began by doing small things to help the people. Soon the neighbors found that Jane Addams was helpful in many circumstances, from caring for a sick child to delivering a baby.

Parents began to bring their children to the newly organized kindergarten classes, and working girls and women came for evening reading sessions and art lectures. The adults were given a New Year's party. Jane Addams and Ellen Gates Starr soon became known as permanent neighbors to those who lived near Hull House.

Much of the work carried on at Hull House through the years is described in Jane Addams's books *Twenty Years at Hull-House* and *The Second Twenty Years*. The settlement house became known for the help provided there to children and young adults. Many of these children and young adults had had to quit school and go to work. After a long day's work in a factory, they needed a place to go where they could read or play. Jane's concern for the children and young adults led to the organization of many types of classes, clubs, and recreational activities. In addition, Jane Addams set up vocational classes that provided training for certain types of factory jobs. She found that the children who took the training classes received better jobs in factories.

There were also dancing classes, teenage social clubs, theater productions, and parties in the holiday season. Jane Addams realized, however, that providing classes, parties, and reading rooms was not enough. The children of the Hull House neighborhood had little time and energy for these things. They had to work long hours, had inadequate schools, and were often in trouble with the law.

Jane Addams felt that one of the most important things she must do was improve working conditions for children. She was horrified when she first learned about the amount of work that young children did. During the first Christmas party at Hull House, before she knew much about child labor, many of the young children refused to eat the holiday candy she offered them. Jane found out that the children had worked six days a week, sometimes thirteen hours a day, to make the candy. The sight of the candy made them sick. Jane Addams met with city officials and state legislators to get laws passed forbidding factory owners to employ children under the age of fourteen. She also tried to improve the working conditions of women so they would not have to work more than eight hours a day, six days a week.

Not many of the children were able to go on to high school. There was usually no high school nearby, and the families needed the wages brought home by the children. The boys and girls who did have to quit school to work could go to Hull House in the evenings and take a variety of courses that included art, music, English, and crafts such as bookbinding.

Juvenile crime was a problem in the Chicago slums. Children were often arrested and put in jail with older criminals. Jane Addams helped these children by going to the police station and pleading for them. She insisted that children should not be put in the same jails as adult criminals. Eventually, Jane Addams and the Hull House group helped get a new law passed that provided the first Juvenile Court in the nation. This was a major breakthrough in the treatment of juvenile offenders.

Typhoid and tuberculosis were common diseases in the Chicago slums. In the Hull House neighborhood, garbage was often thrown in the street and allowed to rot. Rats and flies lived off the garbage. Sometimes the garbage would not be collected for weeks. Nothing was done about this unhealthy situation until Jane Addams launched a campaign for cleaner streets. She was appointed garbage inspector for the Hull House neighborhood. Jane held the position for one year, and in that time, she made sure that garbage was picked up and disposed of properly.

Parents and children living in the Chicago slums seldom had a chance to visit the country. Many of the children had never been out of the slum district; they had never seen a cow grazing in a field or heard birds singing in a forest. Jane Addams wanted to take the children outside the slums. She arranged for her friends outside Chicago to take children and their mothers on visits to the green farm area of the state and to camps along Lake Michigan.

Eventually, a summer campground was established near Lake Geneva, Wisconsin.

Jane Addams also thought that the city children needed a playground. Not far from Hull House, she noticed a few run-down buildings. She asked the landlord if she could have the property, and he agreed. To his surprise, she had the buildings torn down. On the lot, Jane Addams supervised the building of the first public playground in Chicago. Both children and their parents could see grass growing and flowers blooming near their homes for the first time in their lives.

Many little children in the Hull House neighborhood died or were injured when they were locked alone in apartments or were left to play in the streets. Almost all the mothers had to work long hours in factories. In the winter, they locked their small children alone in the rooms; in the summer, when the rooms became too hot, they locked the children out on the streets. Jane Addams and other concerned people in Chicago built a day nursery near Hull House for the children of working mothers. Here, the mothers paid a small amount of money to have their children watched by responsible adults.

Jane Addams grew famous all over the world for her work in the crowded Chicago slums of the 1890s. She traveled widely, both in the United States and in Europe, speaking about social reform. She enjoyed public speaking, but it was her writing as much as her speaking that helped her become famous. In addition to her autobiographies, she published several books and essays about social reform. In 1909, she became the first woman to receive an honorary degree from Yale University. For her work in helping people, Jane Addams won the Nobel Peace Prize in 1931. She was the first American woman to win this award. At her death, thousands of people mourned this woman who had done so much to give others a better chance in life.

In 1963, most of Hull House was torn down to make way for part of the University of Illinois. However, the original Hull mansion and a dining hall were not destroyed. These buildings have been preserved and turned into a museum. Today, an organization called the Hull House Association operates about twenty-two community centers in the Chicago area. The services they provide are similar to those offered during Jane Addams's time. They provide services such as child care and housing. The association continues to carry out the work that Jane Addams began, relieving human suffering, improving social conditions, and providing social, economic, and educational opportunities for those who need them most.

Directions: On another sheet of paper, answer the following questions about Jane Addams.

1. What important contributions did Hull House make? Explain your answer.
2. Jane Addams worked to get laws passed to protect children from unfair working conditions and to protect juvenile offenders from being put in jail with older criminals. Why was this type of social reform necessary? Explain your answer.

WILLIAM E.B. DU BOIS

Scholar, author, civil rights leader, political activist, co-founder of the NAACP; born in Great Barrington, Massachusetts in 1868 and died in Ghana in 1963

For a long time, William Edward Burghart Du Bois did not realize that he was any different than any of his schoolmates. He was born and raised in Great Barrington, Massachusetts. His parents were Albert Du Bois, of French and African descent, and Mary Burghart, of Dutch descent. He was one of about fifty blacks in the town of 5,000 people.

Will, as he was known, went to an almost entirely white school. He was generally accepted by his classmates, although he felt that he was different. At first he thought that this difference was due to his academic excellence. He was very bright. Then, one day, the class decided that it would be fun to buy and exchange visiting cards. When a new girl in the class refused to take Will's card without even explaining her action, Will knew that he was different for another reason. That reason was the color of his skin. This incident provoked a life-long desire in William E.B. Du Bois to prove to everyone that black people could be just as intelligent, and could make just as great a contribution to American society, as white people could.

After Will became aware of the invisible curtain that separated him from his friends and neighbors, his attitude began to change. He began to compete seriously with his classmates. He fought to show that he was better than they were at schoolwork, races, sports, and every other event. He soon found out, however, that many opportunities were not open to him because he was black. Nevertheless, he achieved good grades in high school, and he wanted to go to Harvard to further his education.

Unfortunately, the high school he had attended was not one that met Harvard's standards. Besides, he could not afford to go to such an expensive school. His father had left home soon after Will was born, and his mother had died in 1884. Du Bois had been forced to work to help support himself while he finished high school. He worked an evening shift as a timekeeper at a local mill.

The Congregational Church that Will attended came to his rescue. They and three other churches gave him a scholarship to Fisk University, a mostly black school in Tennessee. Here Will experienced the racism of the South. In the South in 1885, white people treated black people as if they were an inferior race. Black people seemed to accept that treatment. Will had been used to living in the North. Racism existed; however, it was nothing like the racism of the South. Du Bois saw for the first time complete segregation, or separation, of whites and blacks in housing, travel, and social functions. In almost every case, the blacks were poverty-stricken. As a student at Fisk, he worked summers teaching at country schools in Tennessee. These experiences had a great effect on Du Bois. He became aware of the social barriers between whites and blacks in the South. He also became determined to do something about the injustices he saw.

When Du Bois graduated from Fisk University in 1888, he received a scholarship to Harvard. He entered Harvard as a junior and, in 1890, was awarded a bachelor of arts degree. When he went North to study at Harvard, however, it was with a changed outlook. He no longer wanted the friendship of his classmates. He was interested only in what he could learn at Harvard. He got to know one or two of the professors that he thought were particularly intelligent, but he carried on his social life almost entirely among the small black population of Boston. After he received his B.A., he entered graduate school at Harvard. He wanted to study sociology. However, Harvard did not recognize sociology as a science, so Du Bois decided to study history instead. As part of his graduate studies, he went to study at the University of Berlin in Germany for two years.

In Germany, Du Bois found that he was not rejected because he was black. He became less aware of racial problems and thoroughly enjoyed his stay in Europe. At the University of Berlin, Du Bois was influenced by the European emphasis on scientific study. He decided to make a scientific study of blacks in the United States. He became convinced that racism in the United States could be corrected scientifically by studying the problem and making the corrections that seemed necessary. He returned to the United States full of enthusiasm for his new project. He went back to Harvard, and in 1895 he earned a Ph.D. This was the first Ph.D. Harvard had ever awarded to a black person. His doctoral thesis was later published by Harvard as the first volume in the well-known *Harvard Historical Studies*.

Having established a historical background for his social work, Du Bois wanted to change his world by teaching sociology. Unfortunately, Du Bois found this to be an almost impossible task. The only teaching job he could get in the United States was at a small black college in Wilberforce, Ohio where he was asked to teach Latin and Greek. The school repeatedly denied his request to teach sociology. He became increasingly dissatisfied with the direction his life was taking. When the University of Pennsylvania offered him a position studying the social conditions in the slums of Philadelphia, he gladly accepted. He had finally been offered a chance to make an indepth study of black sociology.

Du Bois had always seemed to talk down to other black people because of his superior intellect. He wanted to help blacks achieve a better life, but he thought that they could do little to help themselves. Du Bois thought that the few blacks who were highly educated should take the leadership in improving conditions for all blacks. He called the few educated blacks "the Talented Tenth."

In this attitude, he differed sharply from the famous black reformer Booker T. Washington. Washington believed that each individual could better him- or herself by learning a trade. He encouraged young black students to train for jobs that whites would allow them to have. Washington also believed that the best way to win black equality was by accepting the attitudes of whites until those attitudes could be changed. By peaceful protests, the blacks could try to change and improve conditions for themselves.

In spite of their differences in approach, both men wanted to cure the same problems. Both recognized that the American black population needed to be taught the skills necessary to live successfully in a predominantly white society. By 1905, however, Du Bois had decided that Booker T. Washington's approach might not achieve their common goal. He even thought that Washington's teachings might harm the black population by holding them back from what they might otherwise achieve.

In the face of increased southern cruelty to blacks, Du Bois began to question the worth of his scholarly research. He realized that calm statements of evident facts alone could not discourage or prevent the abuse of the black people. Du Bois began to see a need for active black protests against injustice.

To try to counter the enormous influence of Booker T. Washington, in 1905, Du Bois and other educated blacks founded the "Niagara Movement." These people opposed the teachings of Booker T. Washington. Their purpose was to counteract the teachings they disagreed with and to promote political activity among the black population. The Niagara Movement was opposed bitterly by Washington, who had considerable political power in the Republican party. Because of Washington's opposition and because of ever-present financial difficulties and internal conflicts, the group existed for only five years. During this time, however, the group had made some significant advances. It had demanded for the first time the same civil rights for blacks that other Americans already had, including economic and educational opportunities. It also helped pave the way for the founding of the National Association for the Advancement of Colored People (NAACP) in 1909.

Du Bois was one of the founders of the NAACP, along with white liberals such as Oswald Garrison Villard, Jane Addams, and John Dewey. At the start, most of the top positions in the organization were held by whites, although this changed through the years.

Du Bois became the National Director of Publicity and Research and the editor of the organization's publication, *The Crisis*.

Du Bois saw his position of editor of *The Crisis* as an ideal position from which to spread his beliefs. His scientific studies ceased entirely, and he spent his efforts trying to sway the black population through the publication. He used *The Crisis* to explain his political views and to try to unite blacks to vote for a common purpose. He thought that all of the blacks in America should vote for the same candidates. Then they could make their votes count. Only then, he thought, could blacks begin to have a say in legislature; and only when blacks could have their say could they better the plight of the black American.

Although Du Bois did not have any direct means of controling NAACP policies, he used *The Crisis* to influence policy decisions. Sometimes he even made policy announcements in *The Crisis* in the name of the NAACP but without the prior knowledge of the other leaders. This practice created many enemies for him within the NAACP. In the years before the first world war, the NAACP was considered a radical organization, largely due to the influence of William E.B. Du Bois. Booker T. Washington was still the major voice for black reform, since most of the whites who sympathized with the quest for civil rights for blacks agreed with Washington'smethods.

During World War I, many changes came about in the United States. Booker T. Washington died. At the same time, Du Bois decided that racial conflicts were of secondary importance to the war, and he encouraged blacks to sign up and fight alongside the whites in World War I. For this softer stand, he was criticized by some of his more radical supporters. However, the combination of Washington's death and his own softer stand gained Du Bois a larger following among blacks than he had ever had before.

During the next ten years, Du Bois changed his views on several major issues. Always one to speak out against segregation, he now began to suggest a society in which black laborers used the raw materials supplied by black suppliers to make products that would fulfill the needs of a black upper class. This proposal of "voluntary segregation" amazed both his followers and his critics. By 1934, his views differed so dramatically from those of the NAACP that the other leaders of the organization took partial control of what Du Bois published in *The Crisis*. Although Du Bois ignored the other leaders to a great extent and published exactly what he wanted, by June 1934, he was ready to resign. To the critics who accused him of reversing his point of view, he explained that he was not interested in being consistent; all he was interested in was the truth.

After resigning from the NAACP, Du Bois once again became a teacher. He took a job at Atlanta University, where he had been teaching before he took the NAACP position twenty-four years earlier. He was then sixty-six years old. He also began writing scholarly works once again. He used the Atlanta University *Phylon* to spread his political views.

As his views became increasingly radical, Du Bois took several trips to the Soviet Union and the Eastern European countries. He became more and more impressed with what he saw. In 1944, after Du Bois had openly criticized several of the university's policies, his contract at Atlanta University was terminated. Surprisingly, the NAACP asked him back at this time to direct special research projects dealing with race relations and international affairs. Seeing this as a chance to get back into national politics, Du Bois agreed.

In 1947, Du Bois, the NAACP, and other organizations asked the United Nations to bring pressure on the United States to end racial discrimination. The United Nations took no action. Because the Cold War between the United States and the Soviet Union had already begun, the Soviet Union used the issue of racial discrimination to try to gain communist support in the United States. Du Bois's sympathies were questioned. At one point, he was indicted as an "unregistered foreign agent" and was brought to trial. The judge found him innocent. However, the incident simply proved to Du Bois that he no longer believed in the important principles of democracy.

In 1963, an embittered William E.B. DuBois applied for membership in the Communist Party. In the same year, the president of Ghana invited Du Bois to live in Ghana. He asked Du Bois to supervise the government's research for its *Encyclopaedia Africana*. Du Bois accepted gladly. Then, only six months before he died, Du Bois became a citizen of Ghana.

In spite of the controversy that still surrounds Du Bois, he achieved much for the black population in America. He led an activist movement that demanded equality instead of ignoring or accepting injustices. He gave hope to young black students who wanted a higher education. It is true that he left the United States an embittered man, but he stood for the truth as he saw it. In 1968, Martin Luther King, Jr., summed up the feelings of many: "Dr. Du Bois recognized that the keystone in the arch of oppression was the myth of inferiority and he dedicated his brilliant talents to demolish it."

Directions: On a separate sheet of paper, answer the following questions about William E. B. Du Bois.

1. What do you think Du Bois meant when he said that he was not interested in consistency, only in truth? Explain your answer.
2. Why do you think Du Bois became bitter enough that he decided to leave the United States? Explain your answer.

PART IV: HARD TIMES

The twentieth century began with uncertainty and doubt. By 1914, the unrest in Europe had exploded into World War I. President Wilson wanted to keep the United States out of the war. However, when German forces began openly attacking United States ships, Wilson asked Congress to declare war. Although the United States was not very well prepared, it was still able to help the Allies win the war.

World War I took a dreadful toll on the nation, however. Hundreds of thousands of American troops were killed. The war had also cost the United States more than 33 billion dollars.

By the 1920s, the United States seemed to have recovered. The Jazz Age was firmly established and the invention of radio enabled musicians and politicians to be heard by much wider audiences. These times seemed to be happy. However, by 1929, the United States was on the brink of disaster.

On October 24, 1929, the disaster struck. The stock market crashed, sending rich and poor alike into some of the hardest times Americans had yet seen. During the Great Depression that followed, thousands of people lost everything they had. Many banks closed their doors. Hunger struck the nation because people could not afford to buy food.

The economy had not yet been stabilized when World War II broke out in Europe. The United States again had no intention of being drawn into the war. Then, on December 7, 1941, Japanese forces attacked Pearl Harbor, almost completely destroying the United States Pacific fleet. The United States declared war on Japan and later on all the "Axis powers," which included Japan, Italy, and Germany.

World War II cost the United States the lives of many more of its people, and it was ten times more expensive than World War I had been. However, World War II also had some good effects on the country. It brought the United States out of the lingering Great Depression. As a result, the nation could now direct its attention to lighter subjects, such as the arts, sports, and air exploration.

WILL ROGERS

Cowboy, actor, humorist, and writer; born in Indian Territory in 1879 and died in Alaska in 1935

Will Rogers strolled onto the stage, twirling a rope as if it were the most natural thing in the world. With a bashful grin, he said, "Well, all I know is just what I read in the papers." The audience settled down expectantly. Night after night people came to the New Amsterdam Theater in New York to hear the cowboy poke fun at the rich and famous. They also came to hear his comments on the day's news. For thirty years, through the First World War and through the Great Depression, Will Rogers told the American people the truth about themselves and their times. These were troubled times when millions of people could not find jobs. But Will's humorous comments on national and foreign events helped people to understand what was going on in America and the world. Through his jokes, people could laugh at themselves and the things they could not change.

Will Rogers was born in Oklahoma when it was still part of the area known as Indian Territory. He was the youngest of eight children and the only one of three sons to reach adulthood. His parents, Clem and Mary Rogers, were both part Cherokee Indian. Although Will grew up as a white man, he always bragged about his Indian blood. "My ancestors didn't come over on the *Mayflower*," he said; "they met the boat." Will's father was a wealthy cattle rancher and banker, who was active all of his life in the affairs of the Cherokee Nation.

Roping and riding were important to Will from his early childhood. By the time he was four years old, he could lasso the barnyard turkeys with his rope. He could not remember a time when he could not ride a horse. However, Will and school never did get along. Clem sent him to several boarding schools, but Will was more interested in riding and roping than in book-learning. He could always find classmates who would bend over and run down the hall, making noises like frightened calves, while Will tried to lasso them. Finally, Clem sent Will to Kemper Military School in Missouri. He thought the discipline at the school would be good for Will. At Kemper, Will heard about the sprawling Ewing ranch in the Texas Panhandle. He borrowed ten dollars from each of his three sisters and headed for the Ewing ranch. When he arrived, he told the Ewings he had run away from Kemper and just wanted to visit a few days. Mr. Ewing knew Clem Rogers and wrote to him asking what to do about Will. Clem wrote back telling the Ewings to get as much work out of Will as they could. That was the end of Will's formal education and the beginning of several years of roaming around the world.

In 1902, Will sold some cattle he owned. With the money, he and a friend started for Argentina. They had heard grand stories about what life was like there for cowboys. All they really knew about Argentina was that it was south of the United States. They went to New Orleans, but found out they could not get to Argentina from there. They went to New York, but still they could not find a boat going to South America. At last, they went to England, and from there they finally reached Argentina. They soon found that there were few jobs for cowboys and that even if they could get a job, the pay would be low—only about five dollars a month. Will's friend decided to go back home, and Will spent most of the money he had left to buy him a ticket. Then Will wrote Clem, expecting his father to send him some money. Clem did not send money. Will had to have money to eat, and the only job he could find was on a cattle boat going to South Africa. South Africa was not where Will wanted to be, but it was there he began his career as an entertainer.

"Wild West" shows were very popular in many parts of the world, and one called Texas Jack's Wild West Circus was performing in South Africa. Homesick, Will went to see if Texas Jack was really from Texas. He was, and he asked Will if he knew much about riding and roping. Will said he knew a little about roping. Will showed Texas Jack a complicated rope trick called the Big Crinoline, and Texas Jack hired Will on the spot. It was not until later that Will learned that for five years Texas Jack had been offering a large amount of money to anyone who could do that trick. As an employee, Will could not claim the prize. However, Will gained something more valuable than the prize from his tour with Texas Jack. Years later, Will said that from Texas Jack "I learned the great secret of the show business—*learned when to get off*. It's the fellow that knows when to quit that the audience wants more of." Will always left his audience wanting to hear more.

After spending several months touring New Zealand and Australia with another Wild West show, Will finally got back home in 1904. He arrived just in time to perform in the Wild West show at the World's Fair in St. Louis, Missouri. After the fair closed, Will continued trying to find jobs with Wild West shows and in vaudeville. In 1905, while he was appearing with a Wild West show at Madison Square Garden in New York, a wild steer escaped and ran into the grandstand. The audience panicked. Police and cowboys tried to stop the frightened animal, but it kept charging into the crowd and climbed all the way up the stairs and into the balcony. Will caught up with the eight-hundred-pound steer there and got his rope around its horns, which had a spread of five feet. He managed to lead the unwilling animal back down the stairs into the arena. Will's daring act got a lot of publicity and led to jobs in vaudeville.

Will had worked up an act in which he roped a horse on the stage. It was quite a novelty, but it was hard to convince anyone to book, or hire, his act. Eventually, however, his act was booked to appear on the roof of the Victoria Theater. Getting the horse to the roof on an elevator was one of the trickiest parts of the act. While it is almost impossible to describe what Will's roping act was like, the act was quite a hit.

The first time Will spoke from the stage was to make a simple announcement about one of his rope tricks. The audience thought his southwestern drawl and shy way of speaking were part of the act, and they laughed. Will was very serious about his rope tricks, and he was angry and embarrassed. It was a long time before he could see that laughter was one kind of applause. One night, none of his tricks worked right, and he began to joke with the audience about his skill with the rope. In the middle of one trick during which he was supposed to jump with both feet into and out of a spinning circle of rope, he only got one foot into the circle. He said, "Well, got all my feet through but one." The audience laughed heartily, and thereafter, Will often made "mistakes" in his act. He began to talk to the audience throughout the act, telling short jokes in a conversational manner as he twirled his rope. "Swinging a rope is all right when your neck ain't in it," he said. "Out West where I come from, they won't let me play with this rope. They think I might hurt myself."

He toured the United States, and his act was a hit in some of the largest cities in America. In 1906, he appeared at the most important theaters in Europe—the Winter Garten in Berlin, Germany, and the Palace in London, England. He was as popular in Europe as he was at home.

In 1908, Will married Betty Blake. He had met her nine years earlier and had written letters to her from all over the world. He often asked her to marry him, but Betty always refused. Betty cared for Will, but she did not want to be married to a vaudeville performer. She did not think his career as a performer would last, and it might not have lasted if Betty hadn't made a suggestion that changed his career.

In 1913, Will was appearing in the "Midnight Frolic," a stage show produced by Florenz Ziegfeld, Jr., a man famous for the expensive and elaborate stage shows he produced. The show began at midnight each night on the roof of the New Amsterdam Theater. It was the fashionable place to go, and the same people came night after night. Ziegfeld did not like Will's act and told his manager to fire Will. That same day, Will asked the manager for a raise. He had a new idea for the show, he said. Betty had suggested that he talk about each day's news, since people did not want to hear the same jokes night after night. Since Ziegfeld had left New York right after giving orders to fire Will, the manager decided to give Will another week. The change was such a success that Will's one-week extension lasted for months. He talked with his audiences as if they were all sitting around visiting in someone's living room. He commented on the day's events, the people in the audience, and things that happened while he was on the stage spinning his rope. His act was always the shortest of the "Frolics" acts; he never forget the secret he had learned in Africa, and he always left his audience wanting to hear more.

Will often chose some celebrity from the audience as the subject of his jokes. As often as not, the celebrity was a prominent politician. In 1916, however, the prominent politician was President Woodrow Wilson. Will was appearing in a benefit performance in Baltimore. Shortly before the show was to go on, the cast heard that the President would be in the audience that night. Many of the jokes Will was planning to use were critical of certain actions of the President. Will was not at all comfortable when he walked on stage. He stood still for a moment. Then he grinned bashfully and rubbed his head. "I'm kinder nervous here tonight," he said. This was so obvious to the audience that they all laughed. He moved slowly into the comments he had intended to use. Will and his audience looked nervously toward President's Wilson's box, but the President was leading the laughter.

Will was still appearing nightly in the "Midnight Frolic" when Ziegfeld asked him to appear in his stage show, the "Ziegfeld Follies." The "Follies" were expensive stage shows that featured many beautiful girls in fancy, costly costumes. Will was to provide the comedy in the show. Both shows were at the same theater, and Will prepared new material for each show every day. He read every edition of every newspaper in his effort to keep his comments and jokes up-to-the-minute. Will was no longer a vaudeville performer; he was now an important stage star. The next step in his career was easy.

Movies were brand new. They still did not have sound, but they were increasing in popularity. In 1918, Will starred in *Laughing Bill Hyde,* and he was as much a hit in the silent film as he was on the stage. In all, he appeared in fifty silent films. The most memorable was *The Ropin' Fool,* which he both starred in and produced. He learned that producing movies was not as easy as starring in them. He produced three films, but none of them were financially successful. He owed a lot of money after he finished the three films, and to earn the money to pay his debts, he started two new careers. He began to travel around the country making after-dinner speeches, and he began to write a column for the newspapers.

Each speech he made was unique. Before he made a speech, he learned about the town where he was speaking and about the people in the town. His jokes and comments fitted the place as well as the organization to which he was speaking. Sometimes he insulted people and often he surprised them; they loved him, whatever he said. His newspaper columns poked gentle fun at society and politics. Once he wrote: "It must be getting near Election time; he has commenced taking up all the Babies and kissing them. . . . Mothers, when you see your Baby picked up by someone nowadays it is either one of two men. It's a kidnapper or a Politican." Most of his political attacks were on the party in power at the time. He said, "You folks know I never mean anything by the cracks I make on politics. I generally hit a fellow that's on top because it isn't fair to hit a fellow that's down." He followed no grammar rules except his own. He punctuated, spelled, and capitalized as he pleased. One editor objected to Will's frequent use of the word "ain't." Will responded, "I know a lot of people who don't say 'ain't,' ain't eating."

A year of after-dinner speeches paid off his debts, but Will continued to make speeches and write newspaper columns for the rest of his life. The years from 1929 to 1935 were good years for Will. He appeared in twenty-one films and wrote six books. He traveled in Europe and became friends with the leaders of many countries. He was equally at ease with cowboys and kings. His idea of a vacation was to join a cattle roundup back at the ranch and work as hard at branding calves as any cowhand. His newspaper columns were read by forty million people. He tried to interest Americans in flying, already a popular way to travel in Europe. He often turned his talents to raising money to help people who had fallen on hard times. Whatever he did, he was always just himself: easy-going, good-natured, and full of homey humor and down-home charm.

In 1935 he had some time off and decided to fly to Alaska with his friend Wiley Post, a pioneer aviator who was also from Oklahoma. They thought they might fly over the top of the world to the Orient, but mostly, they just wanted to see Alaska. On August 15, they became lost in bad weather and Wiley landed the seaplane on Walakpa lagoon. There was an Eskimo camp on the shore of the lagoon. One of the Eskimos spoke English and was able to tell them they were near Point Barrow. The plane took off, started to climb, and turned in the direction of Point Barrow. Without warning, the engine went dead and the plane crashed.

Will's humor echoed in the silence of his death. "When I die," he had said in happier times, "my epitaph or whatever you call those signs on gravestones, is going to read, 'I joked about every prominent man of my time but I never met a man I didn't like.' I am proud of that. I can hardly wait to die so it can be carved."

Directions: On a separate sheet of paper, answer the following questions about Will Rogers.

1. How did Will Rogers's skill at roping and riding contribute to his career as a world-famous humorist?
2. What do you think was Will Rogers's greatest contribution to America? Explain why you think so.

MARY MCLEOD BETHUNE

Black educator and leader, born in South Carolina in 1875 and died in Florida in 1955

"Put down that book! *You* can't read!" Mary McLeod, the little black girl, dropped the book. She was outside the Wilson family's big white plantation house playing with the Wilson children. Mary's mother had been a slave of the Wilson family before the Civil War. Now the Wilsons paid her a small amount to do their laundry in her home. When Mary and her mother arrived to pick up the laundry that morning, two little Wilson grandchildren were playing outside. They asked Mary to play with them, so that she could tend their dolls and serve make-believe tea in their doll dishes. Mary was delighted to play the part of the maid. Among the toys was a book lying on a table. Mary picked up the book, and it was then that little Essie Wilson screamed at her. The Wilson children believed that blacks could not learn to read and had no right to touch books.

After her mother had gathered the Wilson's laundry, Mary walked home barefoot in the dust with her mother. The McLeods lived down the road in a cabin in the black section of Mayesville, South Carolina. The cabin had four small rooms. Mary, her mother, father, grandmother, and six brothers lived in the cabin. The older children in the family were born in slavery, but Mary, who came later, was born in freedom. Mary wondered about it the next day as she helped her mother weed out the crab grass from among the cotton plants. Was she really "free" if she could not read and would never get the chance to learn how? There was no school at all for blacks in that part of South Carolina.

Not long afterward, Emma Wilson, an educated young black woman, came to Mayesville. She had been sent by the Presbyterian Board of Home Missions to open a school for black children. Mary walked five miles every day to attend Miss Wilson's classes. The school was in one room of a shack in Mayesville, but to Mary it was a new world. With some of his hard-earned money, Mary's father bought her a gingham school dress, a slate, and a slate pencil. Mary studied at home by the light of a kerosene lamp. Her grandmother, parents, and other brothers watched with wonder as they did their evening chores.

Mary attended Emma Wilson's school for two years. By then, she could read the entire Bible. She learned arithmetic and used it to help her father and neighboring sharecroppers with their accounts. At the end of two years, Miss Wilson held a graduation ceremony for Mary and three other students. Mary received a diploma and an award as Miss Wilson's best student.

Mary McLeod wanted more education, but there was no other school she could attend. That spring the old McLeod mule died. All the children at home had to take turns dragging the plow. There was no money for a new mule, and the fields had to be plowed and planted. Mary worked dragging the plow through the cotton fields for the rest of the summer.

After the Civil War, many Americans thought about the problem of education for blacks. In Denver, Colorado, lived a dressmaker named Mary Chrissman. Miss Chrissman, a member of the Quaker faith, decided to do her part by sending a black girl through school. She gave money to the American Board of Missions, asking the Board to use it to educate a black girl who would be serious about her studies and who might go on to help other blacks. The Board sent this scholarship money to the Scotia Seminary, a mission high school in Concord, North Carolina, where Emma Wilson had gone to school. When Miss Wilson learned about the scholarship, she immediately suggested Mary McLeod as a person worthy of Miss Chrissman's help.

Mary was then twelve years old. Her family and neighbors went to the train station to see her off to Concord, North Carolina. Mary rode on a train for the first time in her life. Concord was a town of only 4,000 people, but it seemed like a large city to Mary. A kind teacher met her at the train station. There were both white and black teachers at the Scotia Seminary. The students lived in a big dormitory. Mary was assigned to a room on the second floor, but she had never climbed any stairs before and was almost afraid to go up.

Mary soon made friends at the school and became a leader among the students. She worked very hard at her studies, eager for the chance to learn new things. The classes in music especially pleased her. Mary had a fine alto voice and soon joined the school choir. She excelled in public speaking, and she took part in plays.

Mary could not go home during summer vacations because she did not have enough money for the train ticket. Instead, she worked as a laundress, cook, or maid, earning money for clothes, books, and paper for the next school year. She spent seven years at the Scotia Seminary. At one time, Mary had heard a lecturer telling about Christian missions in Africa. She learned that the blacks in Africa were not Christians. When her schooling was over, she decided to become a missionary and help spread Christianity in Africa. She applied to a missionary training school, the Chicago Bible Institute, in Illinois. Dwight L. Moody, the founder, was a famous religious teacher. Mary was the first black American who had ever managed to get enough education to apply to the missionary training school, and Moody decided to take her as a scholarship student.

After a short visit to her home, Mary went to Chicago. She was then nineteen years old. Chicago was a big, new city, recently rebuilt after the great Chicago Fire. Very few blacks lived there. During the four years that she attended the Bible Institute, she never met any blacks in Chicago. In her classes Mary learned the things that a missionary needed to know. Along with the other students, she did missionary work in Chicago, often helping people in the city's slums.

Dwight L. Moody trained missionaries, but he did not place them. He sent Mary McLeod to New York to be interviewed by the Presbyterian Board of Missions. They told Mary that they could not use her; there was no opening available in Africa. She was disappointed, but she did not give up. She applied to the American Board of Missions. The members of the Board found Mary to be the best qualified black applicant they had ever had. They decided to give her more training and sent her to Augusta, Georgia. There she would teach at the Haines Institute, a training school for black teachers.

The principal of the Haines Institute was a black woman named Lucy Laney. She inspired Mary with the idea that blacks in the South needed schools just as badly as blacks in Africa. Mary decided that she would someday start a school in the south, just as Emma Wilson had founded the school in Mayesville.

Teaching under Lucy Laney, Mary saved enough money to buy her parents a nice home in Sumter, South Carolina. The house had three large rooms and a bathroom, plastered walls, and glass windows. She also saved enough money to send her two younger sisters to the Scotia Seminary in Concord. Mary's next teaching assignment was at a school in Sumter. A fine young man worked in a store in Sumter, earning money to help his brothers through school. His name was Albertius Bethune. He fell in love with Mary McLeod, and they were married in 1898.

The Bethunes moved to the town of Palatka, Florida, and both Mary and Albertius began teaching school there. One day, Mary heard that a railroad line was being built down the eastern coast of Florida. The tracks were being laid by black workers who came from the cotton-growing areas of the South. Their families were with them, living in shacks built at Daytona Beach by the railroad company. Mary McLeod Bethune got on the train and went to Daytona Beach. She saw families living in windowless shacks. Of course, there was no school. Then and there, she decided to found a boarding school for black girls in Daytona Beach.

Mary had her five-year-old son with her, and she had a dollar and a half in her pocket. She rented a four-room cottage for eleven dollars a month. She went out to talk to the wives of the workers about her school. She enrolled five little girls from five to eight years old. Their parents agreed to pay fifty cents each week for schooling.

To furnish the school, Mary made chairs and desks out of packing boxes. She went around asking for donations of old cooking pots and anything else people would give her for the school. She collected flour, lard, eggs, and sweet potatoes. She used these ingredients to bake sweet potato pies to sell to the workers on the railroad. She bought books with the money she earned.

Mary taught her pupils to read, write, and sing from written music. She also taught her pupils how to make many of the clothes they needed and to cook pies and other things that the railroad workers would buy. The five little girls learned so quickly that many other parents began sending their children to Mrs. Bethune's school. Soon she started a garden, and the children raised vegetables and strawberries to sell. Albertius Bethune came down to Daytona Beach to help his wife.

The school grew. In less than two years, it had 250 pupils. Mary Bethune taught the girls to sing so well that wealthy tourists at a nearby resort came to hear them. One of these tourists was Thomas H. White, who manufactured sewing machines. Mr. White was so impressed with Mrs. Bethune's school that he paid for land and fine new school buildings. Another wealthy man, James N. Gamble, a well-known soap manufacturer, also became interested in the school. Both of these important businessmen became school trustees. Every winter when they came to Florida they arranged to bring sheets, shoes, dresses, and books. Thomas White left the school $79,000 when he died.

Booker T. Washington, the great black educator who founded the Tuskegee Institute in Alabama, came to visit Mrs. Bethune's school. He felt that blacks could best help themselves by learning trades. Mary told him, however, that she wanted to prepare the girls in her school for college. She insisted that blacks must have a college education before they could be treated as equals by white people.

In 1923, Mary McLeod Bethune combined her school with a black college for boys. Her original school in Daytona Beach grew into Bethune-Cookman College, with 300 students enrolled. Today, Bethune-Cookman is a four-year college with an enrollment of 1,900 students. At that time, however, it was a two-year college. Most of the students went out to teach elementary school as soon as they finished their two years. Mary urged her best students to continue their educations. She tried to get them scholarships at big northern universities.

Mary McLeod Bethune became one of the best-known black women in America. She traveled widely, attended conventions, and made many speeches about education. In Los Angeles, California, she met Mary Chrissman, the shy old woman who had once given a part of her dressmaker's income to send Mary McLeod to high school. The Quaker woman had lived to see her investment returned a thousandfold.

When President Herbert Hoover called a White House conference on child health problems, Mary McLeod Bethune was one of the delegates. During this period, the Great Depression hit the entire nation. Blacks were among the first to suffer. They lost their jobs in the cities and on the farms. Those who were attending school could not find the money to continue. In 1933, President Franklin D. Roosevelt tried to find ways to help people during the depression. He did not want young people to leave school, so he created the National Youth Administration (NYA). This organization gave students jobs around school or in social centers and paid them $15 or $20 each month to help them stay in school. Mary heard about the program; however, it provided no money for students in black schools. She went directly to the President, who promised to help young black Americans who were working for a better future.

Mary became First Assistant in the National Youth Administration. During the next nine years, she helped 600,000 black students stay in school with the help of NYA jobs. Students worked at cleaning playgrounds and parks, building dormitories and school buildings, and helping to enforce conservation laws. Under the President's Vocational Training Project, many young blacks from the country and from city slums learned trades such as agriculture, dressmaking, nursing, and child care.

While doing this work in Washington, D.C., Mary became a friend of Mrs. Eleanor Roosevelt. The two women were often photographed together as they worked at planning slum-clearance and school projects. When World War II began, Mary threw herself into work for her country. As Special Assistant to the Secretary of War, she chose many young Black women to enter the Women's Army Corps. She helped President Roosevelt plan the Fair Employment Practices Committee (FEPC) to ensure equality for all races in defense jobs and in the armed forces.

One of the last things President Roosevelt did before his death was to make Mary McLeod Bethune a delegate to the San Francisco conference planning the United Nations. Mary later served with Mrs. Roosevelt as a member of the United Nations Commission on Human Rights.

In 1949, at the age of seventy-four, Mary made one of her last speeches. She spoke to a group of white and black teachers in Columbia, South Carolina. On the stage with her as a second honored guest was another rather old native of South Carolina, Miss Essie Wilson. Miss Wilson had been a missionary in China for many years. Tears streamed down her face when she realized who Mrs. Bethune was. Miss Wilson embraced Mrs. Bethune with great affection and spoke of the honor she felt at being on the same stage with the famous Mary McLeod Bethune. Mary had come a long way since the day Essie Wilson told her, "Put down that book! *You* can't read!"

Directions: On a separate sheet of paper, answer the following questions about Mary McLeod Bethune.

1. Mary McLeod Bethune is considered to be a pioneer in education for Black Americans. In what ways do Mary McLeod Bethune's accomplishments make her a pioneer? Explain your answer.

2. Mary's mother always felt that Mary was "different." In what ways was Mary different from her older brothers? How did this difference affect her life?

ROBERT GODDARD

Pioneer builder of rockets, born in Massachusetts in 1882 and died in Maryland in 1945

One of the most widely read novels in America after the Civil War was *A Trip to the Moon*. Jules Verne, its author, was a French author who wrote novels about inventions of the future. Many of Jules Verne's predictions came true. He wrote a novel called *Around the World in 80 Days,* and before long it was possible to travel around the globe in that amount of time. *Twenty Thousand Leagues under the Sea* told of a vessel that could travel under water. Today there are submarines that prove that Jules Verne's "fantasy" was not impossible. The idea behind *A Trip to the Moon* is no longer a fantasy either. In this novel, the main characters are gunnery experts who form a gun club after the Civil War. Out of an enormous cannon, they shoot a large, hollow aluminum cannonball at the moon. The cannonball travels at a very high speed and is able to overcome the earth's gravity.

One enthusiastic reader of Jules Verne's *A Trip to the Moon* was a fifteen-year-old boy named Robert Goddard. He read all of Jules Verne's novels, as well as a novel by H.G. Wells called *The War of the Worlds*. This science-fiction book told of people on other planets;

it also told of planets that might be reached by projectiles, or rockets, from the earth.

Robert was not interested in science fiction alone. He was also very interested in mathematics and science in general. Robert was a sickly child. When he was fourteen, he had been well enough to attend a regular eighth-grade class, but now his poor health kept him out of school. He was eager to learn more mathematics and science and was disappointed to have to stay at home.

Both Robert and his mother had tuberculosis. On the doctor's advice, the Goddard family went to live out in the country near Worcester, Massachusetts. Here Robert and his mother could rest in the clean country air.

Robert's condition was so bad that he had to spend the next two years in bed. During this time, a fine public high school opened in the town of Worcester. The school had some excellent mathematics and science teachers. When Robert heard about the school, he began to study very hard at home in bed. He studied physics, mathematics, and chemistry. When he was well enough to sit up in bed, he got a portable drafting table and taught himself mechanical drawing. Finally, Robert was well enough to enter the high school as a sophomore at the age of eighteen.

Robert continued to study science, both in school and at home. During the summer, when he was supposed to be resting, he performed scientific experiments on mechanical devices. On October 19, 1899, Robert developed the idea of a rocket that might be able to travel out into space beyond the earth's atmosphere and gravity. He kept careful notes about his ideas and experiments. That day was so vivid in Robert's memory that he referred to October 19 as Anniversary Day.

In school, Robert wrote articles about the motion of stars and the possibility of people living on Mars. These were unusual subjects for high school students at the turn of the century. Robert tried to get these articles published in technical magazines, but the editors rejected them.

Robert Goddard was twenty-one when he finished high school. His health had improved. There was a technical college in Worcester, and Robert decided he wanted to attend it. Unfortunately, he could not afford the tuition fees, which were rather high. His mother was still ill with tuberculosis, and all the family's money went to pay her medical bills. Robert's grandmother, however, was able to borrow some money to pay the tuition at Worcester Tech (now called Worcester Polytechnic Institute).

Robert found the work in college much harder than it was in high school. He learned from his physics professor that many of his ideas for experiments would not work. He did not give up his ideas, however. He still thought about the possibility of sending a rocket into space, but when he wrote papers about it, his teachers and fellow students thought his ideas were very peculiar.

Goddard had many other ideas that sounded strange to people at the time, but that have since become reality. For example, Goddard once wrote a paper for his English composition class about the year 1950, which was almost half a century in the future. He described a train being pulled through a vacuum tube and traveling across the United States in three hours. He later published this paper as a piece of science fiction.

Meanwhile, Goddard continued his studies on the use of a gyroscope for balancing airplanes. A gyroscope is a mounted wheel. When it is rotated at high speeds, the gyroscope can be used to stabilize the course of moving vehicles such as airplanes and ships.

After graduating from Worcester Tech, Goddard did graduate work in physics at Clark University. After receiving his Ph.D., he went to work at Princeton University. During all of his studies, he kept thinking about his space rocket. He thought of a rocket that would carry its own fuel. The fuel would burn at certain times, or stages, and would thrust the rocket forward. Goddard did not have enough money to make such a rocket, but he drew elaborate designs of it. Using his designs, he took out a patent on the rocket in 1914.

When World War I broke out in Europe, Goddard tried to interest the United States Navy in his rocket. The Navy asked for "samples," but Goddard was ill with tuberculosis at the time and could do nothing. Later, with his illness under control and under orders not to work too hard if he wished to remain well, Goddard became a professor at Clark University. He began building a collection of rockets of all sizes. He soon found, however, that this was an expensive project.

Goddard sent drawings with descriptions of his ideas to the Smithsonian Institution, and to his surprise, the agency sent him a grant of $5,000 to use for building experimental rockets. In 1917, the United States entered World War I. The War Department learned of Goddard's experiments and hired him to work for the Signal Corps. Goddard went to California, where he conducted experiments at Mount Wilson Observatory in Pasadena.

In 1923, Goddard met Esther Kisk, an intelligent young woman who was working as a secretary in the president's office at Clark University. Robert fell in love with Esther. After he proposed several times, Esther finally agreed to marry Robert. She also became one of his best research assistants.

Goddard continued to work on his rockets. Finally, he was able to launch his first rocket, a small model. It stayed in flight for 2.5 seconds and went up 41 feet. The rocket traveled a distance of 184 feet during its flight. This is equal to a speed of about 50 miles per hour. A year later, Goddard built a larger model. This model contained a thermometer and a camera. Goddard and his wife launched the larger rocket model from the Massachusetts farm of an old family friend. The model stayed in flight only 18 seconds, but it reached a height of 80 feet.

The rocket made a loud noise when it fell back to the earth. Neighbors called the police and reported an airplane crash. The police arrived with two ambulances and two newspaper reporters. There was a lot of bad publicity, and the Goddards were forbidden to launch any more rockets. Goddard was afraid that he would be forced to stop his experiments, but he received permission from the federal government to use Camp (Fort) Devens, Massachusetts, to test his rockets.

The publicity did one good thing, however. It aroused the interest of the young aviator, Charles Lindbergh, who had flown alone across the Atlantic Ocean in 1927. Lindbergh knew many scientific-minded men who had money to invest in experiments. He persuaded one of them, the wealthy Daniel Guggenheim, to finance more of Goddard's rockets. Guggenheim agreed to give Robert Goddard $25,000 a year for four years. The Goddards moved to Roswell, New Mexico, where there were wide open spaces and good weather conditions.

Goddard set up a machine shop and hired specialists to help him. He planned to build a full-sized rocket. He and his students constructed a 60-foot launching tower. In December 1930, Goddard sent up his first full-sized rocket from the tower. It rose to a height of 2,000 feet at 550 miles per hour.

After this success, Mrs. Goddard tried to get her husband to rest for the sake of his health. She finally got him to go to Europe for a month by simply going ahead and buying the tickets for the trip. Goddard was restless while away from his work, however. When they returned, he plunged back into his experiments. In April, 1932, Goddard launched a multistage rocket. A gyroscope kept it on course, and Goddard directed its flight by remote control from the ground. The launch was successful, but Goddard needed more money for further experiments. Daniel Guggenheim was dead now, and his heirs did not seem interested in financing rockets. The Great Depression had hit the nation, and there were few people willing to contribute money for such experiments. The Goddards decided to return to Worcester, where Robert could resume teaching at Clark University. He closed up his machine shop in New Mexico, and left his old hat inside. Goddard wondered if he would ever see that hat again.

After another two years, Lindbergh persuaded the Guggenheim heirs to renew the grant for the rocket research. The Goddards returned to New Mexico. The first thing that Robert did was to find his old hat, dust it off, and put it on.

This time Goddard's work was interrupted by World War II. During the war, Goddard and his wife moved to Washington, D.C. There, Goddard conducted wartime research for the United States government. Unfortunately, the strain of wartime work brought back his old illness. Doctors then discovered that Goddard had an incurable cancer of the throat.

He lay in the hospital planning new experiments, but he had lost his voice and could not talk about them. Although Goddard knew he would never recover, he thought only of his interrupted work. The research Goddard carried out before his death led to the development of weapons such as the bazooka and to devices such as jet-assisted takeoff planes, multistage rockets, and rocket launchers. Robert Goddard, the space pioneer, would probably not be surprised at the accomplishments of the space program today if he had lived to see it. He knew it could be done.

Directions: On a separate sheet of paper, answer the following questions about Robert Goddard.

1. Why was Roswell, New Mexico such a good location for Robert Goddard's rocket research? Explain your answer.

2. Robert Goddard always kept detailed notes and records of his ideas and experiments. How did this prove helpful to him during his career? Explain your answer.

GEORGE GERSHWIN

Pianist and composer of concert music and popular show music; born in Brooklyn, New York, in 1889 and died in Beverly Hills, California, in 1937

As the lights grew dim in New York's Winter Garden Theater, the audience became silent. The year was 1919. Many people had filled the large vaudeville theater on Broadway to see the Sunday-night show done by the famous vaudeville star, Al Jolson. One of the most popular songs in Jolson's show was a new tune called "Swanee." It was an instant success both for Al Jolson and for the song's composer, George Gershwin. "Swanee" marked the beginning of an exciting career for George Gershwin as a Broadway composer.

George was born in Brooklyn, New York on September 21, 1898. His parents were Jewish immigrants who had come to America from Russia in 1890. They were married in America and settled down in New York. George was the second of four children in the Gershwin family.

During his childhood, George was considered a bit of a troublemaker. He played in the streets with other boys and often got into fights. He liked to roller skate and play street hockey. He used to say that music was for sissies, but music managed to capture his interest early in life. When George was six years old, he heard a player piano in a Harlem penny arcade playing Anton Rubinstein's "Melody in F." The young boy stood there spellbound as he watched the piano play the music. Four years later, he overheard a classmate, Max Rosen, practicing a violin solo for a school assembly. George was so inspired by Max's playing that he began to learn as much as he could about music.

In 1910, the Gershwins bought a second-hand upright piano. Mr. and Mrs. Gershwin had planned to have George's older brother, Ira, take piano lessons. As soon as the piano arrived in the Gershwin house, however, George spun the piano stool down so that he could sit on it. He immediately began to play "by ear" one of the popular songs of that time. From that moment on, the piano belonged to George.

George's first two piano teachers were not very good. As a result, his early training and exposure to piano music was weak. Nevertheless, George continued to learn popular songs of the day.

Charles Hambitzer probably had more influence on George than any of his other teachers. Hambitzer recognized George's talent and knew about his interest in jazz and other popular music. However, he was convinced that George should have a good education in "serious" music before he was allowed to study popular music. George was equally convinced that popular music could be a valid art form if the composer took it seriously and gave it the same amount of thought that a composer would give "serious" music. George and his teacher had many discussions about this point. Much later, George was able to apply what he had learned from Hambitzer to popular music. This resulted in a style that was an immediate hit—and one that was uniquely Gershwin. As it turned out, both teacher and student were correct.

At the age of fifteen, George left high school to take his first job as a pianist for a music publishing company in New York. He also began composing popular songs on the side. Up until 1919, however, George Gershwin was not a well-known song composer. Then, in 1919, he composed "Swanee." The song was an overnight success, and suddenly everyone was talking about George Gershwin, the popular new song composer. In that same year, Gershwin entered the world of musical theater as the composer of the broadway musical *La, La, Lucille*.

From 1919 until his death in 1937, George Gershwin had at least one of his shows running in theaters from New York to London. Some of his most popular songs came from successful Broadway shows. A few examples are "Someone to Watch Over Me" from *Oh, Kay!*; "Strike Up the Band" from *Strike Up the Band*; and "Embraceable You," "I Got Rhythm," "But Not For Me," and "Bidin' My Time" from *Girl Crazy*. In 1931, *Of Thee I Sing* made theater history by becoming the first musical to win a Pulitzer Prize.

On some occasions, Gershwin tunes appeared in more than one Broadway show. One of the most striking examples is "The Man I Love." George Gershwin wrote this song for the Broadway show *Lady, Be Good!* After a week, however, the song was dropped. Later, it appeared in the first rendition of *Strike Up the Band*. This first run was not very successful, but "The Man I Love" was rescued and rearranged for still another Broadway show: *Rosalie*. Due to many last-minute changes in the score, however, it was not used. "The Man I Love" was actually most successful as an independent song. It became so popular that when *Strike Up the Band* was remade in 1929, the song could not be used.

Many of George Gershwin's songs and shows were actually family affairs. While George was composing the music, his older brother, Ira, was busy writing the song lyrics. Ira was a talented songwriter, and the billing "Music by George Gershwin, Lyrics by Ira Gershwin" became a common sight on theater playbills.

In addition to his Broadway shows and popular songs, George Gershwin composed a number of concert pieces. These pieces, in particular, show the influence of Hambitzer. However, they also show the influence of Jerome Kern and other popular composers of the time. George's compositions marked the beginning of a distinctly American style of concert music. His first concert composition, *Rhapsody in Blue,* is one of the first pieces in which jazz harmonies and rhythms appear in a classical setting. It is still one of the most widely played concert pieces in the world.

Rhapsody in Blue was originally written for piano and jazz band. In 1925, Gershwin expanded his concert compositions to a full-size orchestra with the *Concerto in F* for piano and orchestra. The lively rhythms and jazz harmonies brought an exciting new sound to orchestras and concert halls. Three years later, Gershwin composed

An American in Paris. This concert piece for orchestra is probably Gershwin's best-known composition. It is considered to be one of the best examples of American symphonic music in the twentieth century.

Gershwin created another American musical milestone in 1935 with the composition of his folk opera *Porgy and Bess.* When it first opened, the public gave it a mixed reception. People who went expecting another Gershwin Broadway show thought the opera was too ambitious. People who went expecting to see a traditional opera thought it was too much like a Broadway show. The opera was very unique in that it called for a cast made up almost exclusively of black singers. Time has proved that what Gershwin had created was a unique fusion between Broadway and opera. *Porgy and Bess* contains some of Gershwin's best-known music, such as "I Got Plenty O' Nuttin'" and "Summertime." At the same time, *Porgy and Bess* has proved to be the most popular American opera to be staged so far.

With the enormous popularity of sound in motion pictures, George Gershwin moved to Hollywood to work on movie musicals. One of his finest movie scores was *Shall We Dance?,* which appeared in 1937. It featured the dancing talents of Fred Astaire and Ginger Rogers.

Later in that same year, George Gershwin fell seriously ill. Doctors diagnosed a brain tumor and, on July 11, 1937, George Gershwin died in Beverly Hills, California. He left behind a legacy of popular songs, Broadway shows, and a distinctly American style of concert music. The following is a partial discography, or list of recordings available, of some of Gershwin's works.

An American in Paris
  Abravanel, Utah Symphony, Vanguard VBD 10017
  Bernstein, Columbia Symphony, CBS MK–42264
  Previn, Pittsburgh Symphony, Phillips 412611–2PH

Concerto in F
  Previn, Pittsburgh Symphony, Phillips 412611–2PH
  Abravanel, Utah Symphony, Vanguard VBD 10017

Porgy and Bess
  Maazel, Cleveland Orchestra and Chorus London 414559–2 LH3

Rhapsody in Blue
   Abravanel, Utah Symphony, Vanguard VBD 10017
   Bernstein, Columbia Symphony, CBS MK–42264
   Previn, Pittsburgh Symphony, Phillips 412611–2PH

Directions: On a separate sheet of paper, answer the following questions about George Gershwin.

1. In what ways can George Gershwin be considered a pioneer in American music? Explain your answer.

2. George Gershwin wrote many Broadway shows and songs, but only a few concert pieces and only one opera. His concert pieces and opera have become more popular today than his Broadway shows. Why do you think this is so? Explain your answer.

FRANKLIN D. ROOSEVELT

32nd President of the United States, governor, and humanitarian; born in New York in 1882 and died in Georgia in 1945

Born on January 30, 1882, Franklin Delano Roosevelt was the only child of James and Sara Delano Roosevelt. James was the vice president of a large company that owned railroads, coal, and other businesses. Sara was a bright, attractive woman who, as a child, had sailed in clipper ships with her father, a sea captain.

Franklin's childhood was a happy one. The Roosevelt family lived in a mansion at Hyde Park, which is on the eastern shore of New York's Hudson River. There Franklin learned from his father how to fish, hunt, swim, and ride horses. On Campobello Island, off the coast of New Brunswick, Canada, Franklin often went sailing with his father. As a result of these sailing trips, Franklin developed a love of the sea.

Because his parents were so wealthy, they did not feel that Franklin should attend the local public schools. A tutor was hired, and she and Mrs. Roosevelt saw to Franklin's education until he was fourteen years old. As an only child who was not allowed to go to school, Franklin spent many hours alone. He was happy to spend these hours working with his hobbies. He collected stamps from all countries, and he read as much as he could, particularly about the sea. Not only was he a fast reader, but his memory was excellent. By the age of fourteen, he had already read half the dictionary, and he had remembered many word meanings.

During the summer, the Roosevelts often traveled to Europe. Something happened to Franklin on one trip that he would recall for the rest of his life. One night, while a male tutor and he were bicycling in Germany, they rode into a town. There they were ordered to halt by a group of soldiers. It was against the law in Germany to ride a bicycle into town after dark. Franklin thought that was ridiculous. From then on, he believed that laws should make sense and should be made to help people, not to hinder them unnecessarily.

When he returned from Germany, Franklin entered Groton, a school near Boston for boys of wealthy families. This was a big change for Franklin. As a child, he had been sheltered by his parents. Now, he found himself in a school that had many harsh rules and more than its share of bullies. A typical day at Groton began with a cold shower, even in winter. Then the boys were marched off to breakfast, and soon after, to chapel for prayers. Classes lasted until three. At that time, all students had to play football in the fall and winter and baseball in the spring. If a boy refused, he would be called names and possibly be roughed up by the other students.

At the time, Franklin was only a little more than five feet tall, and he barely weighed 100 pounds. Nevertheless, he joined the school's roughest teams. Every day he would be blocked and tackled by players twice his size. Every night he would stagger back to his room to study and sleep.

When Franklin graduated from Groton, he wanted to attend the United States Naval Academy at Annapolis. His father, who was very ill and dying, convinced Franklin that he should not do so. After all, how could he be head of the family while he was on board a ship thousands of miles away? Franklin agreed, deciding to enter Harvard instead.

At Harvard, Franklin was only an average student. His main interest was not in his courses but in the daily student newspaper, the *Crimson*. Franklin wanted to be an editor. One day, to impress the editor for whom he was working, Franklin announced that the

Vice President was coming. He would be speaking at Harvard on the very next day. Since no other newspaper was aware of this, Franklin's editor was very impressed. The editor printed the headline, the Vice President did arrive, and Franklin was on his way to becoming an editor himself. Of course, Franklin had had inside information. The Vice President happened to be his distant relative, Theodore (Teddy) Roosevelt.

While at Harvard, Franklin fell in love with Teddy's niece, Eleanor. Unlike Franklin, Eleanor had had a terrible childhood. Both her parents had died before she was thirteen years old. This and other hardships had made Eleanor very sympathetic toward the poor and the suffering.

Franklin often visited Eleanor in New York. She took him to the homes of the very poor and showed him how the people suffered. These experiences convinced Franklin that, if he ever became a politician, he would have to help these people.

Eleanor and Franklin were married in 1905. They settled in New York City, where Franklin attended law school at Columbia University, and Eleanor had their first child, Anna.

In 1910, the Democratic committee from his home town chose Franklin to run for the state senate. No Democrat had been elected from the Hyde Park area for more than fifty years. Roosevelt campaigned very hard. Day after day he drove his bright red car over country roads, speaking to farmers and townspeople. He told them he would fight for laws to raise crop prices and to keep big businesses from cheating farmers. The people believed him, and he was elected.

In 1911, Franklin moved his family to Albany, the capital of New York. There he became involved in a political fight with a powerful member of his own party. At that time, the two United States senators from each state were chosen by the legislators in their own state. Now they are elected by the people. William "Boss" Murphy, one of the state legislators, wanted a friend of his to be picked, so that Murphy could tell him what to do. Roosevelt and his supporters protested. They refused to attend the senate until Boss Murphy chose a different person. For ten weeks, nothing could get done because so many senators were protesting. Murphy finally gave in, and Franklin had won another major political victory.

Franklin so impressed the members of his party that he was appointed assistant secretary of the navy by President Wilson in 1913. When the United States entered World War I, Roosevelt wanted to join the navy and fight. President Wilson would not let him. Franklin was more important to the country as assistant naval secretary.

After the war, Franklin was nominated by the Democrats to run for Vice President. World War I had not been popular with the American people. Because Roosevelt and his running mate, James Cox, had been supporters of President Wilson, they were defeated in the election.

The following year, 1921, was even worse for Roosevelt. One day, he was sailing off Campobello Island with two of his children. Suddenly, he spotted clouds of smoke coming from a nearby island. Roosevelt went ashore and soon found himself in the middle of a forest fire. For hours, he and others fought the blazes. Finally the flames died out. Then he and his children jogged the two miles back to the cottage. To cool off, they swam in the icy waters of a nearby bay.

That night Franklin became ill. When he awoke the following morning, he could not stand. Then the pain began. Over the next few weeks, doctors diagnosed him as having infantile paralysis, which was caused by the polio virus. Franklin would never walk unaided again. Doctors fitted Roosevelt with leg braces so that he could get around. To do so, he needed to have a cane in one hand and to hold onto somebody with the other.

In 1924, Franklin went to Warm Springs, a resort community in Georgia. Franklin had heard that a polio victim had been cured by swimming in the mineral waters at the resort. As soon as he lowered himself into the pool, Roosevelt felt better. As long as he stayed in, he could move his legs, swim, kick, and float. He would never recover, but at least the warm water made him feel better.

Franklin loved Warm Springs so much that he purchased the old, run-down resort. In time, Warm Springs became an international center for studying infantile paralysis and for treating its victims.

That same year, at the Democratic National Convention, Franklin nominated New York Governor Al Smith for President. Refusing all help, he hobbled toward the speaker's platform on crutches. When he arrived, cheers filled the auditorium. Smith did not receive the nomination, but Roosevelt had returned to politics for good.

Four years later, Smith, who was now the party nominee for President, asked Franklin to run for governor of New York. He felt that Roosevelt was so popular that he would help carry the state for the 1928 Democratic ticket. Smith ended up losing both the governorship of New York and the Presidential election. Roosevelt, however, became governor of New York.

On October 24, 1929, the New York Stock Market crashed. Overnight, fortunes were lost. Factories closed. Millions of Americans lost their jobs. The Great Depression had begun. President Herbert Hoover attempted to deal with the depression, but his efforts were unsuccessful. In the next Presidential election in 1932, Hoover was defeated by New York's governor, Franklin Delano Roosevelt.

Roosevelt's inaugural address was one of the most famous ever delivered. In it, Roosevelt told the people that the United States of America would recover and continue to grow and prosper. He said that the people must be courageous; the only thing they had to fear was fear itself.

In his first 100 days as President, Roosevelt introduced one program after another to help get the country back on its feet. To win the people over to his side, he went on radio. In these "fireside chats," as they were called, Roosevelt spoke directly to the people as if they were his friends. He told the people how the "new deal" he had promised them during his campaign would come about.

One of the New Deal programs was the Civilian Conservation Corps. This created a quarter of a million jobs for young men to help restore America's national parks. The Agricultural Adjustment Act helped improve farmers' incomes. Factory workers were guaranteed the right to form unions by the National Labor Relations Act. The Fair Labor Standards Act improved working conditions by setting a minimum working age and shorter working hours. The Tennessee Valley Authority helped build dams to control floods on the Tennessee River and to develop electrical power.

Roosevelt appointed the first woman cabinet member in United States history. She was the Secretary of Labor, Frances Perkins. In 1934, Roosevelt told Perkins that he wanted all Americans to receive guaranteed retirement insurance. Soon after, the Social Security Act was passed by Congress.

Slowly but surely, America came out of the depression. In 1936, Franklin was reelected for a second term, and in 1940, for a third. No other President in the history of the United States had ever served three terms as President. Many Americans felt that the country needed Roosevelt. Just as the problem of the depression was improving, another, far worse situation developed.

On December 7, 1941, the Japanese launched a surprise attack on the American naval base at Pearl Harbor in Hawaii. Nearly twenty American ships were sunk or damaged. More than 200 planes were destroyed. At least 4,000 American men were either dead or wounded. Roosevelt called it "a day that will live in infamy." Congress declared war on Japan and later on Japan's allies, Germany and Italy. America was now involved in its second major overseas war, World War II.

At first, things looked bad for the United States and its major allies, Great Britain, France, and the Soviet Union. Roosevelt believed that, with the help of the people, the war could be won. America gave Roosevelt its support. Men and women worked long hours in factories, producing guns, tanks, planes, and other war necessities. United States fighting units grew enormously, combining to form the greatest military force of its time. Soon, the Allies began winning major victories.

During the war, Roosevelt met a number of times with British Prime Minister Winston Churchill and also with the Soviet leader, Josef Stalin. One of the results of these meetings was the creation of the United Nations. The three hoped that this organization would help prevent future wars.

In 1944, Roosevelt was elected for a fourth term as President. That year, Allied forces invaded Europe. Although the war would soon be over, Roosevelt would not live long enough to see it. On April 12, 1945, while vacationing at his home in Warm Springs, Roosevelt suffered a massive stroke. Later that day he died. He was sixty-three years old.

Franklin Delano Roosevelt was born into wealth and luxury, and yet he had sympathy for the poor. He suffered with an incurable disease, but he overcame its crippling effects to achieve many improvements for America and the world. He led America out of its worst depression and to victory in one of its bloodiest wars. It is no wonder that most historians consider Roosevelt one of the greatest Presidents of the twentieth century.

Directions: On a separate sheet of paper, answer the following questions about Franklin D. Roosevelt.

1. Franklin Roosevelt had a happy childhood, and he came from a wealthy family. What happened in his life that made him sympathetic to people who were less fortunate than he?
2. Franklin Roosevelt was the first and last President to serve more than two four-year terms in office. He was one of the most popular Presidents in United States history. Yet, as a result of the Twenty-second Amendment to the Constitution, it is no longer possible to serve more than two terms as President of the United States. Why do you think Congress passed the Twenty-second Amendment? Explain your answer.

FRANK LLOYD WRIGHT

World-famous architect; born in Wisconsin in 1867 and died in Arizona in 1969

Frank Lloyd Wright was nine years old when the United States celebrated its one-hundredth birthday. A large fair, the Centennial Exposition, was held in Philadelphia in honor of the anniversary. Frank's parents traveled from Massachusetts to Philadelphia to attend the fair. They saw many wonderful things. Frank's mother was most interested in the educational display. There she bought some colored paper strips and blocks made from maple wood. She took them home to Frank. He never forgot that gift. He spent hours and hours creating patterns and forms. He loved the feel of the shapes and the look of the colors. He knew then that he wanted to build and design things.

Frank Lloyd Wright was born on June 8, 1867, in Richland Center, a small town in Wisconsin. His father, William, was a musician and preacher who traveled from town to town. His mother, Anna, was a school teacher. Frank was the oldest of three children. Through Frank's earliest years, the family moved from Wisconsin to Iowa to Rhode Island to Massachusetts. When Frank was eleven, he and his parents and two sisters moved back to Wisconsin. They went to live near Spring Green, where Anna's brothers were farmers. In the summers, Frank worked for his uncles on their farms. In the winters, he attended school in Madison.

As he was growing up, Frank studied drafting. He wanted to become an architect. Unfortunately, there was no course in architecture at the University of Wisconsin. Instead, he began to study engineering. He heard about architects and their work in Chicago, Illinois. Two terrible fires had nearly destroyed Chicago. Architects were using new designs, materials, and techniques to rebuild the city. Before long, Frank went to Chicago in search of a job. When he arrived, he walked from office to office looking for an architect who needed a drafter.

Frank took a job drawing designs for an architect named J. L. Silsbee. He stayed with Silsbee only briefly. Then he went to work for Adler and Sullivan. Dankmar Adler and Louis Sullivan were two prominent architects. Adler had just secured the massive job of building the Chicago Auditorium—a combination auditorium, hotel, and office tower. Sullivan, the partner in charge of design, needed a drafter, and he hired Frank. Frank did well with Adler and Sullivan. He kept learning and developing his own talents. Soon Frank became the firm's chief drafter. Later, he was put in charge of designing all the firm's houses.

More and more people began to notice Wright's house designs. Occasionally someone went directly to Frank and asked him to design a house without going through the firm. Several times Frank accepted a private job. One day in 1893, Sullivan found out what Frank was doing. Sullivan angrily accused Frank of violating their agreement and fired him. Frank went into business for himself.

Frank and other architects were experimenting with a new kind of Midwestern house, called the *prairie house*. Wright was soon the leader of this movement. The prairie house had large rooms and large windows. It was designed to provide a family with separate spaces for visiting and for privacy. Despite the feeling of spaciousness, the prairie houses were only one or two stories, without basements or attics. They appeared low to the ground, with long sweeping lines. Wright used woods and other natural materials. In the prairie house, and in other kinds of buildings as well, Wright used a great deal of glass. He wanted to fill his buildings with natural light.

Wright's designs were so unusual for his time that they did not please everyone. In 1910, he offended some people by designing a church without a tall steeple. Instead, the church had a sloping roof, which Wright said resembled a person's hands closed in prayer. Critics praised Wright's first big office building: the Larkin Building in Buffalo, New York, designed in 1904. However, Wright's first design for a skyscraper, in 1912, was so bold and daring that it was never built.

By 1910, Frank Lloyd Wright was famous all over the world for his houses, theaters, churches, and office buildings. He was already known as the nation's most modern architect. He was equally famous for his designs and for his use of natural, native materials. A German publishing company invited him to prepare a big picture book of his drawings for new houses.

Wright went to Germany and worked on the book there. Then he spent a year in Italy looking at historic buildings in old cities. He decided not to go back to Oak Park. He did not like suburban life. Instead, he returned to Spring Green, Wisconsin, the scene of his childhood. There he built a house on land his mother gave him. He called the house *Taliesin,* the name of an ancient Welsh poet. Besides the house, Taliesin included farm buildings, offices, and a studio.

Soon after he built Taliesin, Wright allowed some friends to stay at Taliesin while he went to Chicago to work on a project. While he was in Chicago, he received a frightening message from home. He rushed back to Spring Green to find Taliesin destroyed by fire and the friends he left behind murdered. A mentally ill servant had gone on a rampage and then killed himself. Wright was terribly distraught. Soon, however, he rebuilt Taliesin.

About this time, a group of Japanese investors wanted to build an Imperial Hotel near the emperor's palace in the center of Tokyo. They wanted the hotel to be modern and luxurious, but it had to fit in with the surrounding Japanese buildings. The investors searched all over the world for the right designer. As part of their search, they sent a Japanese architect to the United States. When the Japanese architect visited Chicago, he saw some new buildings that pleased him very much.

More than twenty years earlier, Frank Lloyd Wright had seen the Japanese pavilion at the 1893 world's fair in Chicago. Then, in 1905,

Wright visited Japan. He liked the Japanese style of architecture, with its long, low roofs. He agreed with the way gardens were used as part of the buildings. He admired many of the ideas of Japanese architecture, and he used some of these ideas in his own designs. Seeing these designs, the Japanese architect felt very sure that Frank Lloyd Wright's work would please the Japanese investors. They discussed the project. Frank Lloyd Wright agreed to design the Imperial Hotel.

There was one problem Wright had never run across before. Severe earthquakes often hit Japan. Recent earthquakes in Tokyo destroyed some modern office buildings. Even the royal palace was badly cracked from earthquakes. Wright puzzled over the problem and finally thought of a remarkable earthquake-proof design for his hotel. He would construct the foundation of the building in a new way that would absorb the shock of earthquakes. Above the foundation, the construction would have other new features to withstand shocks. Many old-fashioned Japanese disapproved of the design, but the Japanese architect who had brought Wright to Tokyo supported him.

There were to be many courtyards, patios, private gardens, and pools. Every guest room was to be different from every other. There was to be a large, deep pool in the central patio. Some Japanese officials argued that the large pool was a foolish waste of space and money. The Japanese architect defended Wright's plans. The pool remained in the plans. Once the drawings were completed, Wright searched the Japanese islands for native wood and stone. Wright stayed on in Japan, supervising every detail of the building. At last the hotel was finished, and Wright returned home.

On September 1, 1923, the city of Tokyo suffered the most disastrous earthquake in its history. The earthquake caused 100,000 deaths. Fire was widespread. Sixty percent of Tokyo was destroyed. Japanese houses made from wood and paper burned down. Some new Tokyo office buildings crumbled. The Imperial Hotel that Frank Lloyd Wright had built, however, was not damaged. After the earthquake, several thousand frightened, homeless people rushed into Wright's modern hotel. Using relays, people handed buckets of water out from the hotel's central pool to the street. These relays kept part of the royal palace from burning. The hotel pool also gave many refugees drinking water for more than a week, until Tokyo's broken water main was repaired.

Wright's experience in Tokyo gave him many new ideas for gardens, spacious rooms, and the use of native stone material. He admired Japanese architecture, but he was also interested in the architecture of the Western Hemisphere. He studied the Mayan and Aztec temples of Mexico and Central America. These temples were built of blocks of stone covered with elaborate carvings. Wright designed several houses using ideas from Mayan temples. The first of these were for rich people. Then Wright designed a small house that would be inexpensive to build. With his own hands, he made an experimental hollow concrete block, about the size of three average bricks. He decorated the block with Mayan designs. With such concrete blocks, low, flat-roofed houses could be built very cheaply.

Then came the Great Depression. There was little money for building new houses or any other buildings. Wright fell into debt and almost lost Taliesin. Some of his old clients, still pleased with the houses Wright had built for them, loaned him money. They created a company so that Wright could continue working without worrying about money. He built a new school for young architects on the Taliesin site.

The first year, Wright took in twenty-three students to live and work with him. Later he made room for more students. They came from all over the world. It was an honor to work with Wright, to do the inking and coloring for his pencil drawings, to plan room interiors for his spectacular new office buildings.

Later Wright built a winter home in the desert near Phoenix, Arizona. He called it Taliesin West. It was made of desert stone. Its gardens, filled with palms and cactus, seemed to be part of the large, rambling studio house. Every November, Wright and his students migrated from Taliesin in Wisconsin to Taliesin West. They designed many buildings in Arizona, New Mexico, and California.

In 1936, Wright designed one his most famous homes, the house called *Fallingwater*, near Uniontown, Pennsylvania. Wright built *Fallingwater* on a cliff over a waterfall. Here Wright beautifully expressed his basic idea: *Fallingwater* appears to be a natural part of the landscape.

Through the years, Wright found time to write nine books and many articles on architecture. His *Autobiography* is regarded as a fine literary work. In later years, Wright lectured throughout the country. He called his architecture *organic*. He explained that *organic architecture* meant the buildings, the people who used the buildings, and the landscapes all fit together. As he aged, Wright's flowing blond hair turned silver, but his gray eyes shone with youthful enthusiasm. With his face bronzed by the Arizona sun, he never seemed to grow old. He was forever trying new ideas.

Wright died in 1959, two months before his ninty-second birthday. After his death, his students completed many of his unfinished buildings. Of his hundreds of designs, nearly 400 were built. Of those, more than 250 are still standing. Even decades after his death, the students at Taliesin are continuing the work of Frank Lloyd Wright.

Directions: On a separate sheet of paper, answer the following questions about Frank Lloyd Wright.

1. Frank Lloyd Wright had many new ideas about architecture. What were some of these ideas? Explain your answer.
2. If Frank Lloyd Wright were still alive, how might he design a space station? Explain your answer.

RICHARD BYRD

Explorer of the Antarctic continent, born in Winchester, Virginia, in 1888 and died in Boston, Massachusetts, in 1957

Suppose that the first organized exploration team to go to Mars and spend a year there took along a Boy Scout. When Richard Byrd planned an expedition to Antarctica in 1928, he decided to include a Boy Scout in the exploration team. He conducted a contest among Boy Scout troops throughout the nation. Byrd wanted a boy who was interested in science and knew enough about rocks and sea life to be of some real help to the scientists on the expedition. The winner of the contest was Paul Siple.

At the time when Siple first met him, Richard Byrd was already a national hero. Born to a famous Virginian family, Richard attended the Naval Academy in Annapolis, Maryland, in 1908. His desire for adventure and excitement in life began in Annapolis, where Richard trained to be a Navy pilot. Aviation was still in its infancy at this time, and the idea of flying fascinated the adventuresome Byrd.

Byrd became one of the Navy's best pilots. When World War I broke out, he was put in command of the United States Naval Air Station in northern Canada. In 1926, he and his co-pilot, Floyd Bennett, made the first flight of the North Pole. While in Canada,

Byrd made plans for a transatlantic flight. No one had ever crossed the Atlantic Ocean in a plane before, and Richard Byrd wanted to be the first person to do it. As the Navy prepared for the transatlantic flight, Byrd suffered many setbacks. His hopes of being the first person to cross the Atlantic were dashed when Charles Lindbergh made his historic flight from New York to Paris in May 1927. One month later, Byrd realized his dream of crossing the Atlantic. His crossing was historic in another sense. He carried with him the first sack of mail sent from the United States to Europe by airplane. Richard Byrd became the first transatlantic mail carrier.

Byrd's flight across the Atlantic, as well as his flights across the North Pole, made him a national hero. When asked where he was planning to travel to next after the North Pole, the answer was obvious—the South Pole.

The world already knew a great deal about the Arctic. The Antarctic, on the other hand, remained a mystery to modern science. Richard Byrd was determined to take a group of scientists on a well-prepared expedition to set up a permanent base on the shore of Antarctica. Then he would fly small planes out of the base during the well-lighted summer months and make the first accurate maps of the South Polar region.

He assembled fifty-four men for his expedition. There were geologists to study the rocks, biologists to study any living things they might find, and meteorologists to study the weather. Cameramen, radio operators, and airplane mechanics were also needed. Drivers of Norwegian dog teams were along to care for the party's eighty-five sled dogs. Paul Siple, the Boy Scout, was made the taxidermist for the expedition. A taxidermist is a person who preserves the skins of animals by stuffing and mounting them. He was in charge of getting sealskins and seal meat. Hundred of tons of canned foods were collected to supplement the food supply.

Finally, in August, 1928, the expedition team set out. Siple and half the team sailed from New York City in a sailing ship. Byrd and the remaining team members followed in a steel-hulled steamer. These two ships cruised along the edge of the Antarctic ice shelf below New Zealand. The expedition scientists made maps of a coast that had never before been charted. The team cruised on the ships all through the Antarctic summer during the months of November,

December, and January. At the southern end of the world, the sun never sets during these months. Byrd made short flights in a small plane to take photos from the air.

By January, autumn was beginning in Antarctica. The ships had to leave or they would be frozen in the ice for months and their hulls would be crushed by the ice. Byrd's men unloaded the ships and built a base. They made sturdy buildings for sleeping quarters, dog kennels, a radio hut, and storage rooms. They had a gasoline engine to produce electricity for the radio and electric lights. An airplane was safely stored away under the snow for the long winter.

Byrd named this "town" Little America. It had its own radio broadcasting station and sent messages and scientific reports to New York every day. For Americans in 1929, this constant radio contact with the Antarctic was as exciting as reports from a distant planet would be today.

Paul Siple made himself useful in many ways during the winter. When there was no blizzard raging, he joined the scientists studying such things as the life of seal puppies born on the ice. Life at Little America was very hard. The temperature inside the shed was very cold. Outside, the temperature was -50°F (-45°C). The sheer whiteness of the ice and snow outside could make a person lose all sense of direction, so the men planted orange marker flags along the paths between buildings. This would help them find their way.

Spring finally came to Antarctica. The airplane was rolled out and tested. Finally, in November, Richard Byrd made the first flight over the South Pole. He found a wide, high plateau at the South Pole. On the other side, he discovered mountain ranges. Byrd considered this flight over the South Pole, made on November 29, 1929, the most important event in his first Antarctic expedition.

The ships returned for the team in February of 1930. While the expedition team was preparing to leave, word suddenly came that the ships had to leave quickly to avoid being trapped in the ice. Byrd commanded the team to take personal possessions and trek the two miles across the snow and ice to the ship. They left their dinners uneaten on the tables in the mess room in Little America.

After that final trip, Byrd, who was promoted to rear admiral, kept busy speaking, writing, and planning radio programs about Antarctica. He felt that only half of his questions about that mysterious land had been answered, so he devoted himself to raising money for a second expedition.

One of the first persons that Byrd asked to come along on the second expedition was Paul Siple. Now a well-trained scientist as well as a veteran explorer, Siple eagerly accepted. Eighteen other members of the first expedition team rejoined Byrd. Many other scientists and explorers also went along. Three large tractors with special treads were added to the equipment.

On January 17, 1934, the expedition team reached the Antarctic shore nearest Little America. They saw the tops of the radio towers still standing. When they dug down in the snow that had been collecting for four years, they found the bunkhouses just as they had left them. That last meal which they had left lay frozen on their plates, and when they thawed it out it was ready to be eaten.

The new team set to work quickly. One of Admiral Byrd's projects was to set up a scientific observation post called the Bolling Advance Weather Base, 123 miles closer to the South Pole than Little America. There they dug into the snow and built a wood-lined bunkhouse. They also set up weather-recording instruments. Byrd planned to stay at his base through the entire Antarctic winter—and he finally came to the decision that he would stay there alone. He feared that if two men stayed there, they would get on each other's nerves in the cramped quarters.

Supplies for six months were brought in. These included more than 300 candles, two sleeping bags, cooking utensils, kerosene lanterns, a small gasoline stove, and a gas engine to provide electricity for the radio. There was a radio receiver and a Morse sending set. If the power failed, Byrd had a hand-cranked sending set. There were also 792 pounds of vegetables, 176 pounds of canned fruits, and 360 pounds of frozen meat. Byrd had many books to read, a diary to write in, and cards for playing solitaire. Paul Siple was very worried about leaving Byrd alone, but Byrd made Paul promise that under no circumstance would the men at Little America send out a party to him during the long winter. He was afraid that the party would get lost in a storm.

When the rest of the expedition finally left and Admiral Byrd settled down alone at Advance Base, it was the middle of March. The sun came up above the horizon for only a few minutes every day at noon. By mid-April, it never rose above the horizon; Antarctica was completely, constantly dark. Byrd kept his records. At 10:00 A.M. three days a week, he talked by radio with Little America for thirty minutes. By May, Byrd began to feel sick all the time. He did not know that he was being slowly poisoned by fumes from a faulty stove and from the engine that ran the generator. Snow and ice were clogging the cabin's air vents, and there was little circulation of fresh air in the cabin.

Finally, in June, Byrd lost consciousness for several hours. The stove went out, and he almost froze to death. When he came to, he realized that he was ill. He did not want Paul and the others at Little America to know that he was so sick for fear that they would try to come and get him. He explained the loss of radio communication by saying that the gasoline generator had broken. He was so ill that he could barely turn the crank on the hand-generated radio. He got the messages in Morse code all mixed up. The people at Little America knew that something was wrong with the Admiral.

Dr. Poulter, the expedition's second-in-command, then asked the Admiral by radio for permission to take one of the tractors out into the winter night to get better observations on meteors. Without telling Byrd, he planned to drive the tractor all the way to Advance Base. The men took the tractor out and tried three times to drive it to Advance Base. It was the middle of August before they reached Byrd's cabin. By then the Admiral had lost sixty pounds and could hardly speak.

Dr. Poulter cleared the air vents, repaired the stove, and nursed Byrd back to health. They did not return to Little America until the Antarctic dawn came, two months later. The men at Little America were overjoyed to see Admiral Byrd and were proud of the way he kept the records of all the instruments every day, even when he was too sick to stand on his own feet.

In May of 1935, the expedition came back to the United States. On Byrd's two Antarctic expeditions, not a single life had been lost, and only Byrd himself had had a serious illness. Admiral Byrd's account of his scientific findings in Antarctica was published in the *National Geographic Magazine* in October, 1935. He discussed the accurate new maps that had been made of the Antarctic area and the knowledge gained about the rocks in the region.

World War II stopped expeditions to Antarctica. Admiral Byrd, now past fifty, worked at special reconnaissance in the North Atlantic. The fearless admiral was not yet finished with Antarctica, however. He went back three more times before his death in 1957. His pioneering work has provided the basis for further experiments by many Antarctic scientists through the years.

Directions: On a separate sheet of paper, answer the following questions about Richard Byrd.

1. In what ways can Richard Byrd's work in Antarctica be considered pioneering research? Explain your answer.

2. What similarities and differences exist between Byrd's exploration of Antarctica and the exploration of Mars by scientists today? Explain your answer.

LOUIS ARMSTRONG

Jazz trumpeter and goodwill ambassador, born in New Orleans, Louisiana, in 1900 and died in New York, New York, in 1971

Every year in the early spring, the city of New Orleans seems to explode with the excitement of Mardi Gras. Thousands of people jam the streets to celebrate with parades and costume parties. The air is filled with the sound of brass bands playing the music that was born in the heart of New Orleans: jazz. People follow the bands, dancing to the lively rhythms. The sheer joy and love that come from the jazz sound can be felt by everyone at Mardi Gras. People around the world have been touched by the spirit of jazz, and no one has carried the spirit of jazz farther than the great trumpeter, Louis Armstrong.

Like jazz, Louis Armstrong was born in New Orleans, Louisiana. He was born on July 4, 1900. The Armstrongs lived in a crowded, broken-down section of New Orleans called "back o'town," along with many other poor black families. His parents were divorced when Louis was only five. Louis, his mother, Maryann, and his sister, Beatrice, moved into a room near Perdido Street.

His mother cooked for a white family in New Orleans. She worked very hard, but she earned barely enough to buy food for her family. Louis worked as a newspaper boy to help make money for the family. He was always interested in music. After he finished selling his newspapers, he would go to one of the nearby "honky-tonk" nightclubs. He would sit outside and listen to the music. The musicians inside played music that later formed the early basis for jazz.

When he was twelve, Louis formed a singing quartet with three other boys. They called themselves The Singing Fools. The boys earned money by singing in the streets of New Orleans and passing a cap around. On New Year's Eve in 1912, the boys were out singing in the streets. People were celebrating, shooting off Roman candles, and even shooting off guns to ring in the new year. That night, Louis took out a revolver from an old trunk in his house. He loaded the gun with blanks to shoot it at the celebration. In the middle of a crowded street, Louis raised the gun and fired it. The crowd immediately dispersed and before he knew it, Louis was under arrest.

At his hearing, the judge sentenced him to be sent to the Colored Waifs' Home for Boys. At the Waifs' Home, the boys were responsible for everything. They cooked, cleaned, made beds, did laundry, and tended the vegetable garden. They lived by the call of a bugle, which told them when it was time to work, eat, or go to bed. In addition to all of the work, the boys attended classes. One of the classes at the Waif's Home was music. The teacher was Mr. Peter Davis. Mr. Davis had a brass band at the Waif's Home. The boys played in parades in New Orleans.

Louis wanted to be in the band more than anything else. He wanted to play the cornet because he loved the look and the sound of the instrument. Louis worked very hard at the Waif's Home, and finally Mr. Davis asked him to join the band. However, when he went to his first rehearsal, Mr. Davis gave him a tambourine to play. Louis was disappointed at first, but he was so happy to be in the band that he played the tambourine as best as he could.

After a short time, Mr. Davis gave Louis a cornet to play. He practiced it every chance that he had. This made Louis very happy. He had a big, broad smile. The other boys said that he looked like a big open satchel, or carrying bag, when he smiled, so they called him "Satchelmouth."

Louis became a very good cornet player. Mr. Davis made him the leader of the band. When the bugler left the Waif's Home, he also made Louis the new bugler. Louis did not mind being the first one up in the morning as long as he could play.

One of the parades in which the band played passed down Perdido Street. All of Louis's friends came out to see him lead the band. They were so happy to see him and so proud of him that when a hat was passed through the crowd, enough money was collected to buy uniforms for the entire band.

Finally, after a year and a half, it was time for Louis to leave the Waif's Home. When he returned home to his mother and Beatrice, he took a job delivering coal on a mule cart. He worked very hard and saved as much money as he could. When he had saved ten dollars, he went to a pawnshop and bought himself an old, used cornet. Louis brought the horn home and polished it until it gleamed. He practiced every day. At night, he went to one of the honky-tonks where Joe Oliver was playing. Oliver was a cornet player who was considered to be one of the best. People knew him as King Oliver.

One night, King Oliver noticed Louis outside the club and spoke with him. He invited Louis to come to his house and meet his wife. The two became friends and Oliver gave Louis cornet lessons in exchange for running errands for Oliver's wife. Louis was a good student and soon was playing in the honky-tonks himself.

In 1917, the United States entered World War I. Most of the clubs in New Orleans closed. King Oliver went to Chicago to play in a band, and Louis was asked to fill his spot in Kid Ory's band in New Orleans. Two years later, Louis was offered a job playing in Fat Marable's band. The band played on a riverboat that sailed between St. Louis and New Orleans.

Louis's love for jazz was growing, and he was passing that love on to the people who heard him play. Old Satchelmouth, as he was called, could make audiences feel very happy, and the riverboat trips helped to spread his reputation around.

In 1922, Louis Armstrong received a call from King Oliver to come join his band in Chicago. The band was known as King Oliver's Creole Jazz Band, and it was one of the most popular bands in the country. Louis played second cornet, and King Oliver played first cornet. Gradually, Oliver gave Louis more and more solo parts. He was able to improvise well, and each solo was filled with his love for jazz. His loud, brilliant tones rang out wherever he played.

King Oliver's band soon began making records. During one of their first recording sessions, Louis had a solo. He stepped forward to begin his solo, just as he always did in performances. He began the solo, which was brilliant, exciting, and quite loud. Suddenly the recording engineers called for him to stop. They asked him to play his solo about 20 feet behind the band. Louis thought that maybe he was playing poorly, but the engineers told him that the only way they could record the notes clearly was for him to stand behind the band. These early recordings brought the popular sound of jazz into many houses throughout the country. They also made Louis Armstrong a well-known jazz cornetist.

Louis was invited to join Fletcher Henderson's band in New York. This band was playing at the Roseland Ballroom during the winter, and during the summer they toured and recorded. He began singing as well as playing his cornet. His low, throaty voice became as much of a trademark of Louis Armstrong as his cornet.

Around 1925, Louis was introduced to the trumpet. This instrument is similar to the cornet except that it is a little larger. Louis liked the brilliant tones that could be produced with the trumpet, and from that point on he played the trumpet instead of the cornet.

Later in that same year, Louis Armstrong formed his own group, Louis Armstrong's Hot Five. The Hot Five (and later the Hot Seven) made many jazz recordings. During one of the recording sessions when Louis was singing, he dropped the lyrics to the song on the floor. An engineer hurried to pick up the music, but Louis kept on singing. He just made up a bunch of nonsense syllables such as "scoobidy-doo-wah-doo-way." When the session was finished, the record people liked the way this singing sounded, so they left it on the record. This type of singing became known as "scat singing." It is still a very popular style of jazz singing today.

Louis traveled around the country for five years performing and recording jazz. In 1931, he returned to New Orleans and was greeted with a hero's welcome. Eight brass bands met him at the train station. One of those bands was the Colored Waif's Home Brass Band. Mr. Davis was still conducting the band. Louis visited the Waif's Home, and the boys prepared a special program for him. After the program, one of the boys handed him an old, dented bugle. After looking at it for a moment, a tear came to Louis's eye. This was his bugle at the Waif's Home. The boys were still using it. In the years that followed, whenever Louis visited New Orleans, he made sure to stop in at the Waif's Home. He also sent gifts of money to help the boys.

In 1932, Louis went to Great Britain. Jazz became very popular there. The people knew that Louis Armstrong was the king of jazz. When he was introduced during a performance, the announcer had trouble pronouncing his nickname, Satchelmouth. As a result, the announcer ended up introducing him as Satchmo Armstrong. That name has been with him ever since. The audiences liked Louis so much that after his tour of Great Britain, they presented him with a solid gold trumpet.

When he returned from Great Britain, Louis headed for Hollywood to be in *Pennies from Heaven* with Bing Crosby. Louis was to play himself in the picture. The movie was so popular that Louis appeared in four more movies in the next four years.

Armstrong's music was his life. As a result, he had two unhappy marriages that ended in divorce. In 1942, he met Lucille Wilson. She realized that music was important to Louis. She was ready to spend the rest of her life traveling with him and supporting him in his music career. They were married and built a home in New York City. Although they traveled all over the world, they liked no place better than their home in New York.

By 1947, Louis Armstrong was one of the most popular musicians in the United States. He formed a group called Louis Armstrong and His All-Stars. This group was made up of the finest jazz musicians in the country. The All-Stars toured Europe many times during the late 1940s and through the 1950s. In 1956, he made his first trip to Africa. His warm smile and friendly personality established him as a goodwill ambassador for the United States.

Many people were wondering when Louis would retire. Louis, however, had no plans to retire. In 1964 he recorded "Hello, Dolly!" It was an overwhelming success for the 54-year-old Louis Armstrong, and it proved that he still had a lot of music to give to the world.

Louis Armstrong continued to work through his seventy-first birthday. His joy and energy seemed to be endless. On July 6, 1971,

Louis Armstrong died peacefully in his sleep. Millions of people shared a deep sense of loss, knowing that the great Satchmo would no longer be able to fill the air with the music he so dearly loved.

Directions: On a separate sheet of paper, answer the following questions about Louis Armstrong.

1. Louis Armstrong contributed to the world of music in many ways. What were some of his roles as a musician?
2. People say that jazz is the only form of music to come from America. How could you support this statement given the facts about Louis Armstrong's life? Explain your answer.

JACKIE ROBINSON

Baseball player, civil rights leader, and businessman; born in Georgia in 1919 and died in Connecticut in 1972

Before 1947, all of the baseball players in the major leagues were white. Black players had their own separate teams, which were part of the Negro leagues. Major league players traveled on trains and airplanes, stayed in nice hotels, and ate in good restaurants. Players for the Negro leagues went from city to city on buses. Their accommodations were usually in run-down hotels in poor neighborhoods. Meals were often eaten out-of-doors at roadside stands.

Major league baseball was played in brand-new ball parks to large enthusiastic crowds. Players such as Babe Ruth, Lou Gehrig, and Ty Cobb earned sizable salaries and became household names. The Negro leagues produced equally great players, but few of them became famous. They played in modest ball parks before small but enthusiastic crowds. Their pay was low. In 1947, with the help of Brooklyn Dodgers owner Branch Rickey, Jackie Robinson changed all that.

Jackie was born on a small farm in Cairo, Georgia, on January 31, 1919. His family worked on a large plantation. In exchange for their work, they were given a shack and a little farm land.

With a family of seven to support, Jackie's parents found life quite difficult. When Jackie was still very young, his father left to look for work in Memphis, Tennessee. He never returned.

Then Jackie's mother moved the family to Pasadena, California, where they lived with Jackie's uncle. Mrs. Robinson earned a living by cleaning homes for white people and by taking in washing and ironing. In time, she had saved enough to purchase a small house. To help pay for it, she rented out some of the rooms.

As a young boy, Jackie felt the hatred some white people had toward blacks. At movie theaters, Jackie and his black friends were forced to sit in certain sections reserved for non-whites. Blacks were only allowed in city swimming pools one day a week. In school, Jackie was an average student, but he was an excellent athlete. He participated in four major sports—baseball, track, football, and basketball—both in high school and in college. One day, for Pasadena Junior College, he took part in two major sports events in two different cities. First, he participated in a track event, in which he set a broad-jumping record. Then, as shortstop, he helped his baseball team win the league championship.

After completing two years of junior college, Robinson attended the University of California at Los Angeles (UCLA). At UCLA, Jackie became the first person in that school's history to earn letters in four major sports. Although he was a very good baseball player, he was considered better in football, basketball, and track.

Because money was tight, Jackie decided to withdraw from UCLA in 1941. He took a job as assistant athletic director at a government-run work camp for young people. Not long after, he was hired as a player by an all-black professional football team in Hawaii, the Honolulu Bears. At the end of the Bears' season, Robinson worked for a construction company located near Pearl Harbor. On December 6, 1941, the day before the Japanese attacked the United States fleet at Pearl Harbor, Robinson was on a ship heading home.

After enlisting in the army, Jackie was shipped to Fort Riley, Kansas. Although he was intelligent, educated, and a natural leader, when he applied for officers candidate school, he was turned down. Jackie knew that there were openings in the school. The white officers in charge, however, were not admitting blacks. Robinson decided to do something about it.

When black heavyweight boxing champ Joe Lewis was assigned to Fort Riley, Jackie went to see him. After listening to Robinson's complaint, Lewis contacted some friends of his in the government. As a result, Jackie was finally accepted for officer training.

In 1943, Lieutenant Robinson was given command of a platoon attached to the 761st Tank Battalion at Camp Hood, Texas. Despite his lack of experience, Robinson proved to be an excellent officer. His military career was cut short, however, by an unfortunate incident. One evening, Robinson was returning from the officers' club by bus. He was ordered by the civilian driver to sit in the rear. At that time in the South, blacks usually were not allowed to take the front seats. These rules, however, did not apply on military bases. When Jackie refused to obey, charges were filed against him. His commanding officer sided with the driver. Soon, Robinson was given an honorable discharge and returned to civilian life. The army had considered him a troublemaker.

During the following year, Jackie successfully coached the basketball team at a small southern college. Then he was hired as a player by the Kansas City Monarchs, a black professional baseball organization. Robinson's reputation as an excellent college athlete had made him famous. As a Monarch, he helped draw crowds to the ball games. He also attracted the attention of Brooklyn Dodgers' owner, Branch Rickey. For a number of years, Rickey had been planning to introduce a black player into the major leagues. In 1945, Rickey thought the time was right. His candidate for the job was Jackie Robinson.

On August 28, 1945, Rickey and Robinson met. Jackie thought he had been summoned to the owner's office to discuss his chances of making the Brown Dodgers. That was an all-black team that Rickey owned. Instead, Rickey offered Jackie a contract with the all-white Brooklyn Dodgers.

Rickey told a stunned Jackie that he needed a good player who would not lose his temper. Jackie would have to stay calm even when people said and wrote horrible things about him. Most likely, white fans would scream out anti-black statements from the stands. Players on opposing teams would be equally cruel. Sports writers would also be very negative toward him. Through all this, Robinson must have the courage not to fight back.

Jackie always had been a fighter. At UCLA, whenever anyone said anything cruel to him, Jackie made sure he had the last word. Now, whenever he was verbally abused, he would have to remain silent. Despite his misgivings, Jackie agreed to Rickey's offer.

Jackie spent his first year in the major leagues playing for the Dodgers' farm team, the Montreal Royals. Before spring training for the 1946 season began, however, Jackie took care of a personal matter. On February 10, he married Rachel Isum. For the rest of his life, whenever he needed encouragement, Jackie would turn to Rachel.

When spring training began, Jackie was so nervous that he tried too hard. As a result, he performed poorly. The newspapers, players, and other team owners criticized Jackie and Rickey whenever they had the chance. Rather than let Jackie give in, Rickey and Rachel came to practice and tried to lift his spirits. Their efforts paid off. By the start of the season, Jackie was ready to play.

His performance against the Jersey City Giants was an indication of what his entire season would be like. He had four hits, including a three-run homer. He also stole two bases and knocked in a total of six runs. He fielded well at second, and his base running was excellent.

The Montreal Royals won the pennant that year, and Jackie contributed greatly to the team's success. Few incidents occurred to spoil things. There were occasional boos from the crowds, but there was also an enormous amount of cheering from the Montreal fans.

During spring training the following year, it became apparent that Jackie soon would become a Brooklyn Dodger. Some of the members of that team drew up a petition in protest. They did not want to have a black man playing with them. When Branch Rickey found out about the petition, he called the leaders into his office. He told them they either could play with Robinson on the team, or they could quit baseball. The protest ended.

Soon after Robinson arrived in Brooklyn, the Dodgers and their fans accepted him as one of their own. In other cities and with other teams, Jackie was not treated as well. Obscenities and racial slurs were shouted at him by players and fans alike. Opposing pitchers tried to hit him in the head with their pitches. Runners attempted to knock him down. Objects were hurled at him from the stands. He received hate mail and death threats. Through it all, Jackie appeared calm. In reality, he was very angry.

Jackie channeled this anger into his playing. The more cruel his opponents were, the better he performed. At the end of the season, Jackie was hitting an impressive .297. He had scored 125 runs, had hit twelve home runs, and was the team leader in stolen bases. For his accomplishments, Jackie Robinson was named the 1947 "Rookie of the Year."

In 1948, Jackie continued to play up to his potential. Fans both white and black poured into Ebbets Field—the Dodgers' stadium—to see Jackie. They enjoyed watching him—not because he was black, but because he was such an exciting player.

Once, after making an error, he went up to his team's pitcher and apologized. To make up for his mistake, Jackie said that he would win the game for the pitcher. The next inning, Jackie hit a home run, which won the game for Brooklyn.

On another occasion, Jackie was awarded first base when he was hit by a pitch. On first, Jackie shouted out that he was going to steal second. To distract the pitcher further, Jackie kept stepping on and off the bag and taking long leads toward second. Then he went. Safe at second, Jackie repeated the process. Before long, Robinson had stolen his way home, winning a victory for the Dodgers.

By 1949, more black players had entered the major leagues. Although things had improved for them, these men were still the victims of racial prejudice. On the road, they were not allowed to stay in the same hotels or eat in the same restaurants as their white teammates. That year, Branch Rickey released Jackie from his promise to keep calm and quiet. From then on, Robinson spoke out against these injustices.

Jackie had his best year in the major leagues in 1949. He batted .342, had 16 homers, 124 runs batted in, and led the league in stolen bases. He made the All-Star team, and, best of all, was voted the National League's "Most Valuable Player."

Although Robinson played well in 1950, it was a bad year for the left side of his body. In spring training, he twisted his left ankle. During the regular season, he hurt his left knee in a collision with an opposing player. In other games, he pulled a muscle in his left thigh, was hit by a ball on his left elbow, and jammed his left thumb into the ground. In spite of his injuries, Robinson hit .328, slammed 14 homers, and batted in 81 runs.

The following year Brooklyn lost the National League pennant to the New York Giants in a one-game play-off. Brooklyn had won in 1947 and 1949, and were to win again in 1952 and 1953. In each of these four cases, however, the Dodgers failed to win the World Series. It was not until 1955 that the Dodgers would beat their longtime opponents, the American League's New York Yankees, in the World Series.

Jackie had one of his greatest games in the 1951 season. To tie with the Giants, Brooklyn had to beat the Phillies in their last regular season game. Brooklyn fell behind 8-5. Then they tied. The game went into extra innings. In the bottom of the 12th, a Philadelphia player smacked a line drive to Robinson in right field. The bases were loaded, and two men were out. Jackie ran right, stretched, and dived for the ball. He made a spectacular catch. He was injured in the fall and should have been removed from the game. Realizing how much his team needed him, however, he decided to keep playing. In the 14th inning, he hit the game-winning homer over the left field fence.

After ten excellent seasons of major league baseball, Jackie Robinson retired. He was thirty-seven years old. In 1962, he was inducted into the Baseball Hall of Fame. For the remaining sixteen years of his life, Jackie worked to improve the lives of black people. As an executive for a major restaurant chain, he saw to it that black men and women were hired for jobs. He provided budget counseling for his employees and started summer camps for the children of his employees.

Later, he worked for the politicians he felt were most in favor of strong civil rights bills. In interviews, on his own radio show, and in his newspaper column, Jackie attacked racial prejudice in the United States. He also participated in fundraisers and marches in support of his beliefs.

Nearly blind from diabetes, at the age of fifty-three, Jackie Robinson died of a heart attack on October 24, 1972. At the time of Jackie's death, black baseball players no longer had to stay in separate hotels. They could eat in any restaurant they wanted, and play on any team in the major leagues. Three years later, the first black manager in major league history was hired. Jackie Robinson would have been proud.

Directions: On a separate sheet of paper, answer the following questions about Jackie Robinson.

1. For the first several years that Jackie Robinson played major league baseball, Branch Rickey made him promise not to lose his temper when people shouted racial insults at him. Why was it important for Jackie Robinson not to lose his temper during the first years he played in the major leagues? Explain your answer.

2. Jackie Robinson was both a great baseball player and a leading spokesperson for civil rights. How were these two efforts related to each other? Explain your answer.

GEORGIA O'KEEFFE

American artist; born in 1887 in Wisconsin, and died in New Mexico in 1986

When Georgia O'Keeffe was twelve years old, she told a friend that she intended to be an artist when she grew up. At the turn of the century, it was almost unheard of for a woman to be an artist. However, Georgia held fast to her dream and did indeed become one of the first important American women artists. For more than sixty years, she attempted in drawings and paintings to capture the spirit of things she saw. She painted pictures of flowers so huge that people had to stop and look at them. She painted pictures of dry animal bones she found in the desert. She painted pictures of tiny stones and great mountains. She painted pictures of ordinary things in such an extraordinary way that her paintings made people see the world around them in a new way.

Georgia was born on her father's dairy farm near Sun Prairie, Wisconsin, in 1887. She was the second of six children born to Francis and Ida (Totto) O'Keeffe. She wrote in her autobiography that she remembered being taken outside for the first time when she was about ten months old. She never forgot the brilliant sunlight or the pattern of the patchwork quilt on which her mother placed her.

Sunlight and patterns remained important to her all of her life and were consistently reflected in her art.

Georgia began taking art lessons when she was about twelve, and her ability with a paintbrush and a pencil was immediately obvious. Her mother hoped that Georgia might become an art teacher, but Georgia's goal was to become an artist.

When Georgia was about fourteen years old, the family sold the farm in Wisconsin and moved to Williamsburg, Virginia. The move did not prove to be a good one for the family. The O'Keeffes felt like outsiders in the tiny southern town. Georgia went to a boarding school, where she completed her high-school education. In the fall of 1905, she went to live with relatives in Chicago, so that she could study at the Art Institute of Chicago. She was unable to return to Chicago for the fall term in 1906, however, because she was ill with typhoid fever. She had such a high fever that all of her long, straight hair fell out. When it grew back in, her hair was curly.

She still had short, curly hair in 1907 when she went to New York to study at the Art Students League. In January 1908, she went with some other students to see a group of unusual drawings by French sculptor August Rodin. The drawings were being shown at an art gallery known as "291" because it was located at 291 Fifth Avenue. Here, for the first time, Georgia saw Alfred Stieglitz, a famous photographer and the owner of the gallery. There is no record that Stieglitz paid any attention to the dark, quiet girl wearing a black dress. Georgia did not care much for Stieglitz and stood in a corner while the other students talked with him about the Rodin drawings.

That year, her father's business failed, and Georgia was forced to look for a way to support herself. She went again to live with relatives in Chicago, and she earned a living by making drawings of lace and embroidery for dress advertisements. She had to give up the work in 1910, when an attack of measles weakened her eyesight for a time.

Upon her recovery from measles, she found a teaching position at her old boarding school. Then she taught art for a while at a school in Amarillo, Texas. She fell in love with the vast, empty spaces of northern Texas.

In 1915, Georgia accepted a position at a small college in South Carolina. One day, she went into her room and locked the door. She spread out all of her paintings and studied them. She noted which paintings had been done to please teachers or other people. She decided it was time to do work just to please herself. She began making charcoal drawings on the rough white paper. From time to time, she sent some of the drawings to a friend in New York. On New Year's Day, 1916, the friend took some of the drawings to 291 to show them to Alfred Stieglitz. He was very impressed by the drawings and kept them.

That summer, Georgia took some college classes in New York. One day, she heard about an exhibit at 291 by "Virginia O'Keeffe." She went to the gallery to see her drawings, which she considered to be very private, hanging on the walls of the largest room of the gallery. She was angry that Stieglitz had shown them without telling her, and without even getting her name right. She demanded that he take them down; he talked her into leaving them up. The drawings were still on exhibit when she left New York to teach summer school at the University of Virginia.

In the fall, she went to Canyon, Texas, to teach art at West Texas State Normal College. She was inspired by the open spaces and added color to her drawings. She sent drawings and paintings to Stieglitz, and the couple regularly wrote letters back and forth. In April 1917, he opened a show at 291 in which only her work was exhibited.

Georgia began to teach another term at West Texas State, but she became ill and had to give up her classes before she finished the term. Stieglitz became concerned about her and sent a friend to bring her to New York. He arranged for Georgia to live and work in an apartment owned by his niece. In New York, Georgia made many paintings. Views of the city and giant flowers were among the subjects she painted. Stieglitz exhibited and sold her paintings.

Georgia and Stieglitz often visited the Stieglitz family's summer house at Lake George, New York, where Georgia painted landscapes. In 1924, the two were married. Georgia defied custom and continued to use her maiden name; she also refused to wear a wedding ring. The marriage was stormy, and in 1929, Georgia went to visit friends in New Mexico. She stayed there for four months. She liked the open spaces of the Southwest, and she returned year after year. Stieglitz did not like to travel, so he remained in New York while she fell more and more in love with the dry, colorful Southwest.

Georgia took long walks in the desert. Sometimes she picked up dry animal bones and brought them home with her to paint. One morning, she heard a knock at the door as she was holding a rose. Feeling uncomfortable with the rose in her hand, she put it into the eye socket of a horse's skull that was lying on a table. When she walked back into the room, she was so taken with the contrast of the rose against the dry bone that she made a painting of it.

Stieglitz, who was about twenty-five years older than Georgia, died in 1946. After Georgia settled his estate, she moved to New Mexico to live. For almost forty years, she lived in an adobe house in the desert and painted pictures of the colorful landscape, the old adobe churches, and the tiny stones and bones that she found on her walks. Her fame continued to grow, and she continued to paint until she was past eighty and her eyesight began to fail. When she died in 1986, she was ninety-eight years old and widely acclaimed as one of the most important artists in United States history.

Directions: On a separate sheet of paper, answer the following questions about Georgia O'Keeffe.

1. What was Georgia O'Keeffe's earliest memory? How do you think this memory may have affected her decision to become an artist?

2. What do you think was Georgia O'Keeffe's greatest contribution to society?

PART V: BROADER HORIZONS

After World War II, Americans began looking at the United States through changed, perhaps more mature eyes. An interest in international politics replaced the isolationism of pre-war years. Later, as a result of this change of policy, the United States became involved in foreign wars, notably the Korean and Vietnam wars.

In spite of the problems that accompanied these wars, people began to feel more secure than they had since the early 1920s. In their security, people took time to look inward at their own values and prejudices. They viewed minorities—those immigrants of previous decades, as well as American Indians and black Americans—with new interest. In the 1960s, the civil rights movement reached its peak under the leadership of Martin Luther King, Jr. Hispanics began to fight for and receive their civil rights. Women, too, made great strides in becoming equal citizens under the law.

The 1960s also marked the first major commitment to the exploration of space. Astronaut John Glenn was the first American to orbit the earth. Later, the United States succeeded in being the first nation to land a human crew on the moon.

Many of the technologies that arose during the World Wars have now been put to peacetime use. In the last several years, these technologies have been expanded to produce still more conveniences for Americans. Commercial airlines have become commonplace. Radio electronics has provided transistors, integrated circuits, and microcomputers for everyday use. Uses for lasers and new superconductors are being explored. In the space program, the United States is constantly expanding its goals. Spacecraft are being sent to bring more information about other planets in the solar system. Some spacecraft are even being sent beyond the boundaries of the solar system, sending back fascinating information. In every way, the United States is continuing to broaden its horizons: through continuing civil reforms, through technology, and through exploration of the unknown.

JOHN GLENN

Military pilot, astronaut, and United States Senator from Ohio; born in Cambridge, Ohio, in 1921

The man woke up at 1:30 A.M. He was not scheduled to get up for another half hour. It was not often that he had quiet time to himself. He opened his eyes and looked upward as if he were gazing at the stars and the moon. Would today be the day? He could not be sure. Then someone came in to tell him that everything was on schedule. The man jumped down from the top bunk, took a shower, and ate breakfast. Then he climbed into his space suit. When he walked out of the building, it was 5:00 A.M. He was surprised at the number of people behind the roped-off area. He smiled and stepped into a van that drove him to the launch pad. John Glenn was about to become the first American to orbit the earth.

John Glenn was born on July 18, 1921, in Cambridge, Ohio. When he was two years old, John and his parents moved nine miles to New Concord, Ohio, where his father started a plumbing business. The little boy spent many hours "playing airplane." Playing airplane was not a complicated game. John would simply stretch out his arms, run around the yard, and make the appropriate airplane noises. Finally, out of breath, he would flop down on the cool grass and stare at the sky. He sometimes imagined that he was a bird and could glide effortlessly over houses and trees.

A few years later, he and his cousin began building models of World War I fighter airplanes. They spent many hours with the balsa-wood parts, a jar of glue, and instructions, although the instructions usually received only a casual glance. Soon his room was filled with airplane models.

Aviation was not John's only interest. He participated in neighborhood and school football games. During the summer, he and his friends went swimming in Crooked Creek. John was easy to be around and had plenty of neighborhood friends.

John Glenn's high school years were very busy. He participated in football, basketball, and tennis, and earned a letter in each sport. John was also involved in the student council, and during his junior year, he was elected class president. He also found time to play trumpet in the school band and sing in the school choir.

After high school, John entered Muskingum College as a science major. The college was only a few blocks away from the high school he attended. During his sophomore year, John took his first step toward a career in aviation. He and four other students began taking flying lessons in a government-sponsored training program.

John Glenn was a junior in college when the Japanese attacked Pearl Harbor on December 7, 1941. The next day, the United States declared war on Japan. John traveled to Columbus, Ohio to enlist in the navy. He was sent to the Naval Aviation Preflight School in Iowa. He completed that flight training course as well as two others in Kansas and Texas. John worked hard. He did not want to be a good pilot—he wanted to be the best. Later he transferred to the Marines, and on March 31, 1943, a very proud John Glenn became a second lieutenant in the United States Marine Corps and earned the golden wings of an airman. After he became a second lieutenant, he returned to New Concord, Ohio. On April 6, 1943, Lt. John Glenn married Annie Castor, his childhood sweetheart, in a quiet ceremony. After a short honeymoon, John and Annie moved to North Carolina, where he was promoted to first lieutenant.

In June, John was assigned to the Marine Corps Air Station in southern California. While John and his squadron waited for combat orders, they ran practice missions in the desert. Finally, the group received word to move out. They boarded a ship that was headed for the Marshall Islands in the Pacific.

The Marshall Islands were made up of many small islands, and at that time, most of islands were held by the Japanese. The marines were supposed to take back the islands, one by one. John flew a F-4U Corsair fighter-bomber airplane. The Corsair was a long, black, propeller-driven plane. At the time, it was one of the fastest planes built.

Flying in the Marshall Islands was dangerous. The weather could change without warning. Hazardous tropical storms sometimes closed in and pilots lost their way. John often had to fly at treetop level. When he fired his machine gun, the Japanese would often fire back from the ground. Sadly, many planes and lives were lost. On his first flying mission, John saw that a fellow squadron member was in trouble. The plane was hit several times, burst into flames, and fell to the ocean. The tragedy taught John never to take the enemy for granted. John Glenn flew fifty-nine missions in the Marshall Islands, more than any other pilot in his squadron. He was a serious and dedicated pilot.

His most important mission was an attack on Jabor Town, an important Japanese supply base for the Marshall Islands. The marines learned that the Japanese were going to redistribute supplies and build their forces. Three squadrons were ordered to attack Jabor Town. Lt. John Glenn was designated a flight leader for the mission. As John's airplane approached the target area, he noticed the overcast weather conditions. He figured that the bombing mission could be completed, if the planes could safely get low enough. John Glenn figured correctly, and the mission was successfully completed. Soon after this mission, he led another successful attack and earned a medal. In all, John Glenn won two Distinguished Flying Crosses and ten Air Medals during World War II.

In February 1945, John returned to the United States. Not long after his return, he was promoted to the rank of captain. Between World War II and the Korean War, John was stationed in China, flying patrols over the Great Wall. Later, his unit was moved to Guam.

John had a way of putting people at ease and often helped less experienced pilots gain confidence. He pointed out their mistakes and explained flying techniques and strategies that they did not understand. John was not a "hot-shot" pilot, but he was a dependable pilot. He had a reputation of knowing airplanes better than anyone in his squadron. He would spend hours explaining in detail the parts of an airplane. He was always eager to fly missions. John had other interests, particularly music, and he especially enjoyed listening to the opera *Madame Butterfly*.

From 1949 to mid-summer 1951, John Glenn served as a flight instructor in Corpus Christi, Texas. When he was not teaching, he earned flight hours flying jet airplanes. He knew that jets were the aircraft of the future.

Soon Major John Glenn was back overseas and assigned as a jet pilot with Marine Fighter Squadron 311 in Korea. In less than four months, he flew sixty-three fighter-bomber missions. He returned from one mission with 203 bullet holes in his plane.

Finally, John received the orders he had long awaited. He was assigned as an exchange pilot with the Air Force. As a result, he would be involved in air-to-air combat in the Air Force in addition to Marine air support missions he had been flying. One time, while flying over an area, John noticed a convoy of enemy trucks and troops. John and his friend, who was flying in another plane, decided to go after the target. They made one successful run over the convoy and headed back for another. However, his friend's plane was hit and went out of control. There was nothing the man could do but eject. John immediately called back to base for a rescue mission and then circled the area looking for the man. He continued to circle the area until he was almost out of fuel. John turned the airplane back and headed for the base. He ran out of fuel and had to glide part of the way back to the base. John led the rescue mission, but they could not find the man. He had been captured by the enemy. Luckily, a few months later, after the war had ended, he was released. After his release, he learned that John Glenn had risked his own life trying to rescue him.

Back in the United States, John applied to a test pilot school in Maryland. Entrance requirements for the school were difficult, but John Glenn met the qualifications. After six months of intense classroom and flight instruction, he graduated. His diploma authorized him to judge the behavior, stamina, and performance of newly designed aircraft. It was his job to find out if an aircraft was worthy of combat.

John Glenn became a Project Officer at the school, and he worked with many different airplanes, including the Crusader jet. The Crusader was put through numerous tests, but it remained fast and tough. Before the Crusader would receive final approval, it had to pass one more test. It needed to be flown at top speed over a long distance. John Glenn was the pilot chosen to make the flight.

John named the project "Project Bullet" because he calculated that he would be traveling faster than a .45-caliber bullet. He took off from California on July 16, 1957. Less than three and a half hours after his takeoff, he landed in New York. John Glenn flew faster than the speed of sound and set a new coast-to-coast speed record. Two days later, he received another Distinguished Flying Cross Medal.

In 1958, the National Aeronautics and Space Administration (NASA) established a program called Project Mercury. The goal of this program was to send men up in space. Hundreds of men wanted to become astronauts, but NASA needed only seven men.

NASA decided that the men would have to be military test pilots. Therefore, John Glenn's name was automatically placed on the list. Officials sifted through the records of over 400 military test pilots. After they had reviewed the records, the number of eligible men dropped to thirty-two. These thirty-two finalists were divided into groups. Each group traveled to a clinic in New Mexico where the candidates underwent rigorous physical and mental tests. NASA officials had to know that each of the seven men chosen to be astronauts was physically and mentally capable of surviving an orbital flight. After six weeks, all thirty-two test pilots had completed the tests. On April 9, 1959, at a press conference in Washington, D.C., a NASA official announced the names of the seven astronauts. John Glenn's name was on that list.

The first goal of Project Mercury was to send one man into space. If that was successful, then NASA would send one of the astronauts into orbit. Each of the seven astronauts wanted to be the first American in space. John Glenn hoped to have this honor, but Alan Shepard was chosen instead. In May 1961, Alan Shepard became the first American in space. His capsule reached an altitude of 116 miles before it came back to earth. Next, Gus Grissom made a similar flight. Then a chimpanzee, Enos, was sent on a two-orbit flight. Enos returned to earth unharmed. Finally, engineers and scientists felt they were ready to send a man into orbit.

NASA announced that Marine Lieutenant Colonel John Glenn had been chosen to make the orbital flight. When John's family heard the news, his children asked if they could choose a name for his space capsule. His two children, John and Carolyn, chose the name *Friendship 7*.

Americans across the country eagerly awaited the launch. However, there were many postponements. Some of the delays were due to mechanical problems, and some were caused by weather. John remained calm and continued to exercise, read, and run through practice missions.

At last, on February 20, 1962, everything was "go." At the launch pad, an elevator lifted John Glenn to the top of the rocket where he squeezed into the tiny space capsule. Thousands of people lined the beaches near Cape Canaveral, Florida. Millions more watched the coverage on television and listened to the radio. The final countdown began and everyone, aloud or to themselves, counted along. Suddenly, with a tremendous roar, the rocket began to rise. The people looked up and watched the rocket grow smaller and smaller, until it finally disappeared from sight.

Soon John Glenn was many miles above the earth. The rocket dropped off, and he was left alone in his space capsule. In space, John Glenn was weightless and would remain that way for five hours. Doctors were not sure how this would affect him because they could not copy weightlessness on Earth. John enjoyed being weightless and suffered no ill effects. He traveled around the earth three times in five hours. After his third orbit, he fired the rockets and pointed the space capsule toward home.

Although the space flight seemed to be going according to plan, there was concern for John's safety as he started the trip back. During the flight, a flashing light alerted Mission Control that the heat shield on the capsule had come loose. If the heat shield were to come off during reentry, the friction between the capsule and the air would cause the capsule to burn up. John Glenn looked out the window and saw an orange glow. The glow was from the heat around the capsule. Luckily, the heat shield did stay in place. Near the ocean, the parachute was released, and the capsule landed with a loud splash. A ship hoisted the capsule onto the deck. John Glenn stepped out of the space capsule.

After he had taken a shower, he put on a comfortable flight suit and a pair of tennis shoes. Then he sat down, put his feet up, and drank a glass of iced tea. Someone told him that he had a radio-telephone call from Washington, D.C. President John F. Kennedy was calling to congratulate John Glenn.

John Glenn became a hero. President Kennedy presented him with the National Aeronautics and Space Administration Distinguished Service Medal for his contribution to the advancement of knowledge and space technology. He was asked to speak before a joint session of Congress. In New York City, a ticker-tape parade was conducted in his honor. His hometown of New Concord, Ohio also held a parade for him. John was very pleased to learn that the town had decided to name its new school John Glenn High School.

In 1964, John Glenn left NASA. He was proud of his achievement, but he was getting older and wanted to make room for younger people. Since his high schools days, John had been interested in politics, and he decided to run for the office of United States Senator from Ohio. Unfortunately, he was injured in a fall and had to withdraw from the race.

Later that year, he became an executive of a soft drink company. In addition, he hosted a television series about great explorers in history. He also remained active in politics.

In 1970, John again ran for the senate, but lost the election. Four years later, he tried again and won by a large margin. As senator, John Glenn worked to help consumers and people without jobs. In April 1983, he decided to run for President. After a year of campaigning, he decided to withdraw from the race. The other candidates received more support from the voters. In 1986, he ran for reelection to the senate and won. His term will expire in 1993.

John Glenn continues to be active in politics. He has concentrated his efforts on foreign policy and arms control. He has been the author of key laws regarding nuclear weapons. Senator Glenn is trying to prevent the spread of nuclear weapons to other nations and is now involved in broader questions of global defense.

Recently, the sixty-six year old John Glenn was asked if he would be interested in going into space again. He replied that if NASA were to start an astronaut program for people his age, he would be first in line. His smile and optimism are the same as they were twenty-six years ago when he made his historic space flight on the *Friendship 7*.

Directions: On a separate sheet of paper, answer the following questions about John Glenn.

1. It was important for NASA to run extensive physical and mental tests before they made the final decision of who would become the first astronauts. Why do you think this testing was necessary? Explain your answer.
2. Why do you think John Glenn was chosen to be the first American astronaut to orbit the earth? Explain your answer.

JOHN F. KENNEDY

35th President of the United States, Senator, member of Congress, war hero, author; born in Massachusetts in 1917 and died in Texas in 1963

John Fitzgerald Kennedy, the youngest elected President in the history of the United States, was sworn in on January 20, 1961. He was forty-three years old. From the steps of the Capitol in Washington, D.C., he gave his inaugural address. He spoke of the great problems of the United States and the world and how they might be solved. Kennedy concluded his speech with the inspiring words: "And so, my fellow Americans, ask not what your country can do for you—ask what you can do for your country."

Kennedy was born on May 29, 1917, in Brookline, Massachusetts. His family were wealthy Irish Catholics. Joseph Kennedy, his father, was a successful businessman and political figure. His mother, Rose, was the mother of nine children. Although Rose was the center of the Kennedy family, Joe spent as much time as possible with his children.

Joe Kennedy believed in hard work and in competition. From a very early age, the Kennedy children had to compete against each other in work and in play. The Kennedys enjoyed sports, particularly tennis, golf, sailing, swimming, and softball. Joe organized the entire family into teams, and they played against each other. This spirit of competition encouraged the Kennedys to work hard all their lives to make sure that they were winners at everything they did.

At dinner, the conversation had to be about serious matters. Quite often politics was discussed. This was not John Kennedy's major interest as a child. John, or Jack, as he was called, was more interested in stories of medieval knights. His favorite story was about King Arthur and the Knights of the Round Table. Not only did Jack love to read, but he also enjoyed writing stories.

At the age of thirteen, Jack was sent to the Canterbury School in Connecticut. Although he liked football, he was not good enough to make the team. His swimming, however, was excellent.

He did not return for a second year to Canterbury. Instead, he was enrolled in Choate, a school for boys from wealthy families, also located in Connecticut. Jack's older brother, Joe, Jr., was a Choate student, too. Jack and Joe, Jr. had always been very competitive with each other. Unfortunately for Jack, he was neither a better student nor a better athlete than his brother.

This competition continued when both brothers attended Harvard College in Cambridge, Massachusetts. Joe, Jr. was on the varsity football team. Jack did not make the first team; he made the junior varsity. Unfortunately, he hurt his back playing, a condition which would affect him for the rest of his life.

In college, Jack's best sport was swimming. Once, a few days before a swimming meet against Harvard's toughest opponent, Jack became ill. So that he would not miss practice, he sneaked out of the hospital each day. Afterward he would slip back into his hospital room. No one ever caught on to what he was doing.

Jack spent part of his junior year in Great Britain. While he was there, Germany invaded Poland, which began World War II. Jack was disturbed at how unprepared England, Poland's ally, was to fight Hitler. In his book, *Why England Slept,* Kennedy detailed the reasons why Great Britain was so poorly prepared for war.

After graduating with honors from Harvard, Jack enlisted in the United States Navy. He was given the rank of lieutenant and assigned the command of the PT–109. This was a small, fast patrol boat that carried torpedoes. Kennedy and his crew of thirteen were sent to the Solomon Islands in the Pacific. Their mission was to keep Japanese supply ships from getting food to their soldiers on the surrounding islands.

It was so dark on the night of August 1, 1943, that no one on Kennedy's ship could see a thing. Out of the darkness, a Japanese destroyer appeared. When it hit PT-109, the destroyer sliced it in half, killing two of Kennedy's crew. The others dived into the water and began swimming to an island three miles away. The waters were full of sharks, and Japanese planes were in the area. One of Kennedy's men was hurt so badly that he could not swim. Although Jack's back had been injured during the accident, he put the strap of the wounded sailor's life jacket between his teeth. Then he towed the man for four hours until they reached an island.

During the following days, Lieutenant Kennedy swam from island to island looking for help. Finally, his group was seen from a canoe by two island natives. Jack, using a knife, wrote a message inside a coconut. He asked the natives to bring it to the nearest friendly island. Two days later, Kennedy and his crew were rescued. For his courage and leadership, Kennedy was awarded the Navy and Marine Corps Medal.

Jack's back had been injured so badly, however, that he had to return to the United States for an operation. It was there that he learned of the death of his brother. Joe, Jr. had been a navy pilot. In 1944, he was sent on a secret mission over Europe. He never returned. No one ever knew the reason why, but his plane exploded in midair. Jack was now the oldest living Kennedy son.

Joseph Kennedy had dreamed that one of his sons would become President. With Joe, Jr. gone, Jack was next in line to fulfill his father's wishes. At Harvard, Jack had become interested in politics, but he was shy and insecure. His dad finally convinced him that he should run for the United States House of Representatives.

As a Democrat, Jack first had to defeat nine opponents from the Democratic party in a primary. Then he would run against a Republican in the actual election. Jack overcame his shyness early in the race, becoming an excellent campaigner and speaker. As a result, he won both the primary and the general election. At twenty-nine, he became the Congressman from the 11th Massachusetts District. He proved to be so popular in the job that he was reelected twice, in 1948 and 1950.

After three terms in the House of Representatives, Kennedy ran for the United States Senate. As always, his family helped him. All through Massachusetts they went, giving speeches and convincing people that they should vote for Jack. No one worked harder than the candidate. In fact, Jack campaigned so hard that his back problems worsened. He was forced to continue on crutches, but this did not stop him. In the end, he won the election by 70,000 votes.

About that time, Kennedy met Jacqueline Bouvier, a beautiful and wealthy young journalist. The two shared a love of writing and of sports. In 1954, they were married. That same year, Jack returned to the hospital for more back operations. While he was recovering, he wrote a book called *Profiles in Courage*. This was a collection of true stories about people who had had the courage to do what was right. For his efforts, Kennedy was awarded the Pulitzer Prize, the highest literary award given in the United States.

In 1958, Kennedy was reelected to the Senate. This time he won by nearly 900,000 votes. His victory was the greatest in the political history of Massachusetts. By now he was a well-known figure in the Democratic Party, and his fame was spreading throughout the country.

Over the next two years, Kennedy visited many parts of the United States, delivering speech after speech. By 1960, he was so well known and well liked that he won the Democratic nomination for President. The Democrats chose Lyndon B. Johnson of Texas to be Kennedy's running mate.

"All the Way with J.F.K.!" was one of the most popular slogans during the 1960 Presidential campaign. In spite of Kennedy's popularity, however, this would be no easy election. Kennedy faced a tough opponent in the current Vice President, Richard Nixon, who was the Republican candidate. Also, Kennedy was very young. Many voters, both Democratic and Republican, felt that an older, more experienced candidate should be President.

Another major problem for Kennedy was that he was a Roman Catholic. No Catholic had ever been elected President. Many non-Catholics felt that if a Catholic were elected, the Pope would run the country. Very early in the campaign, Kennedy convinced most voters that he believed in the separation of church and state. His religion would play no part in how he ran the country.

Kennedy and Nixon faced each other in a series of debates on national television. These programs were seen by as many as 70,000,000 viewers. Kennedy proved to the majority of the viewers that he was mature enough to be President. He also was better prepared and a better speaker than his opponent.

Even though he did well in the debates, Kennedy still was not assured of victory. In fact, the 1960 Presidential election was one of the closest in American history. When it was over, however, John Fitzgerald Kennedy had been elected President.

Kennedy referred to his Presidency as "The New Frontier." In this "New Frontier," Kennedy's goal was to correct many of the evils in the United States. Poverty and racial hatred would be things of the past. All Americans would be guaranteed a good education and a decent job. Great strides would be made in science and in the arts. Relations with other countries would be greatly improved.

It was during Kennedy's administration that the Peace Corps was started. This organization was responsible for sending American volunteers to Asian, African, and Latin American countries. These volunteers worked to make the lives of the people better in a number of ways. The Peace Corps was so successful that many countries now felt more friendly toward the United States. The Peace Corps also helped make Kennedy one of the nation's most popular Presidents, both at home and abroad.

Kennedy had his share of problems, too. Three months after taking office, Kennedy approved a plan for the invasion of Cuba. Since 1958, Cuba had been a Communist country under the control of Fidel Castro. Because it was only ninety miles away from Florida, many people believed that a Communist Cuba was a definite threat to the United States.

Anti-Communist Cubans made up the army of invasion. On April 17, 1961, these forces landed at the Bay of Pigs. They expected to be helped by anti-Castro Cubans in the country. Instead, they were attacked by Castro's soldiers, and all were killed or captured. The invasion had been a disaster, and President Kennedy was blamed for its failure.

Throughout his Presidency, Cuba was a thorn in Kennedy's side. In September of 1962, the United States discovered something quite frightening. The Soviet Union was shipping missiles to Cuba. These missiles, which contained nuclear warheads, could be sent to destroy American cities. President Kennedy acted quickly. He notified Soviet Premier Khrushchev that he wanted all missiles removed immediately. The United States Navy was ordered to blockade Cuba and to search all ships coming into the country.

For two days, no answer came from the Soviets. The world held its breath waiting for Khrushchev's reply. Finally the Soviet leader backed down. All missiles were removed from Cuba, and Kennedy and the United States had won a great victory.

Kennedy and Khrushchev realized that they would have to work together to avoid war. Between Moscow, the Soviet capital, and Washington, D.C., a telephone "hotline" was set up. Both leaders now could talk to each other in a matter of moments. The two also came to an agreement to ban nuclear tests above ground, in space, and under water. The Soviets for the first time allowed their bases to be inspected by foreigners.

Competition between the two countries was greatest in the exploration of space. The Soviets had been the first to send a capsule into the upper atmosphere. The United States, however, was the first to put a man in orbit around the earth. On February 20, 1962, Marine Lieutenant-Colonel John Glenn's spaceship orbited the globe three times in five hours. Kennedy was overjoyed. From then on, he tried even harder to convince Congress to give more money to support the United States space program.

At home, Kennedy fought for the rights of racial minorities. In many states, black people were denied the right to vote and to attend certain public schools and universities. Kennedy asked Congress to pass a new Civil Rights bill, which would guarantee certain rights to all citizens regardless of race. He also sent federal troops to make sure that the racial integration of schools was achieved.

In the autumn of 1963, Kennedy began thinking about reelection. He decided to make a campaign visit to Texas. On November 22, he and Mrs. Kennedy went with Vice President Johnson and Mrs. Johnson to Dallas. Their hosts were Texas Governor John Connally and his wife. Thousands of Texans lined the streets as the Kennedys and the Connallys drove slowly past in a convertible limousine. The top was down so that people could get a good look at their elected officials.

Suddenly a shot rang out, then another, and a third. They had been fired by Lee Harvey Oswald from a building across the street. President Kennedy was hit in the head and in the back. Governor Connally also was wounded but not as seriously. Both men were rushed to the hospital. Connally recovered, but President Kennedy did not.

Kennedy's body was flown to Washington to lay in state in the Capitol Building for one day. Thousands of people filed past to pay their respects. Burial took place at Arlington National Cemetery, where an eternal flame burns in his memory.

John Kennedy was forty-six when he died. He had come a long way from his boyhood days when he had loved to read adventure stories. He would be remembered by Americans and non-Americans alike for his youth, his courage, and his love for humanity.

Directions: On a separate sheet of paper, answer the following questions about John F. Kennedy.

1. John F. Kennedy's book *Profiles in Courage* contained biographies of a number of American leaders. In what ways were Kennedy's life and political career a "profile in courage"?

2. President Kennedy referred to his Presidency as the "New Frontier." What were some of the programs and events during his years in office that represented "new frontiers"?

MARTIN LUTHER KING, JR.

Civil rights leader, minister, Nobel Prize winner; born in Georgia in 1929 and died in Tennessee in 1968

When Martin Luther King, Jr., was assassinated on April 4, 1968, the country lost one of its finest leaders. Dr. King was a champion of civil rights. He was a great American as well.

Martin was born in Atlanta, Georgia on January 15, 1929. His father, Martin, Sr., was assistant pastor at the Ebenezer Baptist Church and had come from a poor farming family. He had had to work hard for an education. Martin, Jr.'s mother, Alberta, was a music teacher and the daughter of the pastor of Ebenezer Baptist Church, Alfred Daniel Williams. Mrs. King's family was well educated and respected throughout the area.

Martin lived with his parents, his Grandpa and Grandma Williams, and his brother and sister in an attractive house in the city. Martin was very close to his grandmother, whom he called "Mama."

When Martin was twelve, Mama died. His grandfather had passed away years earlier, and his father was now church pastor. On the Sunday his grandmother died, Martin had disobeyed his parents by slipping away to attend a parade. Returning home, he heard the terrible news. Martin felt that his grandmother's death was his fault because he had been disobedient. It took a long time for his parents to convince him that this was not so.

As a young child, Martin had many friends, both black and white. When he reached school age, however, everything changed. Martin's white friends could not play with him anymore. Their parents would not allow it. Martin could not go to the same school as his white friends, either. Blacks were not allowed in white schools.

As Martin grew older, he began to see more and more racial prejudice. One day he and his father went shopping for shoes. The two took seats in the front of the store. A sales clerk asked them to get up and move to seats in the back. Blacks were not allowed to sit in the front of the store. Martin, Sr. said that if the store did not serve black people in the front, then it would not serve him at all. Then he and Martin marched out proudly.

A far more serious racial incident occurred while Martin was in high school. Martin, like his father, was a very good speaker. His speech teacher, Miss Bradley, chose Martin and a few other students to represent their school at an oratorical contest. The event was held in a town a number of miles outside of Atlanta. There was no trouble on the bus ride to the contest. The ride back was another matter. It was late at night by the time Martin and the others boarded the bus. The members of the group all took seats in the rear. With each new stop, more and more white people got on. It was expected that a black person would give his or her seat to a white person.

When the driver told Martin to get up, he refused. The man repeated the order, but Martin would not budge. Then the driver began cursing at the boy and threatening him. Martin still would not give in. Finally, fearing that the boy would be harmed, Miss Bradley asked Martin to move. He did.

These and other incidents made Martin bitter toward white people. Many times he had heard his father preach that a person should love his enemies. Martin did not understand why he should love the white people who were cruel to him.

Martin was always a good student, but his studies did not keep him from playing with his friends. Among his favorite activities were football, baseball, swimming, tennis, and riding his bicycle. Once, when Martin was catching in a softball game, his younger brother Alfred Daniel (nicknamed A.D.) came to bat. A.D. swung wildly at a pitch, missed, and accidentally threw the bat. It hit Martin, knocking him flat on the ground. A.D. kept asking the semi-conscious Martin if he was all right. Finally, Martin sat up. He said that he was okay, but that it had been A.D.'s third strike, and he was out.

After high school, Martin entered Atlanta's Morehouse College. He was only fifteen. At Morehouse, Martin majored in sociology. His father had wanted him to become a minister, but Martin resisted that idea. He wanted to spend his life righting some of the wrongs his people had suffered. Could he do that and be a preacher at the same time? Martin was not sure.

During his college years, Martin read a good deal and listened very closely to his professors. He learned that it was all right to disobey an unjust law, but that disobedience never should be violent. The most important thing Martin learned was that one should hate the sin but love the sinner. Now Martin knew why his father preached love and not hate. Now Martin understood how a minister could follow God's law and still fight injustice at the same time. Upon graduation, at age eighteen, Martin was ordained a minister.

In the fall of 1948, he entered Crozer Theological Seminary in Chester, Pennsylvania. Martin's experiences at Crozer were very different from those at Morehouse. For one thing, he no longer was living at home. More importantly, Crozer was integrated, so students of all races could attend.

Not every white student liked having blacks at Crozer. One evening, while Martin was studying, a young man from North Carolina barged into his room. The student accused Martin of playing a prank on him. He said that Martin had gone into his room when he was not there and had made a mess of it. Calmly, Martin denied everything. Angrily, the Southerner pulled out a pistol and pointed it at Martin. Other students heard the commotion and ran into Martin's room to see what was going on. The young man still had the gun pointed at Martin. Martin, still calm, refused to save himself by lying.

Finally, the others got the pistol away from the angry young man. Charges were brought against him by the faculty and student government. Martin refused to testify against the Southerner, and so the charges were dropped. The young man apologized, however, and soon after he and Martin became good friends.

After graduating from Crozer in 1951, Martin attended Boston University. While in Boston, Martin met Coretta Scott, a talented young concert singer. Martin thought that Coretta had everything he was looking for in a woman: character, intelligence, beauty, and personality. He proposed, and she accepted. The two were married by Martin's father on June 18, 1953.

After receiving his doctoral degree, King accepted the position of pastor at the Dexter Avenue Baptist Church in Montgomery, Alabama. Alabama at that time was even more segregated than Georgia. Soon after the Kings arrived in Montgomery, trouble began. On December 1, 1955, a quiet, 42-year-old black woman boarded a bus and made history. Her name was Rosa Parks. As she was riding home from work that day, the bus she was on began to fill up. The driver told her to give up her seat to a white person. Mrs. Parks refused. The police were summoned, and Rosa Parks was arrested for her refusal.

When the black community heard of her arrest, they asked all black residents to stop riding city buses. This began the Montgomery Bus Boycott. Getting to work was difficult at first, but most people managed. Dr. King was elected president of the strike organization. The organization wanted blacks to be treated courteously and respectfully and not to have to give up their seats on buses. They also demanded that black bus drivers be hired for some routes. The white leaders refused.

Months went by. People from other areas of the country heard of the boycott. They sent money and other forms of support to the strikers. Downtown businesses began to be hurt because blacks no longer went there to shop. Still the white leaders would not give in. Instead, they struck back.

Black workers were told by their bosses that they would be fired if the boycott continued. King and other black leaders were arrested without reason. Worst of all, one night a bomb was dropped on King's front porch. No one was hurt, but the porch and King's living room were almost completely destroyed.

The Montgomery boycott lasted slightly more than one year. Finally, the United States Supreme Court upheld a U.S. District Court ruling that Alabama's bus laws were unconstitutional. Dr. King, Rosa Parks, and the Montgomery strikers had finally won.

By 1960, the King family was living in Atlanta, where Martin was his father's assistant pastor. Two years before, he and the Reverend Ralph David Abernathy had formed the Southern Christian Leadership Conference. The mission of this organization was to foster the cause of civil rights by peaceful means. Now that the bus issue had been settled, it was time to desegregate lunch counters.

On October 10, 1960, Dr. King and dozens of his followers picketed outside Atlanta's department stores. They sang "We Shall Overcome," a song that would become the anthem of the civil rights movement. Some of the picketers sat at store lunch counters, demanding to be served. Soon the police arrived, and the picketers were arrested.

Everyone but King was released shortly after the arrests. Handcuffed and with chains around his legs, he was moved out of Atlanta to a jail miles away. Coretta King feared for her husband's life. However, democratic Presidential candidate John F. Kennedy heard the news, and he and his brother Robert saw to it that King was released. After Kennedy's election, the civil rights movement had an ally in the White House.

By now, Martin was the father of four: two sons and two daughters. One day the older girl, Yolanda, saw a television commercial advertising a new amusement park. The park was called Funtown and it was right outside of Atlanta. Yolanda ran to her father and asked him if he would take her there. It broke King's heart to have to tell his little girl that she could not go. Black people were not allowed in Funtown.

One of the civil rights movement's greatest battles took place in Birmingham, Alabama. The city was violently opposed to integration. Its police chief, Bull Connor, was extremely cruel. When King and his followers picketed stores and marched in protest, they quickly were arrested. King was thrown into solitary confinement and denied the right to see a lawyer. Thanks once again to President Kennedy, King was finally released.

The Birmingham battle was not over. On May 2, one thousand black children of all ages took part in a freedom march through the city. The next day twice that number participated. Conners arrested hundreds of blacks, including children. High pressure fire-hoses were turned on the people. The water sent the little children flying in all directions. Later, attack dogs were unleashed, biting adults and youngsters alike. Through all of this, most of Dr. King's supporters remained non-violent.

Much of the police violence was shown on television throughout the United States. Americans were horrified that this sort of injustice was going on in their country. Even Connor's own men became disgusted and refused to obey his orders. On May 10, the city's white business leaders gave in. Birmingham was about to become an integrated city.

In the summer of 1963, Dr. King led a civil rights march in Washington, D.C. He and 250,000 of his followers, black and white, walked arm-in-arm to the Lincoln Memorial. Standing in front of the statue of Lincoln, Dr. King delivered his now-famous "I Have a Dream" speech. "I have a dream," he said, "that my four little children will one day live in a nation where they will be judged not by the color of their skin but by the content of their character. . . ." On and on he spoke of his wishes for a better America. He hoped someday that blacks and whites would live together in harmony. He prayed that someday all would be able to join hands and sing "Free at last! Free at last! Thank God Almighty, we are free at last!"

The following year Dr. King received the Nobel Peace Prize. He was given this honor for his non-violent efforts in the cause of civil rights. To formally accept the award, Dr. King traveled to Norway. At the ceremony, he was praised for his courage and devotion to the cause of freedom. Part of the prize he received was a check for $54,000. He donated the money to various civil rights groups.

King fought hard to see that the Voting Rights Act of 1965 was passed. This bill was necessary because in many Southern communities blacks were not permitted to vote. Earlier in the year, he and his supporters had marched fifty-four miles from Selma to Montgomery, Alabama. They did so to support the proposed law. The marchers were greeted by police who beat them and tossed tear gas in their paths. Three people were killed. Nevertheless, the march continued until Montgomery was reached. King and his followers had won a moral victory by remaining non-violent. They had also won a real victory: the Voting Rights Act was passed.

Dr. King's last days were spent in Memphis, Tennessee. He went there to support the city's sanitation workers. The workers were striking for decent working conditions. On April 4, 1968, King walked out on the balcony of the motel at which he was staying. A few seconds later a shot rang out. Dr. King was hit in the jaw. He was rushed to the hospital, where he died at 7:05 that night. His assassin, James Earl Ray, was caught, tried, and sentenced to ninety-nine years in prison.

In Martin Luther King, Jr., the civil rights movement had its greatest leader. He had helped make it so strong that even today his cause lives on.

Directions: On a separate sheet of paper, answer the following questions about Martin Luther King, Jr.

1. In 1964, Dr. King was awarded the Nobel Peace Prize. What events in King's life might have convinced the committee that he deserved the award?

2. When he was young, Martin Luther King, Jr., was reckless. As a man, he became courageous. How did his youthful recklessness contribute to his later courage? What other characteristics of Martin Luther King, Jr., contributed to this change?

MARIA TALLCHIEF

Internationally known ballet dancer and founder of the Chicago City Ballet; born in Fairfax, Oklahoma in 1925

The Osage Indians gathered on their reservation in Oklahoma. They were preparing to greet their new princess, *Wa-Xthe-Thonba*. Leaders of the Osage tribe, local community members, and even the governor of Oklahoma gathered to greet the princess. Everybody was proud of *Wa-Xthe-Thonba* because the new princess was, in fact, the internationally known ballet dancer, Maria Tallchief.

Maria Tallchief was born in Fairfax, Oklahoma, on January 24, 1925. Fairfax is a small town on the Osage Indian reservation. Maria's father, Alexander, was a full-blooded Osage Indian, and her grandfather, Peter Big Heart, had been chief of the tribe. Her mother, Ruth, was of Scottish and Irish descent.

As a child, Maria was very interested in music and dance. When she was only three years old, Maria was able to play tunes on the piano. She began piano lessons, and a year later, four-year-old Maria began dance lessons.

In 1933, the Tallchiefs moved to Los Angeles, California. Young Maria began to study music seriously in preparation for a career as a concert pianist. She also continued her ballet lessons. To celebrate her twelfth birthday, Maria gave a concert. For the first half of the concert, she played the piano. The second half of the concert was a dance recital. The concert showed that Maria was a wonderful pianist and a gifted dancer as well. She continued to study the piano and began studying ballet from the famous Russian teacher Bromislava Nijinska (Brahm uh SLAHV uh nuh ZHIN skuh).

Nijinska recognized the great talent that Maria had as a dancer and, in 1940, gave her a leading role in a dance performance at the Hollywood Bowl. After this performance, Maria decided that she should become a professional ballet dancer rather than a concert pianist.

After finishing high school, Maria went to New York and joined the Ballet Russe de Monte Carlo. She danced with the Ballet Russe from 1942 until 1947. During that time, she met the great choreographer George Balanchine. He thought Maria was a brilliant dancer and began to work more and more with her. They worked together very closely and were married in 1946.

Balanchine created many roles for Maria in his dances. In 1947, he and Maria left the Ballet Russe to begin work with the Paris Opera. Maria Tallchief became the first American ballet dancer to perform with the Paris Opera, and she was received enthusiastically by European audiences.

Balanchine and Maria Tallchief continued to work together. Maria became the leading dancer, or *prima ballerina,* for Balancine's new ballet company, the New York City Ballet. In 1949, he choreographed *Firebird,* and Maria danced the leading role of a beautiful, wild bird with magic powers. This role made Maria an international ballet star. She was hailed as one of the world's greatest ballet dancers.

Although her dancing career was very successful, Maria's marriage to Balanchine was unhappy. Maria wanted to have children, and Balanchine wanted her to devote her life to ballet. In 1951, their marriage was annulled. However, she and Balanchine continued to work together for many years.

In 1957, Maria married Henry Paschen, a prominent Chicago engineer. Meanwhile, her dancing career continued to flourish. She gained international recognition as the prima ballerina of the New York City Ballet. Her popularity was so great that during a tour of

Maria Tallchief as the Firebird

Japan in 1958, the New York City Ballet played to sold-out audiences every night. The company went on to tour in Australia without Maria. When the Australians learned that the New York City Ballet had arrived without Maria Tallchief, ticket sales dropped off and few people attended the performances.

Maria did not go to Australia because she wanted to return to Chicago. She wanted to spend more time at home with her husband. Maria and Henry planned to have a family, and three years later, they had a baby daughter, Elise. Maria continued dancing until 1966, when she "hung up her toe shoes," as dancers would say.

Maria's involvement with the ballet world did not end with her retirement. In 1975, she became the director of the Chicago Lyric Opera Ballet. She then went on to become the founder of the Chicago City Ballet in 1981. Today, aspiring young dancers are benefiting from the experiences of a woman who has been considered one of the world's greatest ballet dancers.

Directions: On a separate sheet of paper, answer the following questions about Maria Tallchief.

1. How do you think Maria Tallchief's music training helped her as a ballet dancer? Explain your answer.
2. In what ways can Maria Tallchief be considered a pioneer in the world of dance? Explain your answer.

ROBERTO CLEMENTE

Baseball player and humanitarian; born in Puerto Rico in 1934 and died at sea in 1972

Roberto Clemente was not a political leader, nor was he a war hero. However, to the people of his native land, Puerto Rico, he was both a leader and a hero.

Roberto was born on August 18, 1934. He lived with his parents, five brothers, and one sister in the town of Carolina. Carolina is near San Juan, the capital of Puerto Rico. This Caribbean island has been a territory of the United States since 1898. Its inhabitants are American citizens.

Roberto's family lived in a large, wooden house. The Clementes were not poor. His father worked as a foreman on a sugar plantation. In addition, his family ran a grocery store and meat market, selling their goods to the plantation workers. As a boy, Roberto helped load and unload his father's trucks. In the early morning, Roberto had a second job. He delivered milk in heavy cans to the people in his town. The pay was so low that it took Roberto three years to save up enough for a bicycle.

Roberto attended Julio Vizcarrando High School in his home town. In addition to being a better-than-average student, Roberto also was a fine athlete. For three years, he was an all-star baseball player. That was not surprising to those who knew him well. Up to that time, he had played ball practically every day of his life. When he was not playing, he squeezed a hard rubber ball to strengthen his arms. He also listened to the radio for news of the Puerto Rican winter league games. Often this passion for the sport caused him to miss meals. Mrs. Clemente worried about Roberto. She tried to interest him in other activities, but she soon realized that it was hopeless. There was no way to stop her son's love for baseball.

One of the better teams in the Puerto Rican leagues was the Santurce Crabbers. One day, while the Crabbers' owner was watching a group of amateurs play ball, he noticed a seventeen-year-old in the outfield. This teenager fielded, ran, and hit better than any of the others. After the game, he approached the young man, and asked him if he would like to play for the Crabbers. For a $500 bonus, a $60-a-month salary, and a brand new baseball glove, Roberto accepted.

In the winter of 1953, a scout for the Brooklyn (now Los Angeles) Dodgers visited Puerto Rico. The purpose of his trip was to locate talent for the Dodger ball club. After watching seventy-two young players, he was impressed by only one: Roberto Clemente. He tried to sign Roberto to the team, but Mr. and Mrs. Clemente objected. They wanted their son to finish high school first. The scout agreed to wait.

The following year Roberto signed with the Dodger organization, receiving a $10,000 bonus. Shortly after, another team offered him three times as much. Roberto, however, would not accept it. He had given his word to Brooklyn, and he would not go back on it.

Clemente never played for the Brooklyn Dodgers. His one and only year with the organization was spent with Brooklyn's minor league team in Montreal, Canada. This was an unhappy year for Roberto. He played very few games, and his batting average was only .257.

In 1955, Roberto was drafted by the Pittsburgh Pirates. Unlike the Dodgers, the Pirates were a terrible group of players. The year before, their team batting average had been .248. Also, their pitching staff had given up more runs than any other team in either the

American or the National league. As a result, Pittsburgh fell into last place a few weeks into the season and never improved.

Clemente was unhappy and lonely in Pittsburgh. In the early 1950s, Latin ballplayers were just beginning to be accepted in the major leagues. Many fans, managers, sportswriters, and players were prejudiced against them. In addition, Roberto was black, and he could not speak English. Far away from his homeland and family and among strangers, Clemente was miserable.

At the end of each season, Roberto would return to Puerto Rico. In late 1954, one of his brothers became incurably ill. One day, after visiting his brother in the hospital, Roberto was involved in a traffic accident. Not far from his home, a car, driven by someone under the influence of alcohol, plowed into his car. Clemente suffered a back injury that caused him pain for the rest of his life.

The 1956 season was a much stronger one for Roberto. When it ended, he returned home and purchased a new house for his parents. That winter his back pain became more intense. Often, during the next season, he had to wear a back brace. Even then, running, swinging, and sliding hurt him a great deal.

Clemente spent that winter as a United States Marine. For six months, he fulfilled his military obligation at Paris Island, South Carolina. There he drilled, exercised, ran obstacle courses, and worked harder than he ever had before. Strangely enough, he left the Marines feeling terrific.

The Pirates began improving in the late 50s, but 1960 was their best year yet. It also was a strong season for Clemente. Not since 1927 had Pittsburgh won a pennant. In 1960, they won again. Roberto had been struggling at the plate since 1956. In 1960, he batted .314, his highest average up to that time.

Pittsburgh's World Series opponents were the New York Yankees. In their last series, in 1927, the Pirates had been defeated 4-0 by this same team. Roberto and his teammates hoped things would be different this time.

The Pirates won their first game, but the Yanks slaughtered them in the second (16-3) and in the third (10-0). Games four and five went to Pittsburgh, but the sixth was another one-sided New York victory (10-0). Roberto had had at least one hit in each game so far. His running and fielding also had been excellent.

Game seven was a dramatic game. In the first two innings, the Pirates scored four runs. Later, however, the Yanks scored two. When Yankee catcher Yogi Berra hit a three-run homer in the sixth, New York was ahead, 5-4. Two innings later they scored two more runs. With a score of 7-4 in favor of New York, the Pirates came to bat in the bottom of the eighth. The first two Pittsburgh hitters reached base safely. The third hit a single, knocking in a run. The fourth and fifth players made outs. The sixth hitter was Roberto Clemente. He hit a slow ground ball toward the Yankee first baseman. Before the infielder could tag Roberto out, Clemente had made it safely to first. A run scored, and the Pirates were behind by only one.

That inning Pittsburgh moved ahead, 9-7, but in the top of the ninth, New York tied the game. In the bottom of the ninth, a Pirate home run broke the tie. For the first time in many, many years, Pittsburgh won the World Series.

At the beginning of the 1961 season, Roberto's batting coach gave him some good advice. He told Clemente not to think about hitting home runs. Instead, he should focus on getting singles. Roberto listened and, throughout the year, did as his coach had suggested. At the end of the season, he was hitting .351, enough for him to win his first batting championship.

His fielding always had been strong, but as he got older, it improved. He often fooled runners into thinking he would catch a ball he could not possibly reach. One day, with one man on first, the other team's batter hit a short fly ball into the outfield. Clemente dashed for it, his arms waving to tell his teammates that he had it. The runner, who had been on first, was halfway to second when he saw Clemente going for the ball. Deciding that the Pirate outfielder would make a catch, he turned and raced back to first. The ball dropped, and Clemente scooped it up and threw it to second. Although the batter was safe, the runner from first was forced out.

That year Roberto was chosen to start at right field for the National League All Star team. He was proud because he had received the second largest amount of votes among all players. Clemente usually played well in important games. The 1961 All Star Game was no exception. Not only did he stay in for the entire game, but he also hit a triple and the game-winning single.

Despite his successes, Clemente still had problems with his temper. In one game, Clemente headed toward the umpire to argue a call, and his first base coach got between the two men. Roberto tried to push past his coach. In doing so, his hand struck the umpire. Afterward, Roberto said it had been an accident. Nevertheless, he was thrown out of the game, fined $250, and suspended for five days.

Another worry was Roberto's health. After he started making a good salary, Clemente wanted to give up winter ball. By the time the winter season started, he was worn out from playing with the Pirates. As a result, he often was hurt playing winter ball. His Puerto Rican fans, however, begged him to continue. In Pittsburgh, Clemente was only a great player. In Puerto Rico he was a great hero. How could he disappoint his people?

So he played. In the winter of 1964, while appearing before his Puerto Rican fans, he tore the ligaments in one of his legs. He was rushed to the hospital for treatment. While recovering from a leg operation, he caught malaria. At the same time, he developed a paratyphoid infection. For the entire Pirate season that followed, Roberto was not a well man.

Earlier that year, Roberto had married a lovely, young Puerto Rican woman named Vera Zabala. After their wedding, which took place in Carolina, the couple honeymooned in Europe. Returning from Europe, they settled down in a house near Roberto's parents. The Clementes had three children, all boys.

Although Roberto won four batting titles during his career, his greatest accomplishment was being voted "Most Valuable Player" in 1966. At the beginning of the season, he promised his manager that he would hit for power. To strengthen himself, every day he drank a "health" drink. It consisted of milk, egg yolks, ice cream, sugar, ice, and a variety of fruit. It must have worked. By the end of the season, Clemente had hit twenty-nine home runs, his greatest record ever.

Six more successful seasons lay ahead for Clemente. During that time, Pittsburgh won one more pennant and World Series—in 1971. As in 1960, Roberto got a hit at least once in each game. As before, the series lasted the entire seven games. This time, however, Roberto was the hero. His home run in the final game won the series for the Pirates.

The following year, Roberto set his sights on achieving another milestone in his career—his 3,000th hit. Very few players in the history of baseball had ever done this, but Clemente felt he had an excellent chance. Unfortunately, early in the season, injuries kept him out of many games. In August and September, however, he was playing again and hitting as well as ever. Sadly, Roberto Clemente's 3,000th hit came on what was to be his last time at bat in his major league career.

As he grew older, Roberto spent more and more time helping young people. He visited sick children in hospitals, contributed to numerous charities, and did volunteer work for worthy causes. One of his dreams was to start a sports city. Roberto believed that one way to fight juvenile crime was to get young people involved in athletics. He never lived to see his dream fulfilled.

On December 22, 1972, a major earthquake destroyed large sections of Managua, the capital of Nicarauga. Immediately, Roberto organized a Puerto Rican relief effort. Its purpose was to see that food, clothing, and medicine were brought to the earthquake victims.

On New Year's Eve, Clemente was at the San Juan Airport. He was supervising the loading of the supplies into the airplane which would deliver them to Managua. To make sure that the goods really reached the people, Roberto was going to fly with them to Nicaragua. Vera Clemente warned her husband that flying in an old propeller-driven DC-7 could be dangerous. He laughed and assured her that everything would be fine.

Everything was not all right. The take-off had been delayed a number of times because something was wrong with the plane. Shortly after it finally did take off, it crashed into the sea. Everyone aboard was killed.

Underwater search crews, using giant flashlights, discovered the wreckage of the plane. The remains of Roberto Clemente and the others, however, never were discovered.

Three days of mourning were declared on the island of Puerto Rico. The people, after all, had lost a great national hero. In Pittsburgh, flags were flown at half-mast. The city had lost a dear friend and one of the greatest players in the history of their team. In March 1973, less than six months after his death, Roberto Clemente was inducted, or voted, into the Baseball Hall of Fame. Normally, a player must wait at least five years after retirement before being inducted. After eighteen years of brilliance on the field, Clemente had more than earned his spot.

Directions: On a separate sheet of paper, answer the following questions about Roberto Clemente.

1. To the Puerto Rican people, Roberto Clemente was a great hero. Why do you think they felt that way about him?
2. Roberto Clemente threatened to quit professional baseball a number of times during his career. What do you think were some of the reasons why he did this?

LUIS ALVAREZ

Physicist and winner of the 1968 Nobel Prize in physics; born in San Francisco, California, in 1911 and died in Berkeley, California in 1988

What do dinosaurs, radar, the atomic bomb, the Nobel prize, protons, neutrons, and electrons have in common? Most people would probably say, not much. No one would ever dream that these different things could be interconnected. Yet, they are all related through one person; and that person was the physicist Luis Alvarez.

Luis Alvarez was born on June 13, 1911, to Walter and Harriet Alvarez. Walter Alvarez was a first-generation American; his father was born in Spain. Harriet Smyth Alvarez was of Irish descent. This was the reason, explained Luis Alvarez, that a good-looking Irish man could come by the name Luis Alvarez. Luis was the second oldest of four children. His father was a doctor who practiced in San Francisco. His mother was a school teacher. Early in his life, Luis showed a great liking for mechanical devices. He was a bright student, and his father sent him to Polytechnic High School. His father was then offered a position with the Mayo Clinic in Rochester, Minnesota, and the Alvarez family moved to Minnesota.

Luis finished high school in Minnesota and planned to attend college. His mother and most of her relatives had attended the

University of California, so Luis fully expected to attend there also. Professional colleagues in Minnesota convinced Walter Alvarez that his son would benefit greatly from attending the University of Chicago instead of going out to California. Luis Alvarez entered the University of Chicago as a member of the class of 1932. He planned to study chemistry. He enjoyed studying the theory of chemical reactions. However, when it came to working in the laboratory, Luis was very unsuccessful. He recalls ending every experiment with black residues stuck to the bottom of his test tubes.

During his junior year, Luis discovered that he was really interested in physics. While chemistry was the study of the composition and characteristics of matter, physics involved the study of the forces and energy of matter. After taking an experimental physics course, Luis decided that he would devote his life to studying physics. Chemistry was a thing of the past for Luis.

Luis graduated from the University of Chicago in 1932 and went on to do his graduate work there. He received his Ph.D. in physics in 1936. In that same year, he married Geraldine Smithwick.

Luis and Geraldine Alvarez moved to Berkeley, California, where Luis joined the physics faculty of the University of California at Berkeley. He also worked at the Lawrence Radiation Laboratory at the university. As a physicist, Alvarez worked on a number of exciting research projects. During World War II, at the Massachusetts Institute of Technology, he worked on the development of radar. In 1944, he began work at Los Alamos Laboratory in New Mexico on the development of the atomic bomb.

In 1954, Alvarez became the associate director of the Lawrence Radiation Laboratory. This laboratory was known for its research in particle accelerators. A particle accelerator is a machine that can take a subatomic particle, such as a proton or an electron, and accelerate it to enormous speeds. These speeding particles have a great deal of energy that scientists can use for nuclear reactions.

Subatomic particles are extremely small. Scientists needed a way to see the particles before they could experiment with them. In 1953, Donald Glaser invented the hydrogen bubble chamber, which was used to see subatomic particles. The chamber is filled with liquid hydrogen. When a subatomic particle enters the chamber, it leaves a tiny trail of bubbles in the liquid hydrogen. This trail of bubbles can be observed and photographed for records. It was while using the hydrogen bubble chamber that Alvarez made a startling discovery.

Most scientists in the 1950s knew that atoms were made of protons, neutrons, and electrons. These were the three subatomic particles that made up all matter. Alvarez used a bubble chamber to observe these subatomic particles. While he was experimenting with them, he noticed that some bubbles were appearing in the chamber that did not correspond to any of the three subatomic particles. These bubbles appeared in a consistent manner. Alvarez came to the conclusion that the bubbles were produced by some type of particle other than a proton, neutron, or electron. These particles, he concluded, must be what protons, neutrons, and electrons are made of. Alvarez went on to discover two different types of subatomic particles. His research was so extraordinary that he was awarded the Nobel Prize in physics in 1960 for his work.

His work on subatomic particles opened the door to more advanced studies in radioactivity. Alvarez became very interested in radioactivity and the information that could be learned from studying radioactive decay. He began studying radioactive decay in rock formations. This seemed an obvious place to study radioactive decay, since rock formations are usually very old and the decay processes usually take place over many thousands of years.

In 1980, Alvarez discovered an unusually large amount of the element iridium in the rock formations in Italy. Iridium is very rare in rocks that were formed on the earth. The rocks were formed about 65 million years ago. This was about the time scientists believe that the dinosaurs disappeared from the earth. Alvarez then looked for similar concentrations of iridium in rocks that were the same age in other parts of the world. He found that the rocks all had this high level of iridium.

These findings led Alvarez to develop a hypothesis, or scientific guess, about how the dinosaurs became extinct. He hypothesized that the dinosaurs, and other large animals, died because an asteroid collided with the earth some 65 million years ago. The asteroid may have been responsible for the iridium in the rocks. The collision would have released so much dust into the air that the warmth of the sun would have been blocked for about three years. During this time, plant life would have been reduced, and large animals would have starved.

Alvarez's hypothesis seems reasonable. However, there is much still to be proved before it is accepted widely by scientists. During the last few years of his life, Alvarez and his son, Walter, spent much of their time trying to gather evidence to support the theory. However, on September 1, 1988, Luis Alvarez died of throat cancer. His son and others will continue to devote the time, hard work, and perseverance necessary to provide support for Alvarez's theories about the disappearance of the dinosaurs.

Luis Alvarez looked at science as an adventure. He often did the unexpected, following up improbable clues to make startling new discoveries. He thought of himself as an explorer, covering previously unknown territory. His reward for his scientific efforts was more than just money or fame—his reward was the knowledge itself.

Directions: On a separate sheet of paper, answer the following questions about Luis Alvarez.

1. Although Luis Alvarez studied physics in college, he became somewhat of a scientific "Renaissance man." That is, he became knowledgeable in many different scientific fields. Explain how Alvarez's study of radar, subatomic particles, radioactivity, and rock formations each relates to physics.

2. How could Alvarez's hypothesis on the extinction of dinosaurs be relevant today in view of the nuclear arms race? Explain your answer.

SHIRLEY CHISHOLM

First black woman to serve in the United States Congress; born in 1924 in Brooklyn, New York

As a young girl, Shirley Chisholm loved reading biographies of famous American women who fought to protect the rights of all Americans. One of her favorite heroines was Harriet Tubman, a "conductor" on the Underground Railroad who helped slaves escape to freedom in the North during the 1800s. Two others were Susan B. Anthony, a social reformer who fought for women's right to vote, and Mary Bethune, an educator who founded Bethune College, one of the first colleges for black Americans. One day, Shirley would also become a champion of human rights and join the ranks of these American heroines. She would eventually be nicknamed "Fighting Shirley" and become the first black woman to serve in the United States Congress.

Shirley Anita St. Hill Chisholm was born in a poor section of Brooklyn, New York, called Bedford-Stuyvesant. Her father, who had emigrated from British Giuana (now Guyana), worked long hours in a burlap factory. Shirley's mother came originally from Barbados, a tiny island in the West Indies. She worked as a housekeeper and seamstress to help make ends meet.

Shirley's parents wanted their children to have a good education and a better chance at life than they had. Even though both of them worked long hours, their incomes left nothing for savings for their children's educations. Shirley's parents decided to send Shirley and her sisters to live with Shirley's Grandmother Seale in Barbados.

Shirley was only three years old when she arrived by boat on the lush, tropical island. She was welcomed with open arms by her grandmother, who took her and her sisters to live on her farm. Although they were far from home, Shirley and her sisters were not lonely for family, for there were other relatives living on the island as well. An aunt and uncle and four cousins lived nearby and visited Shirley and her sisters often.

Shirley was happy on Barbados. There was always plenty to do and eat, and the countryside was beautiful. Trees laden with fruit grew in abundance on the island. Some of Shirley's favorite fruits were mangos and pawpaws—melonlike papayas—and plantain, a fruit similar to the banana. In addition, many other crops were grown on the farms, and much of the rolling land was covered with acres of sugar cane and corn. Also, there was plenty of fish to eat, since fishing was one of the island's industries. In particular, Shirley's favorite dish consisted of the island's best-known specialty, the flying fish.

Life on the island was not all pleasure and no work, however. Each morning, Grandmother Seale sent the children to a schoolhouse in a neighboring village called Vauxhall. She wanted to make sure the children received a good education. All the children were required to work at their lessons from 9 A.M. until 4 P.M. Although Shirley may not have realized it at the time, she was receiving a strict but excellent education that would serve her well the rest of her life.

Shirley remained on Barbados until she was ten. Then one day she received word that her parents were coming to take her and her sisters home to Brooklyn. Shirley, her sisters, and her grandmother were excited and sad at the same time. All the family members had been close and it would be hard to leave Grandmother Seale after living with her so many years.

Shirley would never forget the day that she left Grandmother Seale standing on the pier. Etched in her mind would be the sad expression on Grandmother Seale's face as the boat carrying Shirley and her sisters back to America moved slowly from the dock and out to sea. Although Grandmother Seale was happy that her daughter and son-in-law could finally afford to keep their children with them, she wept as the children left.

Once back in America, Shirley was unprepared for the type of life she faced. Nonetheless, she was happy to be with her parents. Although her parents could afford to have Shirley and her sisters stay with them again, they were still poor. They had rented a small apartment in a fairly decent section of the city. However, the apartment had no central heating, even though it did have hot water. During their first winter in New York, Shirley and her sisters were miserable. They were not used to cold weather after living on warm Barbados, and they caught bad colds often.

Shirley had to adjust to New York in several other ways as well. She was not used to seeing such tall buildings and so many cars! She soon realized that if she tried to walk in the roads as she had always done on Barbados, she would surely be run over. In addition, there were miles and miles of stores and hundreds of streets that looked alike. She got lost several times going to the store and had to be brought home by a local policeman.

Eventually, Shirley began to adjust to her new surroundings by concentrating on her school studies. Shirley's teachers soon discovered that this young girl who had lived on a faraway island had received an excellent education. Shirley did so well at her studies that she was advanced one full grade. This was not the only time that Shirley made such an impression on her teachers, however. In another year, she was again advanced one grade.

Shirley was happy that her efforts and achievements in school pleased her parents, but she was saddened to see how worn and tired her parents looked from working too hard. To make matters worse, Shirley's mother had taken on an extra job in addition to doing housework. She was also doing janitorial work to afford an apartment with heating in the same building in which she worked. Shirley liked finally living in a building that had heat and room to spare, but she knew her parents were making difficult sacrifices so that their children could succeed. Shirley promised herself that she would make her parents very proud of her one day.

As the years passed, Shirley kept her promise. She was always serious about her studies and continued to do well in school. She occasionally went to dances, at which she earned a reputation as a wonderful dancer. By the time she graduated from high school, she had been offered scholarships to several colleges. She accepted the one from Brooklyn College, which would allow her to live at home and save money on living expenses.

At Brooklyn College, Shirley's talents shone. Not only did she excel in her coursework, but she also became active in several after-class activities that exposed her talents to others outside the classroom. To Shirley's delight, there was a Harriet Tubman Society at the college, in which Shirley became an active member. She also joined the Debating Society, which eventually became her favorite after-class activity. During college, Shirley soon discovered that she had a talent for persuading people when she talked. She argued and won debates on such topics as whether the United States armed forces should be integrated and whether the United States should abolish capital punishment.

Shirley majored in sociology and was seriously thinking about becoming a teacher. However, several people, including one of the college's professors, thought she had the talent for something else as well. Professor Louis Warsoff of the political science department often listened to Shirley debate. He told her he believed her sincere concern for other people and her talent for speaking would make her a natural for politics.

In 1946, Shirley graduated from Brooklyn College with honors. Although she had remembered well Professor Warsoff's comments about her entering politics, she wanted to get a little work experience in another area first. Shirley's first job after college was as a nursery school teacher in Harlem. In the meanwhile, to improve her skills, she began studying part-time for a master's degree in education at Columbia University. Between working and studying, Shirley had little free time except to attend an occasional dance. It was at one of these dances that Shirley met her future husband, Conrad Chisholm. Conrad and Shirley married a year later and settled in a house in Brooklyn not far from Shirley's parents.

Once Shirley had earned her master's degree, she was appointed director of a nursery school. For six years she worked in this area of education and became recognized as an authority in child care and early education. She also became involved more and more in community activities. From 1959 to 1964 she was a consultant for New York City's Bureau of Child Welfare. She also became a director of the Brooklyn Home for Aged Colored People and was active in the National Association for the Advancement of Colored People. Shirley was rapidly establishing a well-earned reputation for trustworthiness within the black community.

During the early 1960s, the civil-rights movement was running in high gear around the nation. Sit-ins and marches were taking place in the South, and the fervor was spreading quickly in the North. It was a significant time for blacks to make political strides. Shirley's outspokenness for the rights of black and Hispanic citizens in her community was timely. She was popular with the people in her community and they supported her completely. In 1964, she decided at last to enter politics full force. She campaigned for the New York Assembly and won. At the age of forty, she was the first black woman from Brooklyn to win a seat on the Assembly.

Her record in the Assembly proved that Shirley Chisholm had the power to make a difference in people's lives. She was responsible for legislation that provided publicly supported day-care centers and unemployment insurance for domestic workers. She also backed a bill that enabled black and Puerto Rican students who lacked the necessary academic requirements to enter college and receive remedial training. Shirley had to address the New York Legislature many times to fight for what she believed. She became known for never being afraid to debate and fight for what she wanted. In addition, she was well respected for always "doing her homework" and knowing necessary background for each piece of legislation she introduced.

When Shirley decided to make a serious attempt at running for Congress in 1968, she knew she had to run against a popular male candidate. Nevertheless, she felt that the people would support her because she understood what they wanted. On November 5, 1968, "Fighting Shirley" won 2½ to 1 against the other candidate. A black woman had finally been elected to Congress.

As a congresswoman, Shirley fought hard for the rights of individuals. She worked to pass many bills that fought poverty and supported job and educational opportunities for the disadvantaged. She won numerous awards for her contributions and efforts in helping all people, but in particular minorities and women, to have a chance in sharing the American Dream.

Shirley Chisholm did not want to stop her quest to help people at the Congressional level. In 1972 she decided to run for the nation's highest office: President. She campaigned hard for, but did not win, the Democratic presidential nomination in 1972. Even though Shirley was beaten for the nomination, she would continue faithfully serving her constituency in Congress until 1983. Since that time, this vibrant, caring modern-day heroine has been in demand as a speaker around the country. She has maintained her interest in education and served for several years as a lecturer at Mt. Holyoke College in Massachusetts.

Directions: On a separate sheet of paper, answer the following questions about Shirley Chisholm.

1. What experiences in Shirley's youth do you think might have affected the legislation she later backed in the New York Assembly and in Congress?

2. Why do you think Shirley Chisholm wanted to make sure all young people had a chance at a good education?

CESAR CHAVEZ

Labor union organizer and leader of the United Farm Workers of America; born in Arizona in 1927

In 1965, nearly ninety percent of the laborers in the multibillion-dollar California farm industry had incomes below the poverty level. Many of these laborers were Mexican-Americans who worked long hours picking crops, only to find that they had not earned enough money to pay their transportation home. In other cases, workers were cheated out of their pay entirely. As a result, thousands of farm workers lived in substandard housing and had little food to eat. Many of these wrongs were corrected, however, by the efforts of one Mexican-American: Cesar Chavez. Chavez helped organize the farm workers into one large union. Today this union is known as the United Farm Workers of America.

Cesar Estrada Chavez was born on a small farm near Yuma, Arizona, to a poor Mexican-American family. During the Great Depression of the 1930s, Cesar's family lost their farm when it was sold for taxes they owed. Like hundreds of other farm families who had lost their farms during that time, the Chavez family headed west to look for work. With only $40 to their name, the Chavez family, which included five children, packed their belongings into an old

Studebaker car and set out for California. The Chavez family had high hopes for California. They had heard that jobs and land were plentiful and that the land was good for growing crops.

However, as soon as Cesar and his family arrived in California, they realized that the state was not the land of opportunity that they had expected. Thousands of people had moved to the state for the same reason they had: to find work. Competition for jobs was so keen that Cesar and his family had no choice but to work as farm laborers. They soon joined the stream of other farm laborers who worked from harvest to harvest in the California farm fields, going wherever workers were needed. As a result, Cesar had to change schools often. No matter where he lived, he usually attended school half the day and worked the other half on the farm to help his family. By the time he had reached the seventh grade, he had attended more than thirty schools.

Although Cesar's family was able to survive, the conditions under which they lived were terrible much of the time. Cesar and his family often lived in tar-paper shacks in the labor camps in which they worked. Many of these labor camps had no plumbing, and workers had to get their drinking water from irrigation ditches.

In addition, the combined wages of the entire family were so low that the family barely had enough money for food and none for clothing. On more than one occasion, Cesar had to walk to school barefoot because he had no shoes. His old ones had rotted and fallen off. One of his sisters, Rita, stopped going to grade school altogether because she was ashamed that she did not have decent clothing. The situation was made worse by other children, who teased Cesar and his sisters and brothers about their clothing.

Although conditions were bad, Cesar did what he could to help the family survive. For example, to help obtain food, he fished in local canals and picked wild mustard greens. To help his family find clothing, he collected tin foil from empty cigarette packages. Then he sought out junk dealers who would trade clothing for the tin foil. What money he earned, he always gave to his family. He and his brothers and sisters did not work for themselves, but for the family. They pooled their money so that the entire group could survive. However, Cesar could do little to help his family find affordable housing. Some of his worst memories would be the times he and his family were forced to live under bridges as shelter from the cold and the rain.

As the years passed, Cesar and his family planted and harvested many kinds of crops. Sometimes they picked cotton or dug up potatoes. Other times they planted or harvested peas, lettuce, carrots, broccoli, or grapes. The crop that Cesar disliked working with the most was sugar beets. Some of the beets weighed fifteen pounds and were difficult to pull from the ground. Not only did Cesar get sharp pains in his back from pulling beets, he also found that his hands often split open between the thumb and index finger from the constant pulling. Other jobs he found particularly difficult were thinning lettuce rows and planting onions. Both jobs required constant stooping. He could tolerate planting onions if the soil was good. However, he usually had to plant onions in soil that had lots of bullheads, or thorny growths, in it. The bullheads constantly punctured his fingers and made them bleed.

In addition, Cesar and the other workers were frequently exposed to the effects of harmful chemicals. Often he and the other farm workers had to work under vines, which were sprayed with sulphur or other pesticides. There was no way to avoid inhaling the poison or touching the leaves. Cesar believed that that was just one of the reasons the majority of farm workers died before they were fifty years old!

Cesar was also angry to see how the labor contractors cheated his family and other farm workers out of their pay. If the Chavez family picked thirty pounds of cotton, often the contractor would insist that they had picked only twenty-seven pounds. Then the contractor would keep part of their pay. In other cases, Cesar saw his parents cheated when they had to borrow money. For example, if his parents borrowed $5 until payday, they were required to repay $10. In many other cases, the workers were cheated out of their entire paychecks. Once the Chavez family worked seven weeks with the promise of payment. When they went to pick up their pay, the contractor had left town. Cesar realized that the only way farm workers could overcome their unfair treatment would be to unite against such practices.

Cesar and his family also suffered injustice away from the farms. As Mexican-Americans, they were often discriminated against in public places. In particular, they were not allowed inside certain stores that posted "White Trade Only" signs. Once, Cesar was even forced by police to leave a movie theater just because he was a Mexican-American.

When Cesar was in his early teens, his father was in an automobile accident, and for a long time, the father could not work. Cesar's mother worked extra hard to try to help support the family, but her efforts were not enough. At that time, Cesar made the decision to leave school. He and his mother had really wanted him to go on to high school, but that had become impossible. Cesar's father eventually recovered, but Cesar had already begun to take over many of his responsibilities. Cesar was growing up quickly.

Conditions for farm workers did not improve as time passed. Cesar's father joined several small farm-workers' unions and from time to time went on strike. However, the strikes were unsuccessful. Most of the people who struck were too poor to stay away from the field for long. Cesar, who also went along on the strikes, was not a dues-paying member as his father was. However, he watched carefully how these small unions worked.

In 1944, when Cesar was seventeen, he enlisted in the United States Navy. He joined the service to get away from farm work. although he never saw combat, Cesar did not care for Navy life. He found that discrimination against Mexican-Americans in the Navy was just as bad as it had been in civilian life.

After World War II ended in 1945, Cesar returned to the farm fields of California. This time, however, he worked independently of his family. While working in Delano, California, he fell in love with and married a girl named Helen. In just a few years they had two children. However, his life as a farm worker and that of his family was no better than the life he had had when he was growing up. Cesar saw that he was caught in a cycle from which he could not escape.

Then, in 1952, Cesar's life changed. He was invited to work for the Community Service Organization (C.S.O.), an organization formed to help Mexican-Americans help themselves. The members had heard of Cesar Chavez's concerns for farm workers and felt that he would be helpful in recruiting members. At first, Cesar worked as a volunteer for the C.S.O., but later he was paid a modest salary.

As a representative of the Community Service Organization, Chavez helped Mexican-Americans in many ways, from leading successful voter-registration drives to helping farm workers with immigration problems. By 1958, Cesar had been made director of the C.S.O. However, he resigned that post in 1962 when the organization's members voted against his proposal to form a farm workers' union.

Cesar returned to Delano and, with $1,200 of his personal savings, formed the National Farm Workers Association (NFWA). Cesar worked as a ditch digger and his wife worked as a farm laborer while he tried to build the union. However, he and his wife could not make ends meet and found they were unable to feed their children. As a last resort, Cesar turned to begging. Although begging hurt Cesar's pride, he found that many people were sympathetic to his cause and willing to help. The NFWA grew quickly in strength after that.

In 1965, with 1,700 families enrolled as members, Cesar's union began to win pay increases and improved working conditions for farm workers. In September of that same year, Chavez's union united with another union to strike against major grape growers in California. This was the first major *huelga,* or strike, in which Cesar's union participated.

Cesar knew that to make gains for farm workers, the unions needed strong national backing. Cesar asked for and received support from individuals and organizations such as Senator Robert F. Kennedy, Hubert Humphrey, and the Episcopal Migrant Industry. He also won the support of the United Auto Workers, which contributed $5,000 a month to the strikers. The strike and a national boycott against grapes were a huge success. The grape growers finally accepted the bargaining power of the union. By 1973, the union had grown in size and in power, and its name was changed to the United Farm Workers of America.

Picketing during a strike was only one of the many strike techniques Cesar used to fight for his causes. He also participated in sing-ins, a 300-mile march, and fasts, several of which lasted twenty-five days or longer. Cesar presented his strikes as part of *La Causa,* a Spanish term meaning "the cause." To Cesar, *La Causa* was a movement for greater social justice that could be achieved only through a combination of nonviolence and national support.

Over the years, Cesar's protests and strikes have resulted in better wages and working conditions for many thousands of farm workers. His struggles for all farm workers continue to this day, even though he is more than sixty years old. To many people, Cesar Chavez remains a national hero of the first rank.

Directions: On a separate sheet of paper, answer the following questions about Cesar Chavez.

1. When Cesar Chavez was growing up, everyone in his family pooled their money and resources so that the entire group could survive. How do you think this thinking may have affected Cesar's ideas in forming a labor union?
2. Why do you think Cesar Chavez believed in using only nonviolence to achieve social justice?

CHRISTA MCAULIFFE

Teacher, passenger on the space shuttle Challenger; born in 1948 in Massachusetts and died in the skies over Florida in 1986

It was January 28, 1986, and all across the state of Florida, people were watching the eastern sky. They watched from cars parked along roadsides, from windows and lawns, from the roofs of buildings. All over the world, other people were watching television screens or listening closely to radios. Today, a teacher was going into space! The sky was a clear, pure blue that seemed to go on forever. The weather was so cold it was hard to believe it was Florida.

On the eastern coast of Florida, a triangle of land known as Cape Canaveral extends into the Atlantic Ocean. Kennedy Space Center occupies almost all of the Cape. On Launch Pad 39B, the space shuttle orbiter *Challenger* sat waiting to arch into that clear, cold sky. Inside *Challenger* were six trained astronauts and Christa McAuliffe.

Christa McAuliffe was a teacher, not an astronaut. The first of Grace and Edward Corrigan's five children, she was born September 2, 1948, in Boston and grew up in Framingham, Massachusetts. When she was fifteen years old, she met Steven McAuliffe, a classmate, at Marian High School. They fell in love.

A year later, they decided to marry when they finished college. After high school graduation, Christa went to Framingham State College, and Steven went to Virginia Military Institute, 600 miles away. The romance lasted through the separation, and six years after they met, Christa and Steven were married. They moved to Maryland, and Steven began classes at Georgetown University Law School, while Christa began her career in teaching.

After Steven finished law school, he encouraged Christa to become a lawyer, but she wanted to continue to teach. Scott, their first child, was born in 1976. In 1978, Christa received a master's degree in education, and Steven received a job offer as assistant attorney general for New Hampshire. In the middle of a blizzard, they moved into an old Victorian house in Concord, New Hampshire. A year later, their daughter, Caroline, was born, and in 1980, Christa returned to teaching. In 1982, she began teaching social studies at Concord High school. Her favorite course, "The American Woman," was a course she had devised. In all of her classes, she liked to stress the roles that ordinary people had played in history. During her twelve years of teaching, Christa estimated that she taught 1,500 students. Her life was happy, productive, and normal, but the "normal" part was about to change.

In August 1984, President Reagan decided that a teacher should be the first ordinary citizen in space. In November, the national Aeronautics and Space Administration (NASA) issued an "Announcement of Opportunity" to schools all over the nation. When she first heard about the teacher-in-space contest, Christa sent for an application. Day after day, she put off filling out the 25-page application. Steven encouraged her, telling her she should not let the opportunity pass. Christa finally mailed her application on February 1, 1985, which was the last possible day. Each applicant was required to plan a project to be carried out as part of the flight into space. For her project, Christa planned to keep a journal covering the training, the flight, and her thoughts and reactions to the adventure in space.

NASA received more than 11,000 applications. The review board chose two teachers from each state and United States territory. Christa's application was one of the 114 selected. In June, she went to a meeting in Washington, D.C., and learned that she was one of ten finalists. The ten finalists went to Johnson Space Center in Houston, Texas. All of the finalists had to prove they were strong enough physically and mentally to stand the stress of space travel. The test that bothered Christa most was spending ten minutes inside a ball that was zipped shut from the outside. The test was to see whether she could stand being inside a tiny place from which she could not easily escape.

The ten teachers returned to Washington, D.C., for one last interview. Then, on the morning of July 19, 1985, Christa put on a bright yellow jacket and, for luck, clasped her mother's jade bracelet on her wrist. She and the other finalists went to the White House. Early in the afternoon, Vice-President George Bush announced to the world that Christa would be the teacher in space. That was the end of normalcy for Christa and her family.

During the rest of the summer, Christa gave interviews, appeared on talk shows, and charmed everyone with her enthusiasm for the teacher-in-space program. Then she went to Johnson Space Center to begin training to be a "teachernaut," as some people called her. Part of her training was to prepare to teach two fifteen-minute lessons from space.

In November 1985, *Challenger* returned from its ninth trip into space. It arrived at Kennedy Space Center riding piggyback on a Boeing 747 airplane. Experienced ground crews checked the *Challenger* carefully. They replaced worn parts and made sure everything was in good repair. Then *Challenger* entered the 525-foot-tall, eight-acre Vehicle Assembly Building, where it was joined to a new external fuel tank and two solid fuel rocket boosters. Next, the space shuttle and its fuel tanks were moved to Launch Pad 39B.

Launch date was set for January 22, 1986. That date was changed to January 25 because another shuttle returned from orbit later than scheduled. On January 25, a dust storm at an emergency landing strip in Africa caused another "scrub," or delay. January 26, it rained, so the launch was put off again. On Monday, January 27, the crew actually went aboard the shuttle and were buckled into their seats. The countdown reached nine minutes to launch, or T minus nine minutes. It stayed there for four hours because a bolt could not be unscrewed. During the delay, the weather became too windy, and the launch was once again delayed.

Tuesday dawned clear and beautiful, but so cold that there were icicles on the shuttle craft and on its gantry, or support tower. No missile had ever been launched from Kennedy Space Center in such cold weather because it rarely gets so cold in Florida. After considering the situation carefully, however, NASA decided the cold would not cause any problems and decided to go ahead with the launch. The astronauts and Christa got ready to go on board. One of the crews that helped prepare the astronauts for their flight presented Christa with a big, shiny apple. She told them to keep it for her, and she would eat it when she got back.

Now it was time to go into space. The countdown was down to its last seconds. The main engines fired. *Five. . .four. . .three . . .two. . .one. . .* lift-off! *Challenger* cleared the launch pad, riding a 700-foot column of fire, and drew a straight white line into the bright blue sky. Cheers exploded in the crisp Cape air and were echoed all around the world. For seventy seconds the flight appeared normal. Then a cloud of smoke and fire appeared at the top of the cloudy column that marked *Challenger*'s path; cheers began to fade. The cloudy column split into a Y-shape. People could not believe what they were seeing. The cheers died as spectators realized that somewhere in the flames and tearing metal were Christa and the six astronauts.

Investigations indicate that a defective part and the intense cold contributed to the tragedy. Future flights will be safer because of the lessons learned from the *Challenger* disaster. Christa did not get a chance to teach her two lessons from space, but the memory of her enthusiasm inspires others to follow her example.

Directions: On a separate sheet of paper, answer the following questions about Christa McAuliffe.

1. What contributions do you think Christa made to the space program? Explain your answer.

2. What contributions do you think Christa made to the teaching profession? Explain your answer.

SANDRA DAY O'CONNOR

First woman Justice of the United States Supreme Court; born in El Paso, Texas, in 1930

In 1952, when Sandra Day O'Connor graduated from law school and applied for a position as a lawyer, the only job she was offered was that of secretary. At the time, few law firms were hiring women in a field that had been dominated for centuries by men. Little did the lawyers who worked for these firms realize then that this highly intelligent woman would someday sit on the highest court in the United States—the United States Supreme Court.

Sandra was born to Ada Mae and Harry Day in El Paso, Texas. She grew up on a 155,000-acre rural ranch called the Lazy B Ranch, which was situated on the Arizona and New Mexico borders. The ranch was founded in the 1880s by Sandra's grandfather, a pioneer from Vermont. Although the ranch was large, it was also quite modest. The ranch was many miles from schools and stores and had no electricity for many years. However, Sandra loved growing up there. She learned to drive a tractor, ride horses, and round up cattle. She even helped her parents mend fences and fix broken windmills.

Sandra's parents could see that their young daughter was strong, bright, and eager to learn. When Sandra was only four years old, her mother ordered lessons by mail and began teaching Sandra at home. Sandra did well at her lessons and loved having books read to her.

Sandra's parents were proud of their daughter and wanted her to have the best education possible. When she was five, they sent her to live with her grandmother in El Paso, Texas. There she went to a private school called the Radford School for Girls. Although she did well in her studies, Sandra often became homesick for her parents and life on the Lazy B Ranch.

Although Sandra continued attending the private school, she always spent her summers back at the ranch. She loved those special summer days, which were filled with lots of activity. She played with her sister, Ann, and her brother, Alan, and did chores at the ranch, including branding cattle. When it got hot, she and her friends went swimming in a large water tank at the ranch.

She was so happy to be back at the ranch that she sometimes hid when it was time to go back to school. Once she and a friend hid in the water tank. Sandra wanted to make it clear that she preferred to stay at the ranch. Sandra's father eventually had to rope his daughter and her friend to get them out of the tank.

Once Sandra was back at school, she continued to do very well at her studies. However, when she was thirteen, she again became very homesick and asked if she could try going to school closer to home. Her parents agreed, and for one year she attended school near the ranch. She was enrolled at a school in Lordsburg, New Mexico, which was twenty-two miles from the ranch. However, to arrive at school on time each day, Sandra had to leave home at dawn and did not get home until evening. Commuting by school bus proved to be both difficult and tiring. The next year Sandra returned to El Paso, where she again attended the Radford School for Girls. After one more year there, she went on to Austin High School, from which she graduated at age sixteen.

Although Sandra had spent much of each year away from her family and the ranch, she had traveled a great deal with her family on vacations. By the time she had finished high school, she had been to Mexico, Honduras, and Cuba. She had also been to all the state capitals west of the Mississippi River and to several other places in California. Her visits to California may have influenced her later choice to attend Stanford University in California.

Sandra enjoyed attending Stanford University, which has a lovely campus just south of San Francisco. She majored in economics and graduated *magna cum laude,* meaning "with great distinction." Not only did she excel in her studies, she also served as senior class president. Sandra was fascinated with law and decided to continue her studies in this area. She did very well and ended up graduating third in a class of 102 law students. The student who graduated first in her class would someday sit on the highest court in the nation with her. That student was William H. Rehnquist, who today is the Chief Justice of the Supreme Court.

Sandra earned additional honors in law school that suggested she might someday do something great. She was elected to the law school's honor society and was an editor of the *Stanford Law Review*. At Stanford as well as at many other law schools, a position as an editor of the school's law review is given only to the best students. Working on the law review became special for Sandra in another way as well: she met her future husband while editing the review. His name was John Jay O'Connor III, and he was in the law class just behind hers. They married shortly after she graduated.

Sandra had worked hard to become a lawyer. However, after she graduated from law school, she found that people were not anxious to hire a woman for a job traditionally held only by men. When she applied for positions as a lawyer with major law firms in Los Angeles and San Francisco, she received no offers other than to be a secretary. Sandra would not give up, however, She soon tried another route into law and was finally hired to work in public service. She was employed from 1952 to 1953 as county deputy attorney for the city of San Mateo, California. In the meantime, her husband finished his law degree.

For the next three years, Sandra and her husband worked as lawyers in Frankfurt, Germany. John had been offered a position there by the United States government. Then Sandra was offered a position, which she accepted, as a civilian lawyer. Although working overseas was an interesting experience, Sandra and her husband hoped to return home to the western United States, which they loved so well. By 1957, Sandra and John had resettled in the Southwest near Phoenix, Arizona. Sandra gave birth to the first of her three sons there. Although she gave special attention to raising her family, she kept up with her interest in law at least part-time. She opened her own law firm and also participated in many community and professional activities. She served on government committees, such as the Maricopa County Board of Adjustments and Appeals and the Governor's Committee on Marriage and Family. She also worked as the administrative assistant of the Arizona State Hospital.

In addition, Sandra began working with organizations that made special efforts to help people. She served as an advisor for the Salvation Army, a charitable organization that works hard in many ways to improve peoples' lives. She also did volunteer work for a school specifically designed to help black and Hispanic children achieve their potential.

In 1965, Sandra again began to work full-time. Her children were older and in school, and she felt that she could put more effort into her law career again. For the next four years, she served as assistant attorney general for Arizona. Then something unusual happened.

Arizona Governor Jack Williams chose Sandra Day O'Connor to replace a state senator who was giving up her position. The state senator was Isabel A. Burgess, who was resigning to accept an appointment in Washington, D.C. Sandra was pleased with Burgess's appointment, and she was also pleased to be chosen by the governor for a seat in the senate. During the next year, Sandra campaigned enthusiastically to win the senate seat. She won easily over her opponent, who was also a woman.

As always, Sandra worked hard and continued to rise in government. During the five years she was a senator, she impressed many people with what she accomplished. She was admired for her insistence on factual accuracy, which is crucial when making important decisions that affect people's lives. She also gained a reputation for being fair—no matter whether her decisions made her unpopular with some people. In 1972, Sandra Day O'Connor was honored again. She was elected majority leader of the Arizona senate. The position of majority leader is very important in the senate. The majority leader is the most powerful elected senator and influences greatly the legislative program of all the other senators in the same party. Sandra was the first woman in history to hold this position in any state senate in the United States.

Sandra's election to the senate and her successful work in that position might have enabled her to have a career as a politician. Instead, she chose to return to law, the field she loved most. In 1964, she was elected a judge on the Maricopa County Superior Court. Again, she earned an admirable reputation for being stern but fair. In most cases, she did not give light sentences, but she always showed a sincere concern about conditions in the prisons to which she sentenced criminals.

Her growing reputation as an outstanding judge soon led to another appointment. In 1978, Governor Bruce Babbitt asked Sandra to become a judge on the Arizona Court of Appeals. His recommendation came as a surprise to some people, since the governor was a Democrat and Sandra was a Republican. However, when the governor was interviewed about his decision, he said that he really had no other choice. In his opinion, Sandra's intellect and judgment were astonishing. He believed that she was overwhelmingly the best choice for the position.

Sandra's rise in government was not without its occasional problems, however. In 1980, when members of the Arizona Bar Association rated the performance of the judges at Sandra's rank, they rated Sandra only eighth. However, ninety percent recommended that she be retained on the Court of Appeals. This indicated a mix of feelings toward Sandra's work. Her work on the Court of Appeals had dealt with matters such as divorce, worker's compensation, bankruptcies, and appeals of criminal convictions. It was not until 1981 that she had the chance to enhance her reputation by giving her opinions on important national issues.

At that time, Sandra recommended that caseloads in the federal courts be decreased. She believed this could be done, in part, by allowing more of the opinions and judgments made in the state courts to stand. Overall, she wanted to see less intervention of federal courts in state and local matters. As it turned out, these opinions matched those of President Ronald Reagan, who was new to the office and was impressed with Sandra Day O'Connor's ideas and record.

On July 7, 1981, Ronald Reagan nominated Sandra Day O'Connor as an Associate Justice of the Supreme Court. The following September 26, she was sworn into office. Only a few days later she was deciding with the other justices which of the more than 1,000 cases they would hear during the coming term. For the first time in United States history, a woman had become one of the "brethren," a term meaning "brothers" that had long been used in describing the justices on the Supreme Court.

In the last several years, Sandra Day O'Connor has proved to be a well-respected Associate Justice. Even though she has achieved one of the nation's highest appointments, she remains the fair, conscientious person she was in the beginning of her career. To this day, she returns to the Lazy B Ranch for visits with her family whenever she gets the chance.

Directions: On a separate sheet of paper, answer the following questions about Sandra Day O'Connor.

1. As a lawyer and a state judge, Sandra Day O'Connor earned a reputation as being stern but fair. How do you think growing up on a ranch may have helped Sandra Day O'Connor develop these qualities?

2. Sandra Day O'Connor campaigned successfully to become a senator. However, she eventually became a judge rather than a politician. What do you think are some of the reasons that may have influenced her decision to return to law?